# The
# Marketing
# Imagination

## New, Expanded Edition

**Other books by Theodore Levitt**

*Innovation in Marketing* (1962)

*Industrial Purchasing Behavior: A Study of Communication Effects* (1964)

*Marketing* (1964) (with John B. Matthews, Jr., Robert D. Buzzell, and Ronald Frank)

*The Marketing Mode* (1969)

*Marketing: A Contemporary Analysis* (1972) (with Robert D. Buzzell, Robert E. M. Nourse, and John B. Matthews, Jr.)

*The Third Sector: New Tactics for a Responsive Society* (1973)

*Marketing for Business Growth* (1974)

# The Marketing Imagination

## New, Expanded Edition

## Theodore Levitt

**THE FREE PRESS**
*A Division of Macmillan, Inc.*
NEW YORK

Collier Macmillan Publishers
LONDON

The Free Press
A Division of Macmillan, Inc.
866 Third Avenue, New York, N.Y. 10022

Collier Macmillan Canada, Inc.

Printed in the United States of America

printing number
1    2    3    4    5    6    7    8    9    10

**Library of Congress Cataloging-in-Publication Data**

Levitt, Theodore
    The marketing imagination.

    Includes bibliographical references and index.
    1. Marketing.    I. Title
HF5415.L482      1986      658.8      86-576
ISBN 0-02-919180-7
ISBN 0-02-919090-8 (pbk.)

*Credits*

*With many thanks to Rachael Daitch,*
*more than a secretary*

# Contents

# Preface to the New, Expanded Edition

Nobody pays attention to even a well-argued proposition if it's obviously devoid of plausibility. The vigorous global debates ignited by "The Globalization of Markets" (Chapter 2) attest to the salience of the topic and the plausibility of the argument it makes. This chapter asserts that no business, however big or small, however wide or narrow its customer base, is exempt from global competition. The local shoe store or fastener distributor is as much affected as the worldwide seller or globally dispersed manufacturer.

Then why debates? Why controversy? Everybody seems to agree that there is a generalized shift, perhaps even an overwhelming movement, toward global competition. But that's different, so it is said, from "the globalization of markets." Global competition does not require, it is said, that markets must be global in the way some have interpreted this chapter as saying.

These critics say approximately the following:

—There is no evidence of the homogenization of global wants and wishes. The opposite is the case. Indeed, there is increased

intracountry heterogeneity, not just intercountry heterogeneity.

—There is no widespread preference for low prices at acceptable quality. Indeed, there is no evidence of universal price
sensitivity. Besides, standardized low prices can be overpriced
in some countries and underpriced in others. Therefore a
universal low price positioning is not a desirable strategy.

—Since cost of production is often an insignificant component
of total cost, economies of scale in production may provide
little competitive advantage. Therefore the focus on product
standardization to achieve low costs and low prices is mis-
placed. Indeed, flexible factory automation can drive down
the cost of product variety.

—In fact, there are powerful operational obstacles to implementing product standardization among global markets:

1. Government and industry restrictions.
2. Country differences in the marketing infrastructure, such
   as in the availability of promotional media, distribution
   channels, transportation facilities, and the like.
3. Differences in and interdependence of resource markets.
   Thus the availability or unavailability of labor and raw
   materials between nations, and the huge differences in
   their costs, create powerful differences in make-or-buy
   decisions between nations. These factors have impacts
   that not even a generalized drift toward homogenized
   preferences could overcome.

—The ability to standardize globally is seriously hampered by
previous corporate commitments. These include existing plant
locations, established distribution facilities, joint-venture and
partnership agreements, distribution and dealer arrangements,
and banking and exchange agreements.

—There are language and cultural barriers.

The globalization debate emerged initially and still rages most
vigorously among advertising agencies and, derivatively, in
advertising-intensive consumer package goods industries. Having
suggested the rising global homogenization of customer preferences
and tastes in all things, and an economic reason—scarcity—that rein-

forces these, "the globalization of markets" became interpreted as prescribing rigidly standardized communications in support of those preferences and tastes.

This formulation is so obviously untenable that it is hardly surprising that it draws fire, especially from an industry totally structured by and deeply dependent on the proposition that all nations have fixed preferences and conditions. To attack that proposition is to attack the justification of globally dispersed institutions and the livelihoods of their many functionaries.

This chapter nowhere speaks of global brands, though critics are correct and justified in inferring them. Still, these critics now widely accept the inescapability of globalization in some sense, qualifying their acceptance with what might be called the Burger King variation, "Have it your way," with themes such as "Global Vision with Local Touch " and "Think Global—Act Local." Thus they concede the new globalization while insisting on the old localization. One commentator, accepting the need to think globally, insisted by way of contrary example that it's very hard to get middle Europeans to use margarine instead of butter because they have an obsession with freshness. They interpret what's made in a factory as unfresh compared with butter. Hence communications that work in, say, the United Kingdom or the United States don't work in Switzerland. Ergo the error of global branding.

Even if the freshness diagnosis is correct, it does not follow that the product, and communications in its support, cannot be regionalized across the relevant nations. In fact, this diagnosis merely suggests that the communication task is for the time being different in Switzerland from the communication task in Britain. An emphasis on "farm freshness" in packaging and advertising is called for—until that finally becomes no longer a relevant or distinctive competitive feature. If the economics of production, distribution, and communication favor standardization across contiguous national borders, and if there is a reasonable basis for believing that consumers in all the nations in that region have the same basic needs and respond to the same economics of scarcity, it makes sense to use one's imagination and energy to appeal to them in the same efficient fashion.

It is unnecessary to speak to all peoples in their native literary language. Nonverbal communication works with increasing power, especially when facilitated by the powerful capabilities of radio and television. In the so-called higher cultural realms, Mozart, Ming vases, and Rembrandt have always communicated universally. When the Beatles exploded on the scene in the 1960s, we witnessed the beginning of the same universality of meaning and sensibility among the masses.

The Marx brothers' movies are understood universally even if the audiences don't read the subtitles. The message of the heavy-metal music of KISS, whose lyrics, for most listeners, are unintelligible in the cacophonous din, is understood by millions everywhere. Professor Campbell, upon first seeing a dramatization of *Finnegan's Wake,* said, "I don't know what they're saying, but I certainly know what they mean." Nonverbal communication knows no language barrier.

Advertising is a specialty business. Its challenge is to communicate—despite the enormous obstacles of indifference, competition, and restricted time. That's what advertising agencies say they're so good at, so let them prove it by spiting yet another obstacle—as have other creative types like Mozart, Mick Jagger, and Andy Warhol.

Nothing of worth has ever been achieved without serious effort, commitment, and high spirits. Even with these, Sisyphus could not push the rock up the mountain. "The Globalization of Markets" argues, however, that the proletarianization of communication, travel, and transport is flattening the mountain and therefore companies that don't try to push the rock across what is becoming a flatter competitive field will themselves be flattened.

This growing flattening is affirmed even by critics who seek alternatives such as "Global Vision with Local Touch" and "Think Global—Act Local." The flattening of the competitive terrain is also attested to by increasingly vigorous efforts to replace the disappearing natural trade barriers with artificial ones: tariffs, exchange controls, quotas, voluntary restraints, and the like. Their significance is not that they are barriers to the intensification of global competition; rather, they are symptoms of it. They indicate that sellers from some nations are being embraced eagerly by buyers in other nations—

buyers who are drawn to products of reasonably standardized quality whose attractive prices are made possible by the superior economics of large-scale production facilitated by global markets.

What, indeed, is a standardized product? Seiko offers over a hundred different styles of wristwatches. Copying the mass-production, high-quality, low-price innovation pioneered by others and perfected with stylish suitability by Timex, Seiko offers a multitude of designs and models. But it manufactures only a handful of different operating mechanisms. The huge range of designs is simply a matter of low-cost variations in packaging. That's standardization. In some markets, certain packaging styles sell better than others. What else is new? Only that Seiko's high-quality, low-price strategy has succeeded by having targeted a global market large enough to justify investment in the cost-reducing plants that make the strategy work.

Of course, there are insurmountable differences between places. Peanut-cultivating machinery that works in the sandy soil of Georgia does not work in the dense soil of Senegal, West Africa. Only a fool would try to standardize. The argument of "The Globalization of Markets" assumes it speaks to sensible people.

Major national differences in the institutions and practices of trade and in the preference structures of peoples are obvious enough. They are especially obvious to managers who have been assigned to handle separate and discrete nation-based territories and to market researchers looking at the unique characteristics of national markets and customers. The distinctions they see are precisely the distinctions to which they owe their jobs. What they do not see is what they are not assigned to look at: what different countries and regions have in common; how commonality is converging, rapidly and irrepressibly, upon all peoples. Nor do they see what is becoming increasingly possible as to commercial practices everywhere: how imagination, daring, and persistence can tumble old assumptions as to the appropriateness of common commercial practices. What they do not do is cross the boundaries of their cognitions and responsibilities so that they might capitalize on the possibilities suggested by more porous or even absent boundaries.

To list all the ways in which markets clearly differ from one another as proof of the ways in which they cannot be alike misses entirely the ways in which they are becoming increasingly alike. Convergence toward commonality is a fact, if not a finality.

Global convergence does not suggest the total homogenization of everything everywhere. Convergence spells the end neither of distinct markets nor of market segments. As "The Globalization of Markets" says quite clearly, we witness the beginning of the globalization and therefore massification of segments, not the completion. In almost all nations, regardless of differences in language, culture, and tradition, there are identical segments for Bach, Bauhaus, bicycles, pita bread, punk rock, pornography, prestige credit cards, international travel, financial instruments, Chinese food, hamburgers, and beer—to speak only of historically more culture-bound products. What may start out as small, local segments migrate with remarkable speed. Additively, they become gigantically global. That is what convergence is all about: the global transformation of markets into discrete but homogenous segments.

The resulting economics are compelling. Nothing contemplated by flexible factory automation can compete with the possibilities for superior competitiveness that derive from the resulting economies of global scale. An important question is how much people will prefer lower prices over more varied choices. Many will choose choice. Within a preference for choice (that is, within a segment) there remains an accompanying preference for the best price. This is a point the world sees affirmed daily, accounting in part for the insistent cry for trade barriers and import restrictions regarding products in all price categories. These barriers and restrictions may work temporarily, but never in the history of commerce have they succeeded for long.

Whether you prefer a luxury automobile or a utility car, you are still likely to be sensitive to price. Understandably, everybody wants to get the best deal for what they're buying. This is such a persistent and compelling characteristic of human (and therefore organizational) behavior that barriers erected against its realization in the global marketplace have always failed.

Failure has taken a variety of forms:

—Circumvention by shifts of capital, as now when Japanese auto and electronic products companies locate plants in Bri-

tain, Brazil, the United States, and elsewhere or engage in joint ventures with companies located in the target markets
—Companies in target markets shifting investment to lower-cost locales and then "importing" lower-price goods back to their home markets
—The further deterioration of the competitiveness of protected industries until their access to capital (either from the capital markets or via their own cash flows) is so badly diminished that they expire, thus removing the remaining justification for barriers
—Pressure from domestic businesses dependent upon the international earning power of the excluded industries and from domestic companies that do business with the excluded industries in their own or other countries
—Trade-barrier retaliation by the affected nations
—Smuggling, piracy, transshipping, and other, often more elegant, subterfuges
—Of course, the threat and use of force

All of these are open expressions of the natural requirement of a highly interdependent world to keep world markets open—especially to the low-price seller.

New, miniscule segments and niches will certainly continue to arise within the interstices of global homogenization—in the future as in the past. But now the future is almost certainly a new future. The proletarian migrations of communication, travel, and transport bring us all implacably closer in all our ways, and it is our ways that define our behavior and consumption. In their major outlines, those ways increasingly look more alike everywhere. To resist or reject their commercial implications is to repeat the mistakes of proud old corporate names that now lay unrecognized or unremembered in the graveyards of commerce.

The three additional chapters in this new, expanded edition of *The Marketing Imagination* reflect my conviction that companies are insufficiently attentive to the commercial possibilities of using their imaginations and insufficiently aware of the self-limiting consequences of being merely excellent in conventional ways about conventional things.

Excellent quality is not enough. Also required is suitability. In pursuit of wrong purposes, excellence is wrong. Employing gas spectroscopy is overkill when a simple microscope will accomplish the task. Using a simulation model to determine the optimal warehouse network may be excellent management science, but you'll realize it's ridiculous if you just stop to think. Common sense will suggest that you'll need a warehouse in the New York metropolitan area, probably one between Washington and Philadelphia, one around Atlanta, around Chicago, around Houston–Dallas, in Los Angeles–San Francisco, in the Pacific Northwest, and somewhere on a line between Denver and Minneapolis. How much more scientific accuracy do you need? Your imagination can tell you in a moment a great deal more than scientific excellence would have told you at great expense and pretension in a year.

A business is not a person. In a business, maturity, decline, and senescence are not inevitable, and stasis is avoidable. But managing well is no assurance that the right things are being managed. This is emphasized in Chapter 8, "Marketing Myopia," which underscores the catastrophic results of being product-oriented rather than customer-oriented. The chapter probably needs no introduction, appearing here with a retrospective commentary written fifteen years after its original publication. Perhaps more than any other chapter in this book, it speaks for itself about the power of the marketing imagination. It asks the reader to follow a particular simple way of thinking about the simple purposes of a business, and from this draws the most obvious conclusions that the mind naturally comprehends. They are the conclusions of the disciplined imagination.

Chapter 9, "Exploit the Product Life Cycle," suggests, and describes in some applicable detail, ways to extend the so-called product life cycle—to pump life into seemingly expiring maturing products and businesses. It shows how these methods have been used with remarkable effectiveness by some of the world's biggest and most admired old and new companies; how, with a little guidance from a few modes suggested in this chapter, other companies can achieve imaginatively expansive possibilities for the most mundane of products and services.

Chapter 10, "Innovative Imitation," develops in yet another direction some of the ideas of Chapter 9. It asserts that no company can survive on its creative contributions alone or entirely on its own constant leadership in its industry or on its own innovative reach. In a world of eager competitors, there always will be others who on some matters will take the lead in creating new things. While a company may work hard at being a leader and an innovator, it must work equally hard at being quite systematically an eager imitator.

THEODORE LEVITT
Harvard Business School

# Preface to the Original Edition

What's new? By this question people who manage mean, What unnoticed things "out there" can help or might hurt my business or my career, can create opportunities or impose perils? They also mean, What new techniques, new ways of doing things, can help us better do our jobs?

Those who answer professionally, with neatly engineered formulas, elegant strategic paradigms, and finely honed analytical techniques are sure to get an audience in this world of great uncertainty, profound ambiguity, and intense competition. Thus the ubiquity of shamans in business dress.

No manager with a detectable heartbeat does not periodically wonder, What's new?, does not wish for swift and magical solutions to troubling problems, for quick alleviation of daily distresses and the risks of uncertain futures. Managers are enormously vulnerable to the confident claims and plausible promises of outsiders peddling answers.

The uncertainties that concern managers most occur mostly in the market place, whether in the United States, the U.S.S.R., the United Arab Emirates, or the United Way. The market is palpable and inescapable. In its implacable operations the fates of all institutions are finally forged.

But the market place is not autonomous. It merely reflects the results of those who act upon it: those who "buy" in it and those who "sell" in it. They marshal materials, technologies, people, sentiments, wits, and money to their intended ends, meeting head-on in an amalgamating and unforgiving crucible.

*The Marketing Imagination* reflects the conviction that the way to deal with "what's new," as well as what's old and enduring, is mostly by being widely informed and thinking straight. Picking easy formulas or exotic models out of textbooks or other people's heads may be convenient and even occasionally helpful, but it does nothing for your mind or for your ability to deal effectively with the constantly emerging new realities. To "think straight" successfully in a world full of smart, straight-thinking people requires thinking with a special quality, transcending the ordinary and thus reaching imaginatively beyond the obvious or merely deductive. The future belongs to those who see possibilities before they become obvious and who effectively marshal resources and energies for their attainment or avoidance. Nor is anything great ever accomplished without high spirits.

The purpose of a business is to get and keep a customer. Without solvent customers in some reasonable proportion, there is no business. Customers are constantly presented with lots of options to help them solve their problems. They don't buy things, they buy solutions to problems. The surviving and thriving business is a business that constantly seeks better ways to help people solve their problems—functionally better, valued better, and available better. To create betterness requires knowing what customers think betterness to be. This precedes all else in business. The imagination that figures out what that is, imaginatively figures out what should be done, and does it with imagination and high spirits will drive the enterprise forward.

This book continues the stream of work of my most recent prior book, *Marketing for Business Growth* (1974). The chapters in this new book do not presume to tell people *how* to think straight or imaginatively. They simply deal with certain important matters in ways that textbooks, how-to books, and most professors and consultants generally do not. These ways apply to all types of businesses and to all other enterprises.

Chapter 1, "Marketing and the Corporate Purpose," sets the tone. It asserts what I've just said. "Profit" is a meaningless statement of the corporate purpose. Without customers in sufficient and steady numbers there is no business and no profit. No business can function effectively without a clear view of how to get customers, what its prospective customers want and need, and what options competitors give them, and without explicit strategies and programs focused on what goes on in the market place rather than on what's possible in the factory or what is merely assumed at headquarters. A chief executive who does not himself have a sense of the marketing requisites of his business or who does not have chief lieutenants who do is almost certainly headed for disaster. Marketing is, indeed, everybody's business, and everybody had better know it, no matter how deeply buried one may be in faraway R&D or out at the telephone switchboard.

Chapter 2, "The Globalization of Markets," asserts that the traditional multinational corporation is obsolete. It operates just as its name implies, multinationally, not globally. The future belongs to the globally, not multinationally, oriented corporation, because the globe is being homogenized by "The Republic of Technology." More and more, people everywhere are growing more alike in their wants and behavior, whether we're talking about Coca-Cola, microprocessors, jeans, movies, pizza, cosmetics, or milling machines. This means that the world explodes into a gigantic market in place of what used to be thought of as small segments or uniquely national markets. This will make even the smallest company in the smallest town subject to the ravages of global competition—competition based heavily on price. That's the new reality.

Chapter 3 is on "The Industrialization of Service." It asserts that ancient ideas about service are indeed ancient, being now replaced by industrial systems that make service both more efficient and more capable of being carried on in large scale that can be managed professionally and rationally, just like large manufacturing firms. Mom-and-pop services systems (in food, law, banking, repair, maintenance, and the like) will survive, but only just barely. The large, rationally managed service corporation is the new colossus that now affects us all—and all for the better. It takes a new kind of manager and management process.

Chapter 4 is called "Differentiation—of Anything." It asserts that differentiation is the essence of competition; that everything can be and is differentiable, even such "commodities" as steel, cement, money, chemicals, and grain. Success goes to those who differentiate themselves in ways that attract differentiably superior numbers of customers to themselves. It is, in fact, relatively easy to do. The point is to know how, and the chapter tells how, giving examples of how it's been successfully done.

Chapter 5, "Marketing Intangible Products and Product Intangibles," carries on some of the notions of Chapter 4, but with specific reference to what's usually called "service." The fact is, "service" is a central part of even the most massively durable tangible products, like earth-moving machines or a ton of stainless steel. All products have aspects of the tangible and the intangible. To know what these are and how to enhance and manage them gives differential competitive power to those who have this knowledge and do things right.

Chapter 6, on "Relationship Management," asserts that when you have a customer you have, in effect, an asset. That asset has to be managed lest the equity you have in that account be dissipated, lest the customer wonder, "What have you done for me lately?" This is particularly true as more of the world's work is done through long-term contracts or via supplier–customer links that must, of necessity, stretch out over many years. To manage the relationship that inevitably exists requires special care lest the equity in the account be destroyed, lest it decline to the point of vulnerability to a competitor's claims that "We can do more."

Chapter 7, "The Marketing Imagination," shows with specific illustrations much of what's been suggested in the preceding chapters. No amount of modern marketing science or heavy analysis will work without the protean powers of the marketing imagination and high spirits. The world looks for easy fixes and finely engineered programs to solve its problems. So also, these days, do people who manage. That's understandable. But this is a world of hungry and eager competitors constantly thinking up new things to do and new ways to do them, leapfrogging over the present, end-running around the powerfully entrenched. Their imagination is at work, and so must be the imaginations of those strongly established enterprises that got where they are largely via the imagination and enterprise of their managerial predecessors.

My expectation is that the reader will find in these and the remaining chapters much that can be put to immediate beneficial use. My greater *hope* is that the reader's cognitive system will somehow be positively affected, that the reader's marketing imagination will be strongly stimulated and will, as a result, continue to develop and yield great results.

My colleague Professor Abraham Zaleznik, a wise man about many things and modestly professing little knowledge of marketing, said casually one day, "What really drives your field is the marketing imagination." Hence the title.

THEODORE LEVITT
Harvard Business School

# The
# Marketing
# Imagination

## New, Expanded Edition

# 1

# Marketing and the Corporate Purpose

Nothing in business is so remarkable as the conflicting variety of success formulas offered by its numerous practitioners and professors. And if, in the case of practitioners, they're not exactly "formulas," they are explanations of "how we did it," implying with firm control over any fleeting tendencies toward modesty that "that's how *you* ought to do it." Practitioners, filled with pride and money, turn themselves into prescriptive philosophers, filled mostly with hot air.

Professors, on the other hand, know better than to deal merely in explanations. We traffic instead in higher goods, like "analysis," "concepts," and "theories." In short, "truth." Filled with self-importance, we turn ourselves hopefully into wanted advisers, consultants filled mostly with woolly congestion.

I do not wish to disparage either, but only to suggest that these two legitimately different and respectable professions usu-

1

ally diminish rather than enhance their reputations when intruding too much or with too little thought on each other's turf.

How often have we heard executives of venerable age and high repute or entrepreneurs flushed with recent wealth pronounce with lofty certainty and imperial rectitude exactly what produces business success? All they really tell, however, in cleaned-up retrospection, is the story of how they themselves happen to have done it. Listen to ten, and you'll generally get ten different pieces of advice.

Listen to ten professors, and you'll generally get advice by some multiple of ten. The difference is not that professors believe more firmly in abundance. Rather, besides teaching, professors are also paid to think. Hence, lacking direct experience, each is likely to think up several different ways to get to the same place. People of affairs are paid merely to get there, and it is almost certain that when they do they'll think the only way there is the one they have taken, even when their neighbors got there by a different route.

On this score, people of affairs are scarcely unique. Consider the many versions we have heard from successful novelists of the "right way" to work: Sit down and get started, don't wait for inspiration; write when you're ready, not when the schedule says so; write from dawn till noon; write from dusk till dawn; always write in the same place; never stick to the same place for long; write only about what you know, don't invent; only invent, all else is mere confusion. The expert at doing things, obviously, is not reliably expert in either understanding what he does or why it works, certainly not in giving consistently good advice.

As a certified academic who is paid, however paltry the sum, to think, teach, and advise about the practices of those in practical work, of one thing I am totally convinced: the healthy state of business practice in the capitalist democracies. The state of business practice reflects the quality of the executive mind and its effective commitment to the purposes of business itself.

The modern executive mind is in very good condition indeed, especially in the larger and, usually therefore, global corporations. Indeed, awed admiration is what any intelligent and fair-minded analyst will come away with when he studies the large corporation of our times. For he will note its extraordinary efficiency, flexibility, agility, and internal diversity; the dedication and remarkable good spirits of its vast variety of employees; its attention to quality in what it does and to fairness in how it behaves; and the studiousness with which it approaches major undertakings. Notwithstanding all the self-righteousness parading of unpleasant contrary facts these days, no institution of any size or diversity, whether government or private, taking any reasonable combination of desirable attributes, can come anywhere near the large corporations of the modern capitalist democracies. Nor is this merely a matter of their having a head start historically. *Fortune*'s list of "Top 500" U.S. manufacturing corporations changes constantly, as does the list of top financial institutions. Federal Trade Commission studies of "industrial concentration" repeatedly show shifting patterns of leadership in one industry sector after another.

Obviously, being ahead or having gotten a head start counts for not a lot within America's little corner of the capitalist world. But the parallel fact that everywhere the capitalist corporations, as a group, are widening their lead over their lagging imitators in the noncapitalist world is extraordinarily significant. It means that being capitalistic gives them a genetic edge. Capitalism simply works better, and anybody who argues the opposite does just that. He argues. He simply doesn't have the facts.

One of the most interesting of these facts is that those who seek to catch up with the more advanced and achieving institutions of our times invariably seek to do it by some sort of selective imitation of the modern capitalist corporations. ("We'll take your best and ignore the rest.") Traffic in the opposite direction is negligible or nonexistent. Nothing could be more unmistakably meaningful. Nothing is more flattering to capitalism's protean prowess.

Even where this imitation now has a long history, having been generously helped with facilitating patents, designs, machines, control systems, technicians-on-loan, cash, whole factories supplied by the capitalist corporations—as they have

3

been in Soviet Russia ever since Lenin's New Economic Policy first imported Henry Ford in 1923—even when helped with the latest methods and technologies, the beneficiaries quickly fall behind again into inefficiency, sloth, and irrelevance. Why, one must ask, after more than half a century of eager (if grudging) imitation and gifts of capitalist technologies in the factories and on the farms have the Soviets fallen with uncomprehending frustration ever farther behind? Even their much-vaunted advanced fighter plane recently defected to Japan turned out to be advanced only in its packaging. At least they learned *that* much from us—the importance of packaging. This constant failure of helpful imitation to take hold persists also in nations with feudal military dictatorships and in the false democracies of South America, Southeast Asia, and now deimperialized Africa.

By what magic do the large corporations of the capitalist democracies work so well? Is it simply that they're capitalist, that they operate in democratic political environments, or some combination of the two? Or what?

The combination is crucial, emphatically. Being capitalist means the liberating absence of the feudal incubus, traditions that fetter people to their assigned masters rather than to their own chosen purposes. Operating in political democracies means the likelihood of public resistance to constantly advancing governmentalization of society, some reasonable probabilities against a constantly expanding and suffocating bureaucratization of the entire polity. (It is instructive, I think, to note that no dictatorship or tyranny has ever been voted in by people. People, however humble, however limited their education, quite naturally and sensibly resist Caesarism, however elegantly it may be packaged or differently presented.)

Nor is it any more presumed to be a reactionary cliché to say these things, as it once was in Western liberal intellectual circles. The cliché has now become the dismal, tragic truth. The firm belief, held by generations of intelligent and informed idealists, that justice and equality could be wedded through the ministrations of public servants working with diligent selflessness at control central has come a cropper. It's now obvious that the

4

future simply has not worked—not for Robert Owen, Karl Marx, Rosa Luxemburg, Sydney and Beatrice Webb, Rexford Guy Tugwell, or Oscar Lange, not even for Fidel Castro or Lyndon Baines Johnson.

What seems somehow to work best is something we call private enterprise and the free market system of economic organization operating in a political environment we call "representative democracy."

Unfortunately, this explanation is not the whole of it. Although, as we have seen, business enterprises in the modern capitalist democracies as a group outperform all other such enterprises operating under different conditions of political and economic organization, we also have seen that the distribution of this superiority is not symmetrical. Some firms prosper more than others. Some lag, wither, and even die. As I've suggested, the explanations of the superior performance that we commonly get from the most successful practitioners of capitalist enterprise, though perhaps quite accurate in themselves, are seldom more than confessions of particular experiences, offering no comparison with the experiences of others and devoid of serious analytical content. What they lack, moreover, in generality they often compensate with pomposity.

Professors also know something of the ways of pomposity, especially in the line of literary obfuscation masquerading as wisdom. They have dispensed some genuine wisdom as well, particularly about the special reasons why fairly free capitalist enterprises operating in relatively open markets vary in performance and about the characteristics associated with varying degrees of failure and success. That wisdom is, in fact, of relatively recent origin. Essentially it sets forth no more than the following few simple statements about the requisites of competitive success:

1. The purpose of a business is to create and keep a customer.
2. To do that you have to produce and deliver goods and services that people want and value at prices and under

conditions that are reasonably attractive relative to those offered by others to a proportion of customers large enough to make those prices and conditions possible.

3. To continue to do that, the enterprise must produce revenue in excess of costs in sufficient quantity and with sufficient regularity to attract and hold investors in the enterprise, and must keep at least abreast and sometimes ahead of competitive offerings.

4. No enterprise, no matter how small, can do any of this by mere instinct or accident. It has to clarify its purposes, strategies, and plans, and the larger the enterprise the greater the necessity that these be clearly written down, clearly communicated, and frequently reviewed by the senior members of the enterprise.

5. In all cases there must be an appropriate system of rewards, audits, and controls to assure that what's intended gets properly done and, when not, that it gets quickly rectified.

Not so long ago a lot of companies assumed something quite different about the purpose of a business. They said quite simply that the purpose is to make money. But that proved as vacuous as saying that the purpose of life is to eat. Eating is a requisite, not a purpose of life. Without eating, life stops. Profits are a requisite of business. Without profits, business stops. Like food for the body, profit for the business must be defined as the excess of what comes in over what goes out. In business it's called positive cash flow. It has to be positive, because the process of sustaining life is a process of destroying life. To sustain life, a business must produce goods and services that people in sufficient numbers will want to buy at adequate prices. Since production wears out the machinery that produces and the people who run and manage the machines, to keep the business going there's got to be enough left over to replace what's being worn out. That "enough" is profit, no matter what the accountants, the IRS, or the Gosplan calls it. *That* is why profit is a requisite, not a purpose of business.

Besides all that, to say that profit is a purpose of business

6

is, simply, morally shallow. Who with a palpable heartbeat and minimal sensibilities will go to the mat for the right of somebody to earn a profit for its own sake? If no greater purpose can be discerned or justified, business cannot morally justify its existence. It's a repugnant idea, an idea whose time has gone.

Finally, it's an empty idea. Profits can be made in lots of devious and transient ways. For people of affairs, a statement of purpose should provide guidance to the management of their affairs. To say that they should attract and hold customers forces facing the necessity of figuring out what people really want and value, and then catering to those wants and values. It provides specific guidance and has moral merit.

Something over twenty years ago this new way of thinking about business purposes led the more enlightened businesses slowly to distinguish operationally between marketing and selling, just as they now also distinguish between budgeting and planning, between long-range planning and strategic planning, between personnel management and human resources planning, between accounting and finance, between profit and cash flow, between the expected rate of return on investment and the present value of that expected rate of return.

All these are remarkably recent notions, few more than a generation old, developed mostly in our own lifetime. The most effective enterprises tend generally to practice them most conscientiously. They make a difference.

But of all these, the most powerful is the idea of marketing and the marketing view of the business process: that the purpose of a business is to create and keep a customer. There can be no corporate strategy that is not in some fundamental fashion a marketing strategy, no purpose that does not respond somehow to what people are willing to buy for a price. An asset consists of its capacity to generate revenue, either directly by its sale or by the sale of what it helps, finally, to produce. Even a quick, opportunistic raid on Wall Street has an underlying marketing rationale: that there's unrecognized or potential value greater than the value currently seen by others. The value is the asset, and that consists of its revenue-generating capability.

Indeed, those who usually consider themselves farthest removed from the unsavory business of sales and marketing are often its most ardent practitioners. One need only to observe the constant competitive jockeying among Wall Street firms to determine exactly where their names will appear on the printed syndication lists of underwritings. Why, if not for its future revenue-producing value, does so much genteel intrigue occupy the time of such self-consciously proper investment bankers? Even more telling is the Wall Street assumption about the importance of flattery and obsequiousness in its relations with gigantic corporate customers. Special brass-plated, unnumbered side doors quietly admit the impressionable bigwigs with especially sought-after investment banking accounts. Heavily starched linen tablecloths, Waterford crystal, and imported chefs once apprenticed to Paul Bocuse characterize the opulent private dining rooms from which clients and prospective clients may enjoy spectacular views of the bustling city far down below. The packaging in which investment banking firms present themselves to their clients gets all the concentrated care that goes into packaging such other comparably hustled products as toiletries for the teeming masses.

Both practices endure because both work. Both customers buy hopeful expectations, not actual things. The ability to satisfy those expectations is more effectively communicated by the packaging than by simple generic description of what's in the package. Feelings are more important than feeling. How we feel about a car is more important than how the car feels. And so it should be, especially when we consider that in the most important decisions of life, like marriage, for example, we mostly decide on the basis of not the cold figures in our intended's balance sheet but our warm feelings about our intended's figure.

There is, however, a problem. In my 1960 manifesto, "Marketing Myopia,"[1] marketing was elevated to a kind of corporate consciousness-raising. It asserted the intentionally narrow proposition that all energies should be directed toward satisfying the consumer, no matter what. The rest, given reasonable good

[1]See Chapter 8 of this book.

sense, would take care of itself. Nine years later, the manifesto having done its intended work, I offered a more conciliatory and sensible proposition: "The Marketing Matrix."[2] It incorporated some of the more broadly based wisdom about the corporate purpose that I've implied here, specifically, the need to balance, at some acceptable level of risk, the conditions of the external environment (customers, competition, government, and society) with the conditions of the internal environment (resources, competences, options, and wishes).

In "The Marketing Matrix," I asserted that early decline and certain death are the fate of companies whose policies are geared totally and obsessively to their own convenience at the total expense of the customer. The last of some twenty-five criteria offered to describe such companies was: "In setting your company goals, always set the standard in terms of production volume, revenues, profits, and expanded stockholder equity. Never state them also in terms of market factors, customer-need fulfillment, customer-service objectives, or market targets." In the matrix, the first part of this quoted example rated the top ranking of 9 on a nine-point scale of policies oriented entirely to the convenience of the company. The second part of this quoted example ("Never state them also in terms of market factors, customer need fulfillment" etc.) ranked a minimal 1 on a nine-point scale of policies oriented to the customer. This statement described, in short, a "9,1" company. There were examples also of "1,9" companies, "5,5" companies, and "9,9" companies. (The last were hard to find and as hard to imagine. Nobody can be *that* virtuous, not even under expert professorial guidance.)

The problem with the marketing concept was half-suggested in my chapter, "The Limits of the Marketing Concept," which followed directly after the matrix chapter. I am now about to drop the other shoe and suggest the remaining half of what is wrong with it. . . .

[2] Theodore Levitt, *The Marketing Mode* (New York: McGraw-Hill, 1969), Chap. 11, pp. 203–17.

In November 1976 IBM finally unveiled its first venture into the world of minicomputers—officially called Series/1. It did precisely what "Marketing Myopia" said it should: If customers prefer something that competes with your own offering, it is far more sensible for you to give it to them than to let competitors do it. It's better to participate in the destruction of your own market than to let it all be done by others. "Creative destruction," I called it, stealing that ringing phrase from Joseph Schumpeter, who was safely in the grave.

IBM was not the first company to enter the commercial computer business. It was, in fact, a particularly late latecomer. But in what seemed like no time, it captured at least 80 percent of the mainframe segment of what in 1976 was a $20 billion industry. It did so largely by being a singularly dedicated and spectacularly effective marketing company. Right through 1976, in its entire history this master symbol of modern science and technology had never had more than two senior executives who had not come up the organizational ladder primarily via the marketing route; and in that entire history, only one was a scientist. The master symbol of twentieth-century science and technology succeeded largely because of its marketing prowess, claims for the singular advantage imparted by the Forrester memory drum notwithstanding. It had industry managers who developed marketing plans, sales programs, and sales training for specifically targeted industries and companies in them. Its salesmen were as specialized in the industries to which they were assigned to sell as in the hardware they offered for sale. It bundled the software right into the product offering at a single set price, so that the customer was assured that the equipment would indeed be programmed to do the promised job. It designated installation facilities for the customer, redesigned his entire data collection and reporting systems, trained his data processing people, took the shakedown cruise, and then later developed new EDP applications to help the client even more. In the process the client became an even bigger and more dependent customer. Meanwhile the customer had the option of paying the single non-negotiable price either by paying outright for everything or by leasing it with virtually no punitive cancellation provisions. If ever there was a thoroughgoing marketing-oriented professional organization, it was IBM. And it worked like magic.

But in November 1976, with Series/1, all that was chucked. The sales force was made product-oriented rather than customer- and application-oriented. It became a dedicated sales force, dedicated to selling Series/1 hardware, and that's it. No special customer help. Sell, sell, sell to everybody on the landscape. And no more leasing options. Cash on the barrelhead, that's all, in spite of the fact that IBM's easy financial capability of offering the lease option had long given it a powerful competitive edge.

Series/1 is clearly a case of creative destruction—competing with yourself in order to save yourself. Nothing is really new about that. But abandoning marketing, sales, and pricing practices that had proved so effective for almost totally opposite practices, *that's* new.

That same week in November 1976 *Business Week's* lead article on Revlon, Inc., had the following headline and subhead: "Management Realists in the Glamour World of Cosmetics: Flair and flamboyance yield to controls, budgets, planning." We all know enough to guess from that what was in the article. We should also know that in the first year of an entirely new operating style, one that substituted management for mystique, sales rose 18 percent and profits 16 percent. Nine months into the next year sales were up another 23 percent and earnings 25 percent.

Just as successful managers and entrepreneurs who presume to give advice to all others on the basis of their own limited experiences are likely to give advice of limited relevance or utility, so do professors of business administration when their ideas become as rigid as other people's experiences. Series/1 switched to product-orientedness because conditions changed. In the Series/2 family (which was sure to come), customer- and application-orientedness once again became competitively appropriate. Likewise, who is to say that Revlon, no matter how big it gets, will be able always to function effectively and prosperously under its new managerial dispensation? Maybe for some purposes miscegenation will become the mode. In the words of Richard Barrie, the new president of Faberge Inc., "Somewhere along the line the industry has to shake off the old idea of management by mystique, yet still retain the mystique in its marketing." Who's to say?

The world of competitive enterprises openly facing each other in open markets is clearly a world of constant change. The marketing concept alerts us to this fact with the prescriptive injunction that to keep up requires studying and responding to what people want and value, and quickly adjusting to choices provided by competitors. It alerts us especially to the fact that competition often comes from outside the industry in which it finally occurs. Deeply implanted in these ideas is the notion that nothing is more important than the customer. The customer is, once more, King.

Suddenly IBM said in 1976 something that appeared quite different: "Be product-, not customer-oriented." Revlon appears to say, "Run the company, don't just run after the customer." And they're both obviously right. Being a "1,9" company (little company-oriented, highly customer-oriented) doesn't really work. Nor does being a "9,1" company. "9,9" is probably impossible, and "5,5" is probably an invitation to get outflanked on all sides.

The problem with the marketing concept, like all concepts in business, "laws" in physics, theories in economics, and all philosophies and ideologies, is a persistent tendency toward rigidity. They get dogmatized, interpreted into constantly narrower and inflexible prescriptions. In the case of the marketing concept, this is especially dangerous because of marketing's centrality in shaping the purposes, strategies, and tactics of the entire organization.

There is not, and cannot be, any rigid and lasting interpretation of what the marketing concept means in the specific ways a company should operate at any given time. Consider the cases of IBM and Revlon once again, and others.

*IBM*

In Series/1, as in its original entry into the computer business, the company was an imitator, a follower of others that preceded it by many years into the market with the product. But when the computer was a relatively new idea, its manufacturers knew a great deal more about its potential uses and usability than its potential users. The needs of potential users for the product had to be converted into wants. For wants to become purchases, the purchasers had to be carefully educated and guided to the product's uses. IBM had to educate its own sales people in the businesses to which they were to sell. All this was not so different from the creation of a mass market for eye shadow and eye liners just a decade ago. The big cosmetics houses had to establish demonstration counters in the stores to teach women how to use the product.

But once educated, either by the seller or by the mushrooming number of independent schools and courses available elsewhere as the markets expanded, the customer became able to make his own decisions about what he needed and how to use it. Thus the more successful the sellers became in teaching their prospects to want and use their products, the less dependent their users became on their sellers. In the first instance, "the product" being sold was a complex cluster of value satisfactions that included education, training, hands-on help, continuing advice, and quick availability for emergency situations. Later, in maturity, as the customer became more sophisticated, "the product" by definition became much simpler. It became, if not exactly a commodity, certainly not a complex cluster of things. It became, simply, a computer; simply an elegant little dish of eye shadow.

But more. As the computer got involved in more things in the corporation (largely at first with the suggested help of its manufacturers, and later more and more with the help of internal specialists in the user organization), it became a hard-to-manage monster. Different users within the organization made different and often conflicting demands on it. It became a continuing battle as to how to charge different departments and individuals for its use and for the accompanying software, which proved increasingly costly. All this finally created a market for the mini-computer. A corporate department, division, or even individual could now have his own small computer, programmed or programmable the way he wanted it. The invention of integrated circuits and then microprocessors turned a trickle into a flood.

With customers as sophisticated about the product as its sellers, with equipment costs low, and with strongly established competing sellers, the properly marketing-oriented thing for IBM to have done was precisely what it did: sell the simple hardware hard, without the attendant beneficiating clusters of the past. And it worked, like magic, just as did the personal computer a few years later.

### Revlon

As one finally lays down Andrew Tobias's book about the bizarre, coruscating career of Charles Revson, *Fire and Ice: The Story of Charles Revson, The Man Who Built the Revlon Empire,*[1] it is clear enough that toward the end Revson himself began to wonder about the fickle feudal terror with which he ran his empire. His escalating ad hominum hatred of his competitors merely mirrored his uncertainties about his managerial methods. When finally, after several shatteringly disastrous trials with managers of a different breed, he bought Michel C. Bergerac, the elegant French-born head of International Telephone and Telegraph Corporation's European operations, he set into motion at Revlon precisely the same kind of transformation that characterized Series/1. So urgently did Revson feel the need that he paid Bergerac $1.5 million just for signing up with Revlon, added a five-year contract for a salary of $325,000 a year, and three-year options for 70,000 shares of stock.

The problem was that competition had become more professionalized, with some of the biggest cosmetics houses having

[1] New York: Morrow, 1976.

been sold to drug and package-goods companies. The regulatory climate had become tougher. Distribution costs suddenly rose sharply, with competition making it harder to get compensating price rises. The tonnage of what moved out the factory gates suddenly became as crucial as the tone of its colors. Bergerac, whose Continental suaveness assuaged Revlon's hard-eyed glamour merchants, also earned their respect for his ITT management methods. No longer did the merchandising tail so vigorously wag the management dog—things were just as they should be. And it worked, like magic, more recent setbacks not withstanding.

*Allegheny Ludlum Steel*

Not so long ago stainless steel was a specialty steel. As with computers, customers had to be created by being taught and shown how to use it and what might be done to use it more abundantly to give them as well a competitive edge in *their* markets. The most important part of "the product" in those early days was not the steel itself but the design and application services provided by its chief manufacturer, Allegheny Ludlum Steel. Customers who were buying regular carbon steel, often more conveniently and in smaller quantities and with faster deliveries from local independent steel warehouses, now bought stainless steel quite willingly from the factory in larger quantities, with longer delivery times and no price shadings. They needed the factory's help on other matters more than the local warehouses' convenience.

In time, however, the independent warehouse market share of stainless steel rose. Allegheny Ludlum lost market share to competitors who sold more intensively through such warehouses. As in IBM's case, the customer, having been educated, no longer needed the supplier's attendant cluster of benefits— or, at least, needed less of them. Selling had to become less marketing-oriented, in the traditional sense, and more vigorously product- and sales-oriented. The number of warehouses had to be expanded or mill inventories expanded so as to speed up deliveries. In selling, "who you know" became relatively more important than "what you know."

Allegheny Ludlum changed to a new mode. It cannot be said that it scuttled the marketing concept. Instead it adopted a new version, a new marketing mode to deal with different needs and pressures. It did not ignore the customer, did not try to shove down his throat what he did not want. It merely simplified and streamlined "the product" to the customer's new specifications. The marketing concept remained in healthy charge, only now it called for something different from what was becoming, in some places, a rigidly dogmatized version of what it should be. And it worked, like magic.


### Chevrolet

Take, on the other hand, Chevrolet at General Motors. To read Alfred P. Sloan Jr.'s autobiographical *My Years with General Motors,* the advice one walks away with about running a successful company includes the idea that each item in the corporate product line should have a clearly distinctive identity, even though all the products are generically the same. "A car is a car," but not really. A Chevrolet was actually a low-priced entrée car, built for youthful peppiness yet roomy enough for new-family practicality. Next came the Pontiac step-up, a clear rise on the ladder of its owner's maturity and success. The larger, sturdier, more impressive Buick was for the solidly achieving middle manager, solidly on the road to better things. The Oldsmobile confirmed the attainment of those better things, and the Cadillac of the best things. Everybody knew clearly whom the car was for and exactly what its possession signified.

But for nearly two decades Chevrolet has now successfully violated Sloan's sacred dicta. Its *own* line of cars is itself wider than the entire General Motors line during Sloan's remarkably successful tenure as its chief executive officer. Not only is it wider in the sizes and prices of its cars and the options it offers the customers for them, but it even has more brand names of its own than Sloan ever had for the entire corporation. Meanwhile, all General Motors divisions have expanded their lines (up and down) across each other's turfs, and still the Chevrolet division does very well indeed, as does the entire corporation. And there's not the slightest whiff of evidence that it's a fragile castle built up momentarily out of sand.

Only a fool would argue that Chevrolet is not market-oriented or that General Motors is confused or has gone berserk. Certainly Alfred Sloan would approve, though his book implies the opposite. His book was written for times when cars were more important as symbols of attainment or expressions of aspirations. As the customer has changed, so has General Motors. And it's worked, like magic. Now even General Motors is proposing joint-venture production of subcompacts with Toyota. More magic.

### Exxon/Gulf

Finally, contrast Exxon and Gulf in the late 1950s for final proof that not even the luck of sudden riches from beneath the Arabian sands can save one from the necessity of doing things right. Gulf, at that time the biggest beneficiary of all, opted for quick conversion of oil into cash. It vastly expanded its service station network throughout the United States, leasing new lands for grand new stations and, just as fast, leasing marginal old stations in declining places. It even created a subregular grade of gasoline, Gulftane, to be sold along with regular and supreme for a penny less than regular.

Exxon opted for the opposite. It stuck to a policy of careful new-site selection and systematic elimination of older and declining stations. It began to buy the land and buildings of its service stations, thus balancing one type of expanding fixed asset in distant lands with another type "at home" where land values were on a secular rise. Moreover, owning rather than leasing its retail outlets made it easier to modify them to the specifications with which it sought to attract more customers per outlet. It worked harder at selecting and training its service station attendants. And though, like Gulf, it acquired lots more stations, it did so by buying not individual stations but entire companies that were specifically in the retail gasoline vending business. These Exxon upgraded and gradually shifted over to its own brand.

Long before October 1973, when suddenly oil-in-the-ground nearly quadrupled in value, and even before increasing ownership participations and expropriations by the Arab countries had reduced the share of what was physically left in the ground, it became apparent to Gulf that it had made a major error. It proved more costly to sell, in small and declining stations, gasoline made from cheap crude than to sell, in larger, more efficient ones, gasoline made from more costly crude. That discovery was foretold long before by others. But what proved more costly than these expenses alone was the attendant destruction of customers. In this case, as opposed to General Motors, expanding the line downward (Exxon expanded it upward, with a super-premium) and expanding the types of stations and locations produced confusion both within Gulf and among its customers. What little serious brand preference there is among major-brand gasoline buyers almost totally vanished for Gulf. With the greatest cost in money and human spirit within the corporation, Gulf for a decade now has been trying to undo and redo what it did so fast in just a few years before. In the 1950s it suddenly *did* become obsessively product-oriented. And it worked, like magic, in the wrong direction.

These examples tell us something we all know but don't always practice in our thoughts and actions: that to refer to an organization's principal marketing policies and strategies is to refer to that organization's principal overall corporate policies and strategies; its principal overall corporate policies and strategies cannot be shaped absent serious marketing considerations; that there are stages in the evolution of markets that may require policies and strategies that appear, falsely, to be perversely product-oriented; but in all this variation and adjustment and oscillation there must be persistent, remorseless, unforgiving, overriding orderliness and logic, no matter how much things seem to be different or to change. This overriding orderliness is the logic of the marketing concept. The market calls the tune, and the players had better play it right.

. . . When people of affairs in their twilight years presume to tell all others "how to do it" by telling merely how *they* happen to have done it, they may be right for their particular one day of the year but not necessarily for the remaining 364. It may be that it takes a Copernicus or a Kepler to study the entire whole in order for the rest of us to understand the underlying order, the constants that the daily pressures of events keep us from recognizing as constants. Down there in the competitive ring, things seldom look as panoramically clear as up in the stands where the observers sit in detached comfort.

But the fact that things can't be *seen* so well by those in the ring does not suggest that what they say is any less true. Certainly it will be more keenly felt. Nothing is as bracing or as certain as what is directly experienced. . . . The people of affairs, the practitioners out there who fight the bull, have fundamental wisdom. What they experience and feel in the difficult life of directing and managing organizations has to be respected. Only *they* know how it feels, but they know only how it feels in *their* particular circumstances and from the angle of vision provided them *down there* on the turf. Up here in the stands we know little of how it feels but perhaps a lot about how it looks, especially as compared with all the others down there on the turf. And from this comparison it is possible, though generally difficult, to know also what it means.

I see a constant that defines the best. It says that there can be no effective corporate strategy that is not marketing oriented, that does not in the end follow this unyielding prescript: The purpose of a business is to create and keep a customer. To do that, you have to do those things that will make people *want* to do business with you. All other truths on this subject are merely derivative.

# 2

---

# The Globalization of Markets

A powerful force now drives the world toward a single converging commonality, and that force is technology. It has proletarianized communication, transport, and travel, making them easily and cheaply accessible to the world's most isolated places and impoverished multitudes. Suddenly no place and nobody is insulated from the alluring attractions of modernity. Almost everybody everywhere wants all the things they have heard about, seen, or experienced via the new technological facilitators that drive their wants and wishes. And it drives these increasingly into global commonality, thus homogenizing markets everywhere.

The result is a new commercial reality—the explosive emergence of global markets for globally standardized products, gigantic world-scale markets of previously unimagined magnitudes.

Corporations geared to this new reality generate enormous

economies of scale in production, distribution, marketing, and management. When they translate these into equivalently reduced world prices, they devastate competitors that still live functionally in the disabling grip of old assumptions about how the world now works.

The world's aspirations now level simultaneously outward and upward, with increasingly larger portions of its population greedily wanting the modernity to which they are so constantly exposed. This in part explains the spectacular and staggering external debts from which so many nations now desperately suffer—not just the somewhat developed ones like Mexico, Brazil, and Rumania, but also several dozen Third World ones like Togo and Malawi. Each for the past decade has raced with exuberant recklessness toward the acquisition of modernity it could not or would not discipline itself to afford, each driven by the urgent demands of its people for what they knew as the comforts and indulgences of people in the developed nations.

All parts of the world want the most advanced things that the most advanced sectors already have, and no longer will merely the same classes and types of goods and services satisfy them. They also want them in their most advanced states of functionality, quality, reliability, service levels, and price competitiveness. Gone are the days when you could sell in the less-developed world last year's models or the used equipment you took as trade-in at home. Gone are the days when you could count on attractive markets in smaller countries for lesser versions of the advanced products that enjoyed solid markets in the advanced countries. Gone are the days when prices, margins, and profits abroad were generally better than at home.

Gone too, or going rapidly, are the accustomed differences in national and regional preferences regarding product or service features. Now in all respects the world levels up in all places to world-standard commonality.

This means the end of the multinational commercial world, and with it the end of the multinational corporation. The new reality is the globalization of markets, and with it the powerful materialization of the global corporation.

Not every company with a presence in more than one nation professes to be multinational. But some that pretend or seem to be are not that at all. Where the purpose of occupancy in another land is merely to extract or even to process raw materials for use in the home country, the company cannot be sensibly though of as a multinational. To be meaningfully multinational, a company must have an operating presence in the markets of other nations. To be merely an extractor, processor, or buyer of nature's riches elsewhere for use and sale at home, no matter how gigantic or geographically dispersed these efforts might be, is to be merely a multinational buyer, not a multinational business. To be a multinational business requires an operating customer-getting presence of meaningful scale in a variety of national markets. The difference is on the order of that between an international tourist and a committed world citizen.

The multinational and the global corporation are not the same. The multinational corporation operates in a number of countries, where in each case it adjusts with accommodating care and therefore high relative costs to the presumptive special conditions of the particular country. In contrast, the global corporation operates with resolute constancy and therefore at low relative costs as if the entire world (or major regions of it) were a single, largely identical entity; it does and sells the same things in the same single way everywhere.

Which strategy is better is a matter not of opinion but of necessity. Widespread communication and travel pound the same constant drumbeat of modern possibilities into the human consciousness everywhere, particularly the possibilities to lighten and enhance work, to raise living standards, and to divert and entertain. Modernity is not only the wish but actually also the widespread practice, even among those who cling with philistine passion or religious fervor to ancient attitudes and heritages.

Who can forget during the worst of the 1979 Iranian uprisings the televised scenes of inflamed young men in fashionable French-cut trousers and silky body shirts open to the waist, with raised modern weapons, thirsting for blood in the name of Islamic fundamentalism?

In Brazil thousands of eager migrants from the preindustrial Bahian wilderness swarm daily into the exploding coastal cities, quickly to install television sets in crowded corrugated-iron huts before which, next to battered Volkswagens, they make sacrificial candlelight offerings of fruit and fresh-killed chickens to the Macumban spirits.

In the fratricidal war of extermination against the Ibos, daily television reports revealed, for all the world to see, soldiers in remote places, with bloodstained swords, listening to transistor radios and drinking Coca-Cola.

In the isolated Siberian city of Krasnoyarsk, absent of paved streets and uncontrolled news, occasional Western travelers are stealthily propositioned for their cigarettes, their digital watches, and even the clothes off their backs.

A thriving underground trade in modern weapons and military mercenaries reaches deeply into underdeveloped places, exceeded in magnitude only by organizing smuggling of electronic equipment, used automobiles, Western clothing, cosmetics, and pirated movies.

A thousand little suggestive scenes attest to the ubiquity of what is so clearly obvious in well-traveled places elsewhere: the rapid homogenization of the world's wants and wishes regarding the most advanced things the world makes and sells, and the ways in which these are made and sold. Daniel J. Boorstin, Librarian of Congress and author of the monumental trilogy, *The Americans,* has characterized our age as driven by ''The Republic of Technology,'' whose ''supreme law . . . is convergence, the tendency for everything to become more like everything else.''

In business this has clearly translated into global markets, with global corporations selling the same single standardized products—autos, steel, chemicals, petroleum, cement, agricultural commodities and equipment, industrial and commercial construction, banking, insurance, computers, semiconductors, transport, electronic instruments, pharmaceuticals, and telecommunications, to mention only a few of the obvious—largely in the same single ways everywhere.

Nor is the sweeping gale of global competition confined

merely to so-called commodity or high-tech products, where standardization is facilitated by customers and users who speak the universal language of science and engineering. The transforming winds whipped up by proletarianized communication and travel enter every crevice of life everywhere. Boorstin wrote: "The converging forces of everyday experience [that 'The Republic of Technology' has ushered in] are both sublingual and translingual. People who never could have been persuaded to read Goethe will eagerly drive a Volkswagen. . . . Technology dilutes and dissolves ideology."

Commercially, nothing confirms this so much as the booming success of McDonald's everywhere from the Champs Elysees to the Ginza, of Coca-Cola in Bahrain and Pepsi in Moscow, and of rock music, Greek salad, Hollywood movies, Revlon cosmetics, Sony televisions, and Levi jeans everywhere. Thus "high-touch" products are as globalized as high-tech. Indeed, globalization goes even further. The Princeton sociologist Suzanne Keller notes that everywhere that's touched by industrialization and urbanization is characterized by rising divorce rates and two-paycheck marriages, declining birth rates, and a generation gap in sexual mores.

Both the high-tech and the high-touch ends of life's continuum merge into global commonality, gradually consuming the undistributed middle into the orbit of cosmopolitanism. Nothing is exempt, and nothing can stop it. Everywhere everything gets more like everything elese, as the world's preference structure gets pressed into homogenized commonality.

Ancient differences in national tastes and preferences, in modes of doing business and the institutions of commerce, fall before the homogenizing modernity everybody experiences via the new technological facilitators. The global commonality of what's preferred leads inescapably to the global standardization of products, of manufacturing, and of the institutions of trade and commerce. Small nation-based markets are transmogrified and expanded into large global-sized markets, with accompanying economies of scale in production, distribution, marketing, and management. This leads to growing world competition based on efficiency in production, distribution, marketing, and management. Inevitably this generates worldwide competitive intensity focused powerfully on price. With price therefore once again the dominant basis of world competition, the way to be the most effective price competitor is to incorporate superior quality and reliability into the price offering. This converges finally into world-standardized product lines that compete on the basis of appropriate value—the best combinations of price, quality, reliability, and delivery for products that, in respect to design, functionality, and even fashionability, are globally identical.

That, and little else, explains much of the surging success of such a vast variety of Japanese companies dealing in such a vast variety of products around the globe—both tangible products like steel, cars, motorcycles, hi-fi equipment, farm machinery, robots, microprocessors, carbon fibers, and now even textiles, and intangible products like banking, shipping, general contracting, and soon, certainly, computer software. Nor are high-quality and low-cost operations incompatible, as argued unanimously with vigorous vacuity for nearly twenty years until 1982 by varieties of data engineers and hustling consulting organizations. The reported data are incomplete, wrongly analyzed, and contradictory. "You can observe a lot just by watching," said Yogi Berra. To "observe" means to put your mind to what the eyes see. The observing mind apprehends everywhere that low-cost operations are the hallmark of superior managerial cultures whose superiority requires and produces superior quality in all that they do and touch. High quality and low cost are not opposing paths. They are the necessary compatible identities of superior practice.

To deny that Japan's case fits the definition of global practices with glib references to certain facts—that at home Japanese cars have right-side drives but they export left-side drives to the United States and the European Continent, that they will sell office machines through distributors in the United States but direct at home, that Japanese bankers speak Portuguese in Brazil, that in France Japanese products and packages are labeled in French—all this is to mistake a difference for a distinction. The steering wheel locations are different, and so are the distribution channels and the language. What is distinctive about Japan is the unrelenting drive for economizing and value-enhancing distinction. And that spells everywhere and in everything a drive for global standardization at high-quality levels.

The governing theory is that with reasonably restrained concern for suitability, if you force costs and prices down and push quality and reliability in all things up, everywhere around the world customers will prefer your world-standardized generic offerings in rising proportions, regardless of what conventional market research and even common observations may suggest about the existence of different national and intranational tastes, preferences, needs, and institutions. In this theory the Japanese have been repeatedly vindicated, as was Henry Ford with the Model T in his time. And they have been repeatedly copied with remarkable success by companies in South Korea (television sets and heavy construction), Malaysia (personal calculators and micro computers), Brazil (auto parts and tools), Colombia (apparel), Singapore (optical equipment), and yes, even in the United States (office copiers, computers, bicycles, castings), Western Europe (automatic washing machines), Rumania (housewares), Hungary (apparel), Yugoslavia (furniture), and Israel (pagination equipment).

Of course, not even large companies that operate only in a single nation or even in a single large city standardize everything they make, sell, or do within their chosen markets. That's why they have product lines, not just one single product version, and multiple distribution channels and the like. There are neighborhood, local, regional, ethnic, and institutional differences even within large cities. But all that is beside the point. Though companies always customize for specific segments, success in a world whose wants become more homogenized requires of such companies strategic and operating modes that search for opportunities to sell to similar segments throughout the globe to achieve the scale economies that keep their costs competitive.

Seldom these days is a segment in one country unique to that country alone. It is found everywhere, thus available to sellers from everywhere. Small local segments in this fashion become globally standardized, large, and therefore subject to global competition, especially price competition.

The globally oriented competitor will constantly seek opportunities to achieve global scale by globally standardizing everything he does in order to maintain his cost competitiveness. The otherwise globally oriented competitor who digresses from this mode does so at his peril, and only after having exhausted all possibilities of standardization while retaining good profitability with segmentation. Meanwhile, having digressed and diverged from standardization, he will push constantly for its reinstatement instead of drifting further into minuscule scale diseconomies.

This does not mean the end of choice or market segments. It means the beginning of price competition for quality products aimed at fewer but larger global market segments.

Increasingly in our homogenized world trouble will stalk the company that lacks a clarified global focus and is inattentive to the simple economics of simplicity and standardization. The most endangered companies are those that produce largely for, and dominate, relatively small domestic markets with high-value-added products for which there are small markets in all countries. With transportation low proportionately to their total costs, and in any case relatively cheap, competitors with global reach, with products produced more cheaply under modern scale-efficient conditions, will successfully enter the distant sheltered markets to which provincial producers have become complacently accustomed. This means the end of domestic territoriality—certainly for products with these characteristics. No matter how diminutive they may otherwise seem, the globe is their competitive crucible.

The new Republic of Technology homogenizes world tastes, wants, and possibilities into global-market proportions, which allows for world-standardized products, giving the global producer powerful scale advantages. When his lower costs are offered to the international multitudes, markets are expanded doubly, as previous holdouts for local preferences in product features, design, and functionality sacrifice these to the superior

27

attractions of price alone. Thus the strategy of standardization not only responds to world homogenized markets but actually expands them with aggressively low prices.

In this way the new technological juggernaut taps into an ancient motivation: to make one's money go as far as possible. And that is something no one has ever suggested is anything but universal.

The difference between the hedgehog and the fox, in distinguishing between Dostoevski and Tolstoy, Sir Isaiah Berlin explained, is that the fox knows a lot about a great many things, but the hedgehog knows everything about one great thing. The multinational corporation knows a lot about a great many countries, and congenially adapts itself to their supposed differences. The global corporation knows one great thing about all countries, and lures them to its custom by capitalizing on the one great thing they all have in common. The global corporation looks to the nations of the world not for how they are different but for how they are alike. While it recognizes the presumed need to be globally competitive as well as nationally responsive, it seeks constantly in every way to standardize everything into a common global mode. And it does this, to repeat the point, by capitalizing on what, increasingly, is the one great thing all nations and people have in common.

The one great thing all nations and people have in common is scarcity. Nobody takes scarcity lying down. Everybody everywhere wants to get out of the inescapability of his insufficiency as much as possible. Everybody wants more. Even those blessedly gone hippies who sought, for a decade, escape in communal penury, proclaimed unctuously that "less is more." They too wanted more—their kind of more—in exchange for the scarcity they could not escape and would not abide.

Almost nowhere is anyone totally self-sufficient. Hence we have everywhere some sort of trade, barter, and money. Division of labor and specialization of production are the means by which people and nations optimize their benefits via trade, barter, and money. Experience teaches everyone the three special qualities of money: scarcity, difficulty of acquisition, and transcience. This explains the reluctance with which people part with it and the care they exercise in doing so. It also explains part of the "one great thing" the global corporation knows: If you can get the price low enough, the increasingly homogenized world will increasingly take your world-standardized offering, even if it isn't exactly what your old mother said was suitable, what immemorial custom decreed as right, or what market-research fabulists asserted was preferred.

The implacable truth of all modern production—of tangible as well as intangible products—is that the more standardized product costs less than the less standardized product, and that the large-scale production of standardized products or components is generally cheaper within a wide range of volume than small-scale production. It is cheaper to do things one or two ways, rather than three, four, or five ways. Hence if the world is treated as one or two distinctive product markets, it can be more economically served than if it is treated as three, four, or five product markets. The global corporation strives to treat the world as fewer standardized markets rather than as many customized markets. It actively seeks and vigorously works toward global convergence. That is its real distinction. Modernity is its mission and price competition its mode, even when it sells top-of-the-line, high-priced products. By contrast, the multinational corporation willingly accepts obvious vestigial national differences, questioning not the possibilities of their transformation, recognizing not how the world is ready and even eager for the benefactions of modernity, especially when the price is right. The multinational corporation's accommodating mode to visible national differences is medieval, and so are its offerings and its prices.

As I have said, global convergence is not the special case of technologically and scientifically advanced products, of high-tech as opposed to high-touch. Consider once more the amazing cases of Coca-Cola and Pepsi-Cola, which by any conceivable criteria are globally standardized products sold globally with standardized communications, and welcomed eagerly by everybody everywhere. Most extraordinary is the fact that both are a product that is ingested through the mouth, crossing to everybody's satisfaction multitudes of taste buds trained immemori-

THE MARKETING IMAGINATION

ally to an enormous variety of preferred and deeply ingrained local differences as to flavor, consistency, effervescence, and aftertaste. Yet everywhere these two invariant products are successfully and expandingly sold in the same way. So too with cigarettes, especially American-made cigarettes, which make year-to-year inroads almost everywhere on hitherto powerful preferences for other tobacco blends. These are not special incidents. They are examples of the general drift toward world homogenization, even in high-touch products, of the means by which all products are distributed and financed, of the way they are priced, and of the institutions through which and the ways by which they are sold.[1] Nothing is exempt. The products and methods of the industrialized world play a single tune for all the world, and all the world eagerly dances to it.

The world moves inexorably forward to greater global convergence in all things, propelled by the technological forces that shape our times. Such differences as remain are vestiges of the hardened inherited past as to cultural preferences, national tastes and standards, and the institutions of business itself. Some yield gradually, while others actually themselves expand globally. That explains, for example, the growth of so-called ethnic markets the world over—specialty segments in foods, clothing, entertainment, and even retail institutions such as delicatessens, boulangeries, and antique shops. These are not denials or contradictions of global homogenization, but rather its confirmation. Without the generalized homogenization of tastes and preferences there would be no distinction in ethnicity or specialization. To have the latter requires the dominant presence of the former. The global growth of ethnic markets confirms the greater presence of global standardization in all else and is itself an example of the global standardization of segments. Everywhere there is Chinese food, pita bread, country and western music, pizza, and jazz. The global pervasiveness of

[1] In 1968 Robert D. Buzzell published a landmark article ("Can You Standardize Multinational Marketing?", *Harvard Business Review*, November/December 1968), in which he catalogued the conditions that facilitated and inhibited standardization. Regarding the latter, he pointed out, even then, the rapidity with which barriers to standardization were falling—and in all cases they fell to the better economics and alleviations of more advanced ways of doing things.

ethnic forms represents the cosmopolitanization of specialty segments. Again, globalization does not mean the end of segments. It means, instead, their expansion to worldwide proportions.

Vast differences in products and product features remain between different nations that have a heavy presence of multinational corporations. And there remain vast differences in how these corporations conduct business in those nations. But many of these differences merely reflect the respectful accommodation of multinational corporations to what they believe are fixed local preferences. They *believe* things are fixed not because they are, but because those who believe this have a fixed habit of thinking and acting multinationally rather than globally. They simply have not pressed at all, or have not pressed properly, for global standardization.

I do not mean to advocate systematic disregard of local or national differences. I maintain, rather, that sensitivity to them does not require one to ignore the possibilities of doing things differently or better. There are, for example, enormous differences among the Middle Eastern oil countries. Some are socialist, some monarchies, some republics. Some take their legal heritage from the Napoleonic Code, some from the Ottoman Empire, some from the British Common Law, and all are influenced by Islam. But in all, to do business there means to personalize the business relationship in an almost obsessively intimate fashion. It requires respecting national holidays, which means, during the Ramadan, a month of starting business discussions after ten o'clock at night, when people are tired and full of food. One almost never has the option of going without a local partner or co-venturer. A local lawyer is a must, as are irrevocable letters of credit. But, as Coca-Cola's Senior Vice President Sam Ayoub said recently, "Arabs are much more capable of making distinctions between cultural and religious purposes on the one hand and economic realities on the other than is generally assumed. Islam is compatible with science and modern times." [2]

Nor are barriers to modernity confined to countries such as these. There are legal and financial impediments to the free

[2] In a speech given in summer 1982 at Pebble Beach, California.

transfer of technology and data across the boundaries even of European Common Market countries. There is resistance to radio and television interference (i.e., "pollution") among proximate European countries. But the past is a good guide to the future on these matters—namely, that with persistence and appropriate means, in the past barriers against superior technologies and better economics have always fallen. It is very much a matter of time and effort.

Many companies that have made the effort tried to standardize world practice and tried to export wholesale, without accommodation or change, products and practices to other nations, and failed miserably in the process. Such failures have generally been seized upon as evidence of bovine stupidity in the face of abject impossibility. Advocates of the possibility of global standardization have used such failures as examples merely of failures of execution. The result is a standoff.

Still, poor execution explains many failed attempts to standardize world practices and products. Horror stories are abundant, too obvious to merit recitation for our education. What are far more instructive are stories of failures to conceive of the global possibilities, and more especially of failure of nerve.

Consider the case of fully automatic home laundry equipment in Western Europe at the time when few homes had even semi-automatic or even manual machines. Hoover, Ltd., with its parent company headquartered in North Canton, Ohio, and a long, prominent presence in England as a vacuum cleaner producer, had also established a strong presence there with its Hoover-branded washing machines, and to a lesser extent also with washers on the Continent. Its large washing machine plant in England operated uneconomically far below capacity, with little possibility of filling it with production for the U.K. market alone. It needed substantially greater sales on the Continent for either its semi-automatic or its fully automatic machines. Thinking itself properly market-oriented, it conducted carefully professional competitive and consumer-preference studies in Great Britain and in each of the major Continental countries. The research proved clearly enough, as Exhibit 1 shows, what product features were preferred in each country.

EXHIBIT 1.  CONSUMER PREFERENCES AS TO AUTOMATIC WASHING MACHINE FEATURES, BY COUNTRY

| Features | United Kingdom | Italy | Germany | France | Sweden |
|---|---|---|---|---|---|
| Shell dimensions[1] | 34" & narrow | Low & narrow | 34" & wide | 34" & narrow | 34" & wide |
| Drum material | Enamel | Enamel | Stainless steel | Enamel | Stainless steel |
| Loading | Top | Front | Front | Front | Front |
| Front porthole | Yes/No | Yes | Yes | Yes | Yes |
| Capacity | 5 kilos | 4 kilos | 6 kilos | 5 kilos | 6 kilos |
| Spin speed | 700 rpm | 400 rpm | 850 rpm | 600 rpm | 800 rpm |
| Water heating system | No[2] | Yes | Yes[3] | Yes | No[2] |
| Styling features | Inconspicuous appearance | Brightly colored | Indestructible appearance | Elegant appearance | Strong appearance |
| Washing action | Agitator | Tumble | Tumble | Agitator | Tumble |

[1] 34" height was in the process of being adopted as a standard work-surface height in Europe.

[2] "No," because most U.K. and Swedish homes had centrally heated hot water.

[3] "Yes," because Germans preferred to launder at temperatures higher than generally provided centrally.

The incremental variable unit costs of customizing to just a few of the preferences of each national market were as follows:

| | |
|---|---|
| Stainless steel vs. enamel drum | £1.00 |
| Porthole window | .10 |
| Spin speed of 800 rpm vs. 700 rpm | .15 |
| Water heater | 2.15 |
| 6 vs. 5 kilos capacity | 1.10 |
| | £6.10 = $18.20 at the exchange rate of that time. |

The costs of customizing to the other preferences would have involved considerable plant investment, as well as additional variable costs. At the time the lowest retail prices (in pounds sterling) of leading locally produced brands in the various countries were:

| | |
|---|---|
| U.K. | £110 |
| France | £114 |
| Germany | £113 |
| Sweden | £134 |
| Italy | £ 57 |

Unfortunately, product customization to the preferred specifications of each country would have put Hoover into poorly price-competitive positions in each of those countries, owing partly to these product extras but also substantially to the higher manufacturing costs incurred simply by having short production runs of machines with each separate feature. Since this was before the Common Market tariff-reduction programs became effective, Hoover also suffered from the additional competitive disadvantage of tariff duties in each Continental country.

Yet an imaginatively systematic analysis of actual automatic sales in each of these countries would have revealed the following incongruities:

1. Italian automatics, small in capacity and size, low-powered, without built-in heaters, with porcelain-enamel tubs, but aggressively low-priced, had substantial market shares in all countries, including Germany, and everywhere they were gaining share rapidly.
2. The by far best-selling automatics in Germany were ideally suited to the indicated German preferences but also were by far the highest-priced machines available in that country. They were also by far the most heavily advertised machines, by a factor of 3 to 1 over the next most-promoted brand.
3. Italy, with the lowest penetration of washing machines of any kind, was rapidly going directly to automatics, skipping over the pattern in other nations, where people went first to hand-wringer manually assisted machines and then to semi-automatic and finally to automatic machines. First-time Italian machine buyers generally bought the aggressively priced small fully automatics.
4. Cold-water and tepid-water laundering was just beginning to be promoted by detergent manufacturers, as had been successfully done in the United States by both detergent and machine manufacturers.

The growing success of small, low-powered, low-speed, low-capacity, low-priced Italian machines, even in Germany against the remarkable success of the preferred but most highly priced and most highly promoted German brand, contained a message that would not be noticed by people wedded confidently to a distorted version of the marketing concept—that you provide the customer with what is wanted rather than blindly with what you want to produce.

The message was clear enough for anyone with imagination and effort to see: In prevailing conditions people preferred, as in the case of the Italian equipment, the low-priced automatic over the manual or semi-automatic equipment, and certainly over higher-priced automatics, regardless of the failure of low-priced automatics to fulfill all their expressed preferences as to features. This was true even of the supposedly meticulous and

35

uncompromising Germans, though the low-priced machines violated strong German preferences as to superheated water temperature, spinning speed, and size of equipment. And equally clear is that people were profoundly subject to promotional influence when it came to automatic washers, for in Germany, again, the most heavily promoted "ideal" machine was also by far the most highly priced and had the highest market share.

The combined message of these two facts is also clear enough: People wanted automatic rather than manual or semi-automatic home laundry equipment. There were two ways in which they were influenced to buy that preference—by low price, regardless of other preferred product features, and by heavy promotion, regardless of price. Both helped homemakers get what they most wanted, the superior benefits bestowed by fully automatic machines.

The message for Hoover should have been obvious: produce only the simple, high-quality machine preferred by the British and sell that same machine aggressively on the Continent at the powerfully competitive low price afforded by the 17 percent cost reduction that the elimination of £6.10 worth of extra features made possible. Suggested retail prices could have been somewhat under £100, with a sufficient extra pool of funds "saved" from the then unneeded plant modifications to support a service network and to launch aggressive media promotions on the Continent. The media message should have been that *this* is the machine that "you," the homemaker, *deserve* to have, and by means of which your relentlessly repetitive heavy daily household burdens are reduced, so that *you* may spend more constructive time for more elevating attention to your children and more loving attention to your husband. Indeed, communications should have targeted wife and husband jointly so as to implant in the latter, preferably in the presence of the former, a sense of obligation to provide an automatic washer for her even before an automobile for himself.

An aggressively low price, made possible by European standardization, combined with heavy promotion to the common global desire for alleviation from menial and repetitive work, and the common desire for enhanced familial and connubial relations, would have overcome all previously expressed preferences as to special equipment features. Such a program would have reflected understanding of the "one great thing" about everybody: People everywhere want their burdens lightened, and they will pay to do so if they can afford it and are told how.

No matter how good the execution of a country-customized product strategy would have been, it would certainly have been suboptimal, and probably a failure. The issue was not execution but conception; not to do things right, but to do the right things.

The whole project got off on the wrong foot. It asked people what they wanted in the way of features alone rather than seeing what they visibly wanted as to life itself. The idea of a responsively responsible line of products tailored attentively to each nation not only would have been dumb but, even worse, would have been thoughtless. Unconscious of its dumbness and thoughtlessness, it would have asked, with erroneous pride in having practiced the marketing concept to its fullest, the wrong questions. In actual fact, it practiced that concept not at all. It merely looked at data and applied to them neither thought nor imagination—like the anthropocentrists in the Middle Ages who with everyday clarity saw the sun revolving in predictable ellipses around the earth, as opposed to Copernicus, who interpreted a more compelling reality, having no more data than they, but a more searching mind.

With much effort and imagination, Copernicus, like the hedgehog, knew everything about one great thing. The one great thing that distinguishes the global from the multinational corporation is that it accepts the reality of modernity, in which the republic of technology drives everything relentlessly toward global convergence, for better or for worse—toward the alleviation of life and the expansion of discretionary time and spending power. The new role of the global corporation is, in that respect, profoundly different from what has been the role of the ordinary corporation in its brief, turbulent, and remarkably protean history. The role of the global corporation is to orchestrate commercially the irresistible vectors of technology and globalization into benign benefactions for all the globe's inhabitants. It is a

37

role created not by fate or nature or God, but by the necessity of open commerce itself, a necessity that compels action in which only the fit and the brave prosper and survive.

In the United States that necessity imposed itself on two of the nation's industries long before they became consciously aware of it. After more than a generation of regular and acrimonious industrywide labor shutdowns, there has not been an industrywide strike by the United Steelworkers union since 1959 or by the United Automobile Workers union of General Motors (which would shut down two-thirds of U.S. production), since 1970. Both reflect the realization that these industries had become global, that shutting down U.S. manufacturing would not shut out U.S. customers. Overseas suppliers helped keep customers in operation and reduced domestic competitive viability. Globalization of competition compelled domestic adjustment to realities to which the unions accommodated before the companies themselves.

Since the emergence of the marketing concept a quarter of a century ago, the more managerially advanced corporations of the Western world have been driven by a responsive eagerness to produce for customers what they clearly wanted rather than merely trying to sell them what was being produced. This has been accompanied by the creation of awesomely large and costly marketing departments complete with ponderously professional market researchers. It has also resulted in extraordinary product-line and operations proliferations—highly tailored products and delivery systems for many different markets, market segments, and nations.

We have witnessed also, more recently, the extraordinary success of Japanese companies all around the globe. Significantly, they operate almost entirely without marketing departments or market research of the kind so prevalent in the West. Yet, in the colorful words of John F. Welch, Jr., General Electric's chief executive, the Japanese, coming from a small chain of resource-poor islands on the other side of the globe, from an entirely alien culture, with an almost impenetrably complex language, have "cracked the code" of western markets. They have

38

done it not by looking with mechanistic thoroughness at how markets and customers are different, but rather like Copernicus, by searching for meaning with a deeper wisdom. This has led them to discover the one great thing all relevant markets have in common. That is the overwhelming desire for dependable, world-standard modernity in all things, and at aggressively low prices, even "low" in the higher-priced product categories and customer segments.

The lower the price the greater the likelihood that the world will accept standardized modernity in all its major sectors and segments rather than insist on higher-priced customization to inherited preferences and ancient practices. The more world standardization and lower prices expand world markets, the lower the production and delivery costs with which to push prices down and expand markets further. This is an old truth clearly recognized during the early stages of the Industrial Revolution, when the British textile industry dominated world markets even in their most inaccessible and primitive backwaters. And today the Japanese typically deliver value that is irresistible everywhere, even to people and places that market-research technocrats conclude with superficial certainty have proliferated varities of product and delivery preferences that push costs and prices ever upward and increasingly out of customer and competitive reach.

To speak of global convergence and commonality is not to ignore the persistence of important differences between nations, areas, and cultures. But this requires making some distinctions. The difference between a distinction and a difference is that differences are perfectly consistent with fundamental underlying and surrounding samenesses. Persistent differences can complement rather than simply oppose the advancement of commonalities—in society and business no less than in physics and space. There is, simultaneously, matter and antimatter. The earth is round, but for most purposes in everyday life it's sensible to treat it as flat. Space is curved, but not much for most purposes here on earth.

The Chinese are different in a whole variety of visible ways from the Germans and the Zimbabwe, but still all three are remarkably alike regarding love, hate, fear, greed, envy, joy, patriotism, pornography, material comforts, mysticism, and the role of food in their lives. The world is driven and held together by the common bonds that unite its differences. Increasingly, modern times create new bonds of commonality that, in themselves, cause lots of problems and raise lots of questions. But how problematical are those problems, how quizzical those questions? Consider Maine and California. It takes no special talents to see the differences—the differences between the socially avant-garde and the socially rear guard; between L. L. Bean and Frederick's of Hollywood; between Silicon Valley and the Penobscot Valley; between Bar Harbor and Muscle Beach or the Mendocino coast.

Yet with all these persistent differences, consider the persuasive evidence of the homogenizing character of American life. If a large nation can be so thoroughly homogenized by the combinative forces of tradition, technology, aspirations, and communications, and yet retain powerfully persistent and significant differences within its borders, then it's reasonable to suggest that commonality can also advance and thrive among disparate nations and regions.

The wider a company's global reach, then the larger the number of differences it is likely to encounter as to national and regional preferences regarding product features, distribution institutions, promotional media, and the like.

Nor is there any presumption, as we have seen, that differences in preferences as to product features, tastes, and market arrangements are largely confined to high-touch products. Evolution does not move linearly along perfectly parallel lines in all parts of the world's disparateness, even in this world of microprocessor modernity. In the United States almost all manufacturers of microprocessors check them for reliability and functionality by what's called the parallel testing system. In Japan, the preference is almost totally for the much different sequential testing system. The result is that Teradyne Corp., the world's largest producer of microprocessor test equipment, makes one line for the United States and one for Japan. That's easy. What's not so easy, and is equally problematic for other firms facing similar situations, is how to organize and manage the marketing effort. The possibilities are to organize by product, by region, by function, or by some matrix combination. Thus, one might have separate marketing organizations for Japan and for the United States, the former obviously specializing in parallel test equipment and the latter in sequential test equipment. Or one might organize by product, the one group ending up working largely in Japan and the other in the United States. A single manufacturing facility might produce both systems, with a single marketing operation that sells both, or a separate marketing operation for each, and the like. If the system is organized by product, should the group that handles the parallel system, whose major market is in the United States, also attempt a sales effort in Japan, thus competing with the sequential group that is focused solely on the Japan market? And vice versa? If the effort is organized regionally, how do the regional groups divide their efforts between pushing (should they?) the parallel system and pushing the sequential system? If the company is organized by function, how do you get commitment in marketing, for example, for one line as against the other?

The point is obvious enough. A major problem in a world of increasing global commonality is how to organize and manage in the face of persistent differences in the context of a generalized drift toward and preference for standardization.

There is no formula to answer that question, not even a satisfactory contingent one. What may work well for one company in a given situation may fail for another in that very same situation. The reasons have to do with the capabilities, the histories, the reputations, the resources, and even the cultures and spirits of the two organizations. In that respect the governing determinants of success are no different from those of success in love and courtship. Even limited experience in such matters affirms that under identical conditions different people will perform differently, that what works for one person in that situation may not for another. The contingencies that prescribe what's important do not predictably define what's appropriate. Not even specific knowledge of the specific actors is enough to assure the appropriateness of the advice. As one would not, in affairs of love, give in a specific situation the same advice to Marcello Mastroianni as to Woody Allen, so also one would not in affairs of commerce give the same advice in a specific situation to Olivetti and IBM, or to Banco di Roma and Credit Lyonnais.[3]

Differences persist. The distinction between the past and the future is that technology and economics favor commonality, forcing onto the modern corporation, regardless of size, the necessity constantly to reach out for adaptation to what's new while functioning effectively with what remains unchanged and abides.

One of the most powerful yet also least celebrated ways in which commerce is being driven toward global standardization is via the monetary system and the international investment process.

In today's times money is simply electronic impulses. With the speed of light it gets moved effortlessly between distant money centers (and even lesser places). A change of ten basis points in the price of a bond will cause an instant and massive shift of money from, say, London to Tokyo. This has profound effects on how companies throughout the world operate. Even Japan, with its high debt-to-equity balance sheets that are "guaranteed" to the banks by various presumptions in that society regarding the superior virtue of "the long view," or "guaranteed" in other ways by government policy—even there, upward shifts in interest rates in other parts of the world attract capital in proportions that are powerfully felt. This accounts for the rising proportion in recent years of Japanese global corporations going to the world's equity markets for funds. Debt is simply too remunerative in other high-yielding countries to keep enough at home to feed the Japanese need for capital. And as

---

[3] For some recent evidence of the contingent nature of all this, see Christopher Bartlett, "MNCs: Get off the reorganization merry-go-round," *Harvard Business Review,* March/April 1983; and C. Bartlett, Y. Doz, and C. K. Prahalad, "Global Competitive Pressures and Host Country Demands: Managing Tensions in MNC's," *California Management Review,* Spring 1981.

interest rates rise, equity becomes for the issuer a more attractive option. The effect on Japanese enterprise will be increasingly transforming. As the equity proportions of Japanese companies' capitalizations rise, so will their need to respond to the shorter-term investment horizons of the equity markets. Thus the much-vaunted Japanese corporate advantage of being able, because of their capital structures, to take "the long view" rather than requiring early results will gradually disappear. Driven thus increasingly to respond to the equity market's demand for early results, so the world will also increasingly be driven toward a common convergence in the forces that influence how business is conducted, not just in how business responds to its markets.

On all fronts, globalization converges into a common coalescence. The differences that persist affirm a fixed and ancient dictum of economics—namely, that the world is driven by what happens at the margin or at the appendages, not at the core; that significance attaches not to the common or typical or average condition but rather to the edges of events. Thus, in ordinary competitive analysis, economics affirms that what's important is not the average price but the marginal price, the price at the unstable interface of newly erupting conditions. What counts in commercial affairs is not what's predominantly happening but what's happening at the cutting edge; not the persistent and predominant differences among nations regarding tastes, preferences, and practices, but the underlying similarity of what happens increasingly to them all at the margin, forces that cumulate everywhere into an overwhelming and predominant commonality.

Nor is it useful to refer in contrast to the persistence of a vast variety of trade and tax barriers that block the globalization of markets. Economic nationalism and various philistine reinforcers are not likely to disappear. They have a powerful persistence. But, as in the case of the globalization of investment funds, the world gets shaped by more than the past alone. It does not remain a fixed paradigm, dominated unyieldingly by immemorial custom and derived attitudes, regardless of the intervening forces of technology and realism. Cosmopolitanism is

43

no longer the monopoly of the intellectual and leisure classes. It has become the established property and defining characteristic of business society itself. Gradually and irresistibly it breaks down the walls of economic insularity, nationalism, and chauvinism. What we see today as escalating commercial nationalism is simply the last violent death rattle of an obsolete institution.

The successful global corporation does not abjure customization or differentiation for the requirements of markets that differ in product preferences, spending patterns, shopping preferences, and institutional and legal arrangements. But the global corporation accepts and adjusts to these differences only reluctantly, only after relentlessly testing their immutability—after trying in various ways to circumvent and reshape them, as we shall see with some examples shortly.

Different market segments and institutional arrangements will always remain the world over, as they do within single countries. That's not the point. The point is that there is increasing and rapid global convergence in all the big things that drive commerce and industry. The world's inherited old varieties of distinctive national economic institutions and practices, its inherited old varieties of distinctive national preferences as to product characteristics and features, and all its other inherited old varieties of culture-bound national attributes that have historically required the almost total domestication of international corporate activities to the requirements of each separate nation —all these rest now on increasingly shaky ground. The world is becoming increasingly informed about the liberating and enhancing possibilities of modernity. The persistence of the past rests uneasily on increased evidence of, and restlessness regarding, its inefficiency, costliness, and confinements. The historical past and the national differences respecting commerce and industry it spawned and fostered everywhere are now subject to relatively easy transformation. It will take only imagination, effort, and persistence by those who accept the truth about the one great thing that dominates life everywhere and who therefore set out with standardized products and practices, and with aggressive prices, to create world-scale markets eager for modernity. In this regard, Henry Kissinger observes, in his book

*Years of Upheaval,* of the continued Japanese economic successes the world over, "What could be more effective than a society voracious in its collection of information, impervious to pressure and implacable in execution?"

There is an opposing argument about how technology can now drive the world. My argument for the growing globalization of markets clearly rests on two premises regarding customer behavior: (1) the homogenization of the world's wants, and (2) people's willingness to sacrifice specific preferences in product features, functions, design, and the like for lower prices at high quality. Lower prices, I have argued, are facilitated by the scale economies of production, transportation, and communication that massive global markets will make possible.

The counter argument is not trivial. It says that the rapidly growing development of flexible factory automation will enable plants of massive size to change products and product features quickly, even without actually stopping the manufacturing process, so that they can produce broad lines of almost customized products without sacrificing the scale economies that come from long production runs of standardized items. Indeed, computer-aided design and manufacturing (CAD/CAM), combined with robotics, will create a new equipment and process technology (EPT) that will make small plants located close to their markets as efficient as larger ones located distantly, hastening ever faster the competitive superiority of Professor C. Wickham Skinner's famous "focused factory." It will not be economies of scale that will dominate, but rather economies of scope—the ability of either large or small plants to produce great varieties of relatively customized products at remarkably low costs. And if that happens, the counter argument says, customers will have no need to abandon in the market place their special preferences. These preferences can be satisfied at the same low prices as standardized products—perhaps at even lower prices, because the new flexible factories are newer and more efficient simply because they are new, not only because they are different.

I will not deny the power of these possibilities, or even the suggestion that the economics of the Industrial Revolution will be replaced by the new economics of the digital revolution. But possibilities do not probabilities make. There is no conceivable way in which flexible factory automation dedicated to producing many customized lines of a specific product can achieve the scale economies of an equally modernized plant dedicated to the massive production of narrow standardized lines of that product. The new digitized equipment and process technologies are available to all. This will enable those with minimal customization and narrow product-line breadth to drive their costs, as in old-fashioned mass production, far below those with more customization and wider lines.

Combining this fact with the global homogenization of taste and preferences that is in such obvious ascent, and with everything we know about the one great thing we all have in common everywhere—namely, the necessity of our insatiable wants to accommodate to our limited financial capabilities—it follows that people will prefer in overwhelming numbers lower-priced, more-or-less standardized quality products over higher-priced customized products. That has been true throughout the recorded history of humankind. It is not reasonable to suppose that the microprocessor, for all its fabulous fungibility, will change what's so powerfully built into our immemorial genes.

It will be said that even though the world moves relentlessly toward product commonality, this does not hold true for the institutions through which products flow. There is a strong prevailing belief in the immutability of distribution channels, for example, and their accompanying institutions that vary so widely in kind, structure, and stages of development around the world. It is known, of course, that things can and do change over time. But the belief in immutability remains strongly entrenched, modified only to the extent of belief also in evolution and gradualism.

What is seldom even imagined are the possibilities of vigorous and yet patient intervention to modify, transform, or bypass established channels and practices. There is abundant evidence that this is both possible and effective. Not that there have not been horrendous setbacks or failures. In Japan, Revlon unnecessarily alienated retailers and confused customers by first selling world-standardized products only in elite outlets and then tried rapidly to recover with low-price world-standardized products in broader distribution, again rapidly followed by changing the Japanese company president and making distribution cutbacks as costs rose faster than sales. The problem was not, as some have argued, that Revlon didn't understand the Japanese market. The problem was irresolution and impatience. By contrast, in Europe the Outboard Marine Corporation, by imagination, push, and persistence, not only collapsed long-established three-step distribution channels (primary, secondary, dealer) to a more controlled and focussed two-step system, and against the overwhelmingly knowledgeable and foreboding advice of local trade groups, but also vastly reduced the number and types of its retail outlets. The result was major improvement in credit and product-installation service to retail customers, major cost reductions, and major sales advances.

In its highly successful Japanese introduction of Contac 600 (the time-release anticongestant), SmithKline Corporation distributed to all forty-seven prefectures via only thirty-five wholesalers instead of the thousand or more somewhat unruly ones that established practice was presumed to require. This was accompanied by certain special daily contacts with the wholesalers and key retailers, also in violation of established practice, but it worked.

Similarly, Komatsu, the Japanese manufacturer of world-standardized lightweight farm machinery, being denied access to established distribution institutions in the United States, successfully entered the market by selling through over-the-road construction equipment dealers in rural areas of the Sun Belt. It went to a part of the United States where farms were smaller and equipment needs less muscular, letting product appropriateness and price attract customers to uncommon distributors. In a vast variety of electronic office equipment and retail checkout registers, the Japanese sold, at the outset in the United States, not through conventional channels using established methods but through electrical repair shops with no previous experience in either the equipment or in sales.

In all these cases supposedly immutable institutional arrangements were circumvented, shattered, or transformed by the combination of product modernity and reliability, strong and sustained support systems, aggressive low prices, aggressive sales-compensation packages, and often these generally combined with audacity and implacability. Instead of producing resentment or disreputability in the entered markets, they produced admiration and awe.

Divergences of these kinds from established practice actually happen all the time everywhere, but they seem natural when done by home-country companies at home. The multinational mind, warped into circumspection and timidity by years of horrific stumbles and stories about transnational troubles, now rarely contemplates departure from presumptively fixed practices in other lands. Indeed, too often it considers even the thought of such departure as mindless, disrespectful, impossible. It is the mind of a bygone day.

In only one significant respect are a company's activities around the world important, and that is what and how it produces and sells. Everything else is derivative from, and subsidiary to, these activities. What is produced and how it is sold represent what is uniquely the corporate purpose.

The purpose of business is to get and keep a customer. Or, to use Peter Drucker's more demanding construction, to *create* and keep a customer. The business does this by being wedded constructively to the ideal of innovation, seeking constantly to offer better or more preferred products in such combinations of ways, means, places, and at such prices as to make prospects *prefer* in some acceptable proportion to do business with itself rather than with others. Preferences are constantly being shaped and reshaped. The significance of modern times resides in how technology is shaping the world's preferences into homogenized commonality—into global standardization. Within that commonality enormous variety constantly asserts itself and thrives, as can be seen within the world's single largest domestic market, the United States. But in the process of the world's being shaped into the kind of homogenizing commonality I have been talking about something else clearly happens, namely, the expansion of modern markets into cost-reducing global proportions.

Thus, two vectors operate simultaneously to drive the world: the vector of technology and the vector of globalization. The first helps powerfully to shape human preferences. The second shapes economic realities. With preferences converging, regardless of how much they constantly evolve and also diverge, markets are shaped into magnitudes that allow great economies of scale and therefore reduction of costs and prices.

The modern global corporation, as contrasted to the aging multinational corporation, "impervious to pressure and implacable in execution," seeks constantly to hasten the consummation of what already occurs, to force suitably standardized products and practices onto the entire globe, because that is, indeed, exactly what the world will take, especially when aggressively low prices are linked to quality and reliability.

Given what is everywhere the purpose of a business, the global business, in the spirit of the hedgehog, will shape the vectors of technology and globalization into a great, single strategic fecundity for itself. It will systematically push these vectors toward a converging center, where optimization of high-quality global standardization produces optimally low costs, optimally low prices, and therefore, in combination, optimal patronage at optimal profits for itself. Reciprocally, this means companies that do not adapt to the new global realities will become the victims of those that do and prosper.

# 3

---

# The Industrialization of
# Service

The service sector of industrially advanced nations has been in proportional ascent for nearly three-quarters of a century. In the United States in the past twenty years alone, the non-goods-producing sector of the nonagricultural labor force rose 40 percent faster than the goods-producing sector.

It would be redundant to recite once more the growing share of the nation's GNP that the so-called service sector occupies. Nor is it just the expanding proportions taken up by the multiplicity of government, school district, and other public employments that have produced this increase, though civilian public employment alone rose nearly four times faster in the past twenty years than goods-producing employment.

Actually, there is a massive hidden service sector: that proportion of nominally "manufacturing" industries whose expenses and revenues largely represent pre- and postpurchase servicing in the form of systems planning, preinstallation support, "software," repair, maintenance, delivery, collection, bookkeeping, and the like.

As the industrialization in the rest of the world gradually catches up with the more advanced nations, some say, the advanced nations will lose their relative advantage. The shift in the developing nations from craft to industrial labor, from hand work to machine work, produces great vaulting increases in productivity. Meanwhile, in the already industrialized nations affluence and discretionary spending shift demand increasingly into low-productivity, labor-intensive service activities—automotive repair, travel, commercial lodging, entertainment, restaurants, shopping, insurance brokerage, medical care, education, and the like. The result, so the argument goes, is that the advanced nations lose their advantage even faster than the developing nations expand their manufacturing industries.

In the advanced industrial nations this has of late produced a paradoxical paranoia—the proposition that their expanding service appetites shift consumer and industrial demand in directions that are little susceptible to the employment of mass-production efficiencies, which, in time, leads to rising general price levels and finally to retarded (even reduced) living standards. Since it costs more to buy the less efficiently produced services, one's money doesn't go as far. Moreover, for the nation intent on maintaining some sort of world trade competitiveness, it will have to tighten its belt, which reduces living standards even more.

Those are the supposed cybernetics of world economics: Advantage leads ultimately to a demand for costly service amenities while producing a parallel no-frills catch-up effort among the less advantaged, who finally not only catch up but surpass the original leaders because, for one thing, their technology is more modern.

Japan, Germany, and Hong Kong are dramatic examples of no-frills catch-up. Britain is a dismal example of having been caught up on and now left pathetically behind.

51

## THE END IS NOT IN SIGHT

But Britain is also a particularly apt example for showing that the fears of accelerating disadvantage in the developed world and of retarded living standards in the more advanced service-intensive industrial nations are not necessarily justified. Britain shows, particularly by comparison with the United States, that the rising proportion of GNP devoted to so-called service activities need not necessarily produce a parallel and equivalent decline in either absolute or relative national productivity.

In the United States the service sector has demonstrated a remarkable capacity to improve productivity, while in Britain it has exhibited the polar opposite, an almost obsessive persistence of ancient service practices that drain the economy of competitive vitality. In Britain, "to serve" remains to this day encrusted with immemorial attachments to master–servant pretensions that dull the imagination and block the path to service efficiency. In spite of spectacularly rising British retail prices, laws have been passed to resist the construction and growth of that new marvel of retailing efficiency, the hypermarché (the superstore). More efficient even than the American supermarket and the general-merchandise mass marketer, the hypermarché has been effectively resisted by coalitions of small personal-service retailers and local and national politicians.

This British resistance to retailing efficiency reflects the traditional insularity of the petty bourgeoisie. It is, in fact, a profoundly persistent cultural manifestation with ancestral roots in distant centuries. Historically there have always been class distinctions, and not just in Britain. The lower classes have always been obliged to serve and fawn for the benefit of those above them. "Service" took the form of one person's labor for the benefit of another—the butler, the footman, the parlor maid, the upstairs maid, the solicitor, the butcher, the greengrocer, the tailor, and the cook, all performing one-on-one, highly personalized service, whether laying out the clothes or cutting the roast just right to the exacting specifications of each familiar customer in the shop. To this day, with Britain teetering precariously on the economic edge, even moderately priced restaurants are redundantly populated with paid factotums in frayed sartorial imitations of the past, each specializing in a separate and costly triviality, like opening doors, removing and carrying coats to the cloakroom (there manned by yet another), removing dirty ashtrays from tables but not dirty dishes. And in offices, the prodigality of worn-out and outworn retainers ever present to run errands and perform menial personal services is visible everywhere, doing questionably required work that incurs unquestionably real expenses and serves no real purpose. The purpose served is purely ceremonial: keeping up, with senile thoughtlessness, with appearances that have no merit save that of decayed grace and mannered tawdriness. Things add up, not only in their measurable pecuniary costs, but also in the way people think about the work to be done and how to do it.

As long as we cling to preindustrial notions about what service is and does—the idea that to serve means to humble oneself before another, to toady and to acquiesce, to respond to orders and custom rather than think about the function to be performed and how it might be accomplished with the new tools that are available and the new systems that are possible—as long as we think of service as being next to servility; of "serving" as a synonym for thoughtless obedience; of service as a lower occupation (when it comes to work) or a higher occupation (when it comes to the elite professions, like the clergy and the military, where the premium is on ecclesiastical faith and marshal obedience, not on thought or independence), as long as these sterile notions of a vanished world dominate our own thoughts and attitudes, none of the applied rationality that has produced such magnificently thrusting efficiencies in the industrial system will be brought to bear on what remains today an unconscionably retarded maze of inefficiencies in the service sectors that surround that system.

The foregoing examples of service wastefulness still present in modern Britain illustrate a general rule about endurance: Things may be obsolescent though not obsolete. All this may be less so in the United States, but in the case of the ancient fetters that enthrall our attitudes toward and shape the quality of our service work, everywhere their endurance carries a common presumption that service literally means, and will be best, when one person directly and personally attends another, much as a servant attends the master. As long as this presumption reigns, service will forever be limited in efficiency, reliability, and quality.

Opportunities for service improvement lie all around, and yet in the United States, where much improvement has already occurred, it has gone vastly unnoticed. We celebrate the glamorous work of heroic astronauts in distant places, accomplishing through science and technology deeds of speculative merit. But we ignore the practical accomplishments of people who daily all around us produce with lesser tools, simpler methods, and less elaborate organization, a constant stream of productive service results of more mundane but immediate merit. We shall see in the following pages exactly how amply we are benefited daily by so much we daily see but don't apprehend—and how these benefactions are the result of what I have called "the industrialization of service."

There is little reason why an industrialized but increasingly service-intensive economy should advance less rapidly than newly industrializing economies, though one may concede that technologically advanced economies may have some disadvantage regarding the rate of future productivity improvement. But I hope to show by concrete example that service activities are so enormously lagging behind existing potentials for improving their efficiency and productivity that a case can actually be made that advanced industrial nations can improve their overall productivity even more rapidly than the lagging developing nations that are so aggressively adopting modern industrial machinery and systems.

## THE NEW SERVICE FECUNDITY

Go back to the hypermarché. Its forerunners in the United States are supermarkets and mass-merchandising discount stores. They are self-service stores, and that helps explain their

54

superior efficiency. Instead of a clerk behind the counter responding to each customer's special requests for items that must then be individually fetched, weighed, and bagged, the customer now does most of the work himself, and lots faster. The corner grocery store in which the clerk was, like Benvenuto Cellini, a careful craftsman personally putting the whole grocery list together and doing all the work associated with the customer's trip to the store has been largely replaced by the supermarket assembly line. The customer alone assembles the purchase, moving through the aisles and filling a cart from the store inventory much as an automobile frame moves along a line and gets assembled from the plant inventory.

The supermarket and the mass-market discount store represent the industrialization of ancient craftsmanship. In both cases there are tremendous economies, great efficiencies, and, I would insist, a much better product. The modern automobile *is* better—more uniformly reliable, cheaper, more durable and yet still highly customized to the special specifications of millions of individual buyers throughout the land, each with his own private preferences that are rather satisfactorily served at remarkably low costs. The independent craftsman might have constructed a more uniquely personalized and interesting car, but also probably a more idiosyncratic one, embellishing the whole project with elaborate little pirouettes expressing his own personal style, perhaps quaintly ornamented or disastrously experimental. And so with the butcher at the older store. He might have cut the roast more lovingly (or, as the case may be, more shrewdly) and perhaps augmented it with the self-serving weight of his own thumb on the scale—a more personal production, certainly, but also less predictably reliable and certainly more painfully costly.

The supermarket represents the industrialization of service. It combines more space and capital in larger but fewer aggregates. Gone, for the most part, are the ancient modes of "service" it displaced with new efficiencies, lower costs, and greater customer satisfaction, altogether an efficient act of creative destruction.

There are numerous other ways in which service has already been industrialized. Most of us regularly see them at work; few of us are aware of them. Even fewer fully appreciate their revolutionizing importance for our lives and businesses. Only he without fresh air to breathe and food to eat fully appreciates their importance. It is worth a long look at the industrializing modes that already help make service more abundantly productive than it has been in the past. It will help focus effort and energize activity toward the use of these principles in other service activities.

Service can be industrialized in three ways: via hard technologies, soft technologies, and hybrid technologies.

The hard technologies are the most obvious. They substitute machinery, tools, or other tangible artifacts for people in the performance of service work. Thus:

1. The electrocardiogram reliably substitutes a lower-paid technician for the high-paid doctor listening unsteadily and unreliably with a stethoscope.
2. The consumer credit card and CRT credit and bank-balance checking machine replace a long and embarrassing manual credit check for each purpose.
3. Airport X-ray surveillance equipment replaces a long, messy, and embarrassing manual rummaging through baggage.
4. The automatic car wash replaces the uneven quality and personality-destroying work of individuals washing by hand.
5. The Polaroid Land Camera replaces film that must be returned and processed in an essentially people-intensive plant.
6. Automatic toll collectors at bridges, subway entrances, and elsewhere replace human collectors.
7. The home is full of hard technologies replacing people: automatic washers, precooked convenience foods, never-needs-ironing clothing, and chemically treated dirt-resistant clothing, floor covering, and upholstered furniture.

Soft technologies are essentially the substitution of organized preplanned systems for individual service operatives.

Often these involve some modification of the tools (or technologies) employed, but their essential feature is the system itself, where special hardware or routies are specifically designed to produce the desired results:

1. Supermarkets and other self-service establishments like cafeterias, restaurant salad bars, open tool rooms in factories, open-stack libraries.
2. Fast-food restaurants: McDonald's, Burger Chef, Pizza Hut, Dunkin' Donuts, Kentucky Fried Chicken, and the like. I have elsewhere explained these in detail. There I pointed out the intricate planning these systems require, the division of labor that's entailed—some workers prepare only the meat for the hamburger in a central commissary, some only the buns, some the salads, and so forth. At point of sale the same rational system of specialization is rigorously followed to produce speed, quality control, cleanliness, cheerfulness, and low prices.
3. Prepackaged vacation tours that obviate the need for extensive and time-consuming personal selling, extensive tailoring of the product to numerous different kinds of customers, and a great deal of price haggling. American Express probably has the largest variety of packages, handsomely presented, described, and promoted in a brochure of magazine proportions. Significantly this, too, is like an assembly line in principle. American Express seldom creates or operates the tours. That's done mostly by others. American Express mostly assembles and packages the information and sells the product for those who deliver it.
4. Off-the-shelf insurance programs, packaged and unalterable, except via the selection of other packages. Allstate Insurance was the mass-market pioneer, though preceded by the old "industrial" insurance salesman who sold door-to-door and collected weekly, and more recently imitated by off-the-shelf insurance-by-mail.
5. Mutual funds, as against one-at-a-time stock selection, the latter filled with ambiguities, uncertainties, and repetitive reselling and reeducation with each transaction.

6. Christmas Club and payroll-deduction savings systems, both one-time selling and one-time deciding situations, and thereafter automatically and routinely and cheaply executed.
7. Bank-by-mail systems.
8. Carefully planned routing systems for salesmen to reduce travel time and maximize sales and service time.
9. Fully systematized, production-line, yet personalized income tax preparation service on a walk-in basis, performed at remarkably low cost with remarkable accuracy and guarantees. The pioneer and master merchant is, of course, H. & R. Block.

Finally, there are the hybrid technologies. They combine hard equipment with carefully planned industrial systems to bring efficiency, order, and speed to the service process:

1. Computer-based over-the-road truck utilization and routing. By careful programming for types and grades of roads, location of stops, congestion of roads, toll-road costs, and mixing-point access, it optimizes truck utilization and minimizes user cost. Its most extensive and complex incarnation is Cummins Engine's "Power Management Program."
2. Radio-controlled ready-mix concrete truck routing, rerouting, and delivery, pioneered early and to an advanced state by Texas Industries of Dallas.
3. Development of unit trains and integral trains that carry, over great distances, a single commodity (coal by the Baltimore & Ohio Railroad and grain by the Illinois Central are common examples) with few or no intermediate stops, thus providing fast long runs at such enormous efficiency that they can deadhead back and still save money. The system requires enormous logistical synchronization at point of origin, at destination, and in between. Its value? In the case of the B&O, its original unit train reduced the round-trip time between West Virginia's coal fields and Baltimore from twenty-one days to seven.

4. Preorder shipment of perishables at long distances, for example, sending trainloads of lemons in California (pioneered by Sunkist) east before orders have been placed, using weather forecasting services for intermediate routing and dropoffs in time to reach cities where expected high temperatures will raise the consumption of lemonade and Tom Collinses. Any lost hot day is a lost day of sales. Weyerhauser pioneered a similar system for shipping lumber east, in this case to provide it with an inventory-free "instant" delivery capability to distant customers.

5. Limited-service, fast, low-priced repair facilities, such as national muffler and transmission shops, originally pioneered by Midas. High volume, specialization, and special-purpose tools combine to produce fast, guaranteed results.

6. In order to assess the degree of risk and determine the terms of a proposed financing service with its potential clients, a major financial services company routinely sent teams of auditors to its prospects to evaluate each individual account in their accounts receivable ledgers. The field auditors made and checked all entries by hand. When these auditors were equipped with portable computing systems, the result was an 80 percent reduction in the number of man-hours required for field transactions, including the generation of immediate bids for the jobs on the clients' sites.

These are fairly familiar, though seldom acknowledged, examples of the substitution of hard, soft, and hybrid technologies (that is, of machines and of organized systems of work, or combinations thereof) for ancient, preindustrial modes of work that was always done as an extension of the craft culture, either one-on-one by servant for master or in a primitive industrial fashion that merely substituted a more powerful or efficient machine (say, the locomotive or the steam shovel) for a weaker or less capacitous predecessor (say, the horse or the spade.) Fortunately, there is a huge array of additional possibilities, some of them not nearly so obvious as to potential, and many considerably more promising than even their visible potential at first suggests. The failure of so many of us to recognize that these opportunities exist, or even to appreciate where applications have already been made or to appreciate that these represent a profound divergence from and improvement upon preindustrial concepts of service—that failure is a measure of how firmly we remain tethered by the confining fetters of an ancient heritage. Even when we invent profoundly significant new things, we remain unaware of what we have achieved and therefore unalerted to the possibilities of the application of those same disciplines to what yet remains to be done.

## THE SPECIAL CASES OF SPECIAL OPPORTUNITIES

"You just can't get reliable repair service any more"—so goes the national refrain. It is such a persistent refrain that we are immediately justified in automatically doubting its veracity. When the General Electric Service Corporation's clean white radio-dispatched repair truck pulls into my driveway, I *know* I'm going to get better and more reliable TV service than in the bad old days of the underinventoried, questionably trained, variably priced (what the market would bear, usually), soiled serviceman in his used pickup truck. I am considerably more confident at the Exxon Repair Center with twelve fully equipped, fully lighted, temperature-controlled work stations, with uniformed certified mechanics, where prices are posted, estimates made clearly in advance, and where the completed work is ready as promised when I return at five o'clock.

Yet it is precisely these kinds of service activities that have room for the most improvement. They require as a precondition to high efficiency and low cost precisely the same sorts of disciplines and strategies that make modern manufacturing so efficient and low-cost. They require (1) the application of industrial modes of thinking to the organization of the service effort and (2), often, large amounts of capital.

For the Exxon Repair Center to be efficient it requires, first, division of labor. A trained transmission expert worth $10 an hour must not work at such minimum-wage jobs as changing transmission oil. Nor would one let a minimum-wage transmission-oil-changer try to repair the transmission. In order to enjoy the advantages of division of labor, one needs a lot of volume. That requires a large plant occupying lots of land; fully equipped with costly new labor-saving tools and diagnostic and repair machinery; professionally managed; and promoted and advertised with sufficient frequency and persuasability to draw large numbers of motorists from a wide area. This would, in turn, probably require pickup and delivery services to make up for the inconvenience of motorists having to come long distances. All this is costly. Thus, efficiency in service can require as much investment in plant, equipment, and promotion as has been historically associated with efficiency in manufacturing. It can require as much planning, organization, training, controls, and capital as produced the original car at the outset. It requires, in short, a different way of thinking about what service is, what it can be made to be, and how it must be financed.

The key point is "volume"—magnitudes sufficient to achieve efficiency, sufficient to employ systems and technologies that produce reliable, rapid, and low-unit-cost results. And that, in turn, requires the kind of managerial rationality seldom seen or, indeed, needed in a small shop.

This same principle of magnitudes applies in other highly promising areas where its employment is now in its infancy.

1. Specialized, highly automated medical diagnostic clinics. The Damon Corporation operates 125 such clinics throughout the nation, which with the help of modern machines, 125 salaried M.D.'s, 22 Ph.D's, and 1,400 medical technologists perform a wide range of diagnostic tests that formerly required patients to visit several doctors and clinics at costs in time and money several multiples above Damon's.

2. Prepaid health service centers, comprising a wide range of specialists who can be kept fully employed at their

specialties. Pioneered by the Kaiser Foundation in Oakland, California, there are several hundred HMOs (Health Maintenance Organizations) all over the country whose members prepay annual "dues" for easy access to medical specialists and technicians working in central clinics equipped with the latest technologies and employed full time, without intervening administrative burdens, at their respective specialties, and only their specialties. Nor is low-cost, rapid, convenient health care confined to outpatient services. Since the formation of the first one in Phoenix, Arizona, in 1970 there are now more than a hundred ASFs (Ambulatory Surgical Facilities) in the United States. They typically are equipped to do some 125 low-risk operations on the healthy, low-risk patient. The typical facility has two or more operating rooms, a recovery area, and a diagnostic center. The patient comes in—say, for a tonsillectomy —undergoes tests and surgery, rests, and goes home, all in one day. At Northwest Surgicare, a for-profit ASF in the Chicago area, the total tonsillectomy bill a few years ago was $169, as against $548 at Chicago's nonprofit Michael Reese Hospital. The Metropolitan Insurance Company, which honored twenty-two ASFs under group insurance policies, estimates it had saved $1 million in three years.

3. Word processing stations, the system of centralized typing for offices, including the use of computerized self-correcting typewriters. Instead of numerous erratically busy secretaries scattered throughout a large company's offices or secretaries engaged in typing where their value is greater for other purposes, a great deal of routine typing is centralized into fully busy word processing centers where the fastest equipment becomes justified and scheduling and supervision become sensible.

4. Centralized food preparation commissaries that provide fresh and tasty delicatessen foods and sandwiches to large numbers at small convenience stores, private clubs, offices, and the like. In some cases (Steward's

Sandwiches Co., for example) these commissaries have route delivery systems and provide infrared and microwave ovens to their customers.

The second "special opportunity" category of service improvement resides in the design of products that often require postpurchase servicing. We shall call this the product/repair interface. Perhaps the best-known "solution" to the repair service problem is Motorola's (now Quasar's) highly advertised "works in a box" television design. Instead of emphasizing improved repair capability via improved repairman training (the ancient idea that to get better service requires getting better or better training of servicemen), Motorola simply eliminated the serviceman, or nearly so. Designed as a modular assembly, the television set is capable of "instant" repair by simply removing and replacing a major module that contains a defective part. A direct imitation of the military's concept of "third echelon maintenance," it emphasizes *fast restoration* rather than reliable repair. The military was clear enough about its needs: fast and reliable return to urgent duty at the front. So was Motorola: Get it working reliably fast. By designing the product originally with that in mind, it not only produced great sales appeal but discovered that this very orientation and intention enabled it to design a quite efficient and low-cost television set. Yet even the most cursory examination of industrial equipment tells a prodigal tale of minuscule attention to the postpurchase repair and maintenance problem. One suspects that the question seldom ever arises. No wonder "service costs so much." No wonder "service takes so much time." No wonder "service is so awful."

In the same fashion, I have elsewhere cited the case of Honeywell, which redesigned its room thermostats to employ far fewer and far more easily replaceable parts and in the process was able to eliminate all its field warehouses and persuade its distributors to carry full parts inventories for faster service both to its customers and to repairmen working on competitive products, for which many Honeywell parts were designed for interchangeability.

## EXAMPLES OF SPECIAL
## RECENT ACHIEVEMENTS

Ideas and concepts are often easier understood in principle than translated into actuality. Some translations are easy enough to recognize and, in retrospect, easy enough to comprehend as representing the industrialization of service. A few less obvious examples are worth a look.

### The paperwork problem

The Transamerica Title Insurance Company receives thousands of title insurance applications each week from numerous small field offices on the West Coast and in the Southwest, Colorado, and Michigan. Clerks and "escrow officers" prepare these applications, for which careful title searches through ancient property records must be made. Escrow officers finally begin preparing preliminary insurance policies, which guarantee the buyer (and protect the lender) against postpurchase claims against the seller, such as faulty property surveys, outstanding liens, unpaid taxes, discovery of subsequent wills that invalidate some seller's presumed title, and the like. The preparation of these preliminary policies requires endless telephone calls, a constant and irregular stream of documentation, and frequent calls for speed, clarification, complaints, and help from the many parties to any single transaction—buyer, seller, listing real estate broker, selling real estate broker, lender, tax collector, surveyor, termite inspector. In all this maelstrom of noise, activity, and push, exact calculations must be made regarding the allocation of credits and debits for pro-rated proportions of remaining taxes, interest, and other assessments. Instructions must be issued regarding each party's remaining duties and where and how these are to be discharged. All this must be done cheerfully, efficiently, rapidly, errorlessly, and for numerous accounts by each escrow officer all day long, all week long. That is, until now.

Now Transamerica has systematically industrialized much

of this complex, pressure-cooker process. By careful analysis of the various functions to be performed and by classifying them by degree of importance (e.g., the extreme importance of thoroughness of title search, and the extreme importance of absolutely error-proof operation in the final "closing" of the transaction and in the final insurance policy), the work was divided into several distinct parts. Instead of having each office person do everything or almost everything, separate installations have been created where some specialists do only title searches, some only the auditing, some only the typing of the "closing" papers, and some only the final policy issuance. Productivity and accuracy improved dramatically. Computerization of the financial calculations and typing helped even more. Meanwhile, in order to guard against the erosion of standards and workmanship that the routinization of work so often produces, systems of work-assignment rotation have been installed and career ladders have been created to give the various specialized workers opportunities for advancement and self-development.

## The shoe repair problem

D. Hilston Ryan, product manager of an American package goods company in Europe, grew impatient with a two-week wait to have new heels put on a pair of shoes. He and an associate designed a fast-service shoe repair facility. With no equipment available to meet the needs as they visualized them, they persuaded a manufacturer to produce equipment to their specifications. It was designed to apply new heels and soles on two shoes in less than two minutes. They persuaded the largest department store in Brussels to put their fast-service, while-you-wait, 40-square-foot-shop into the store window on opening day. Lines formed for two blocks. In four years they had 1,400 leased installations in department stores, railroad stations, and supermarkets all over Europe. What was the secret? First, they invented a system to produce speed; not only did they design the equipment, but they also devised its layout, the quality and work-rate standards, the selection and training of workers, the location of inventory relative to the location of the specialized equipment that was used, the type of adhesives and sewing machinery, the seating arrangement for the while-you-wait customers so they could see the work being done, and, of great importance, the low-noise nature of the machines and automatic dust collectors that prevented polluting either the work area or the surrounding store. And the prices charged the customers? Lower, of course.

## The selling problem

Few things trouble the business community more than the alleged high and accelerating "cost of selling," especially personal selling. There are, of course, solutions, and I have mentioned some: self-service stores, which simply eliminate the personal selling function; mutual funds, which substitute one sales call for many; packaged travel tours, which substitute pre-planned itineraries for negotiated ones; and, in industrial selling, a plentitude of item and parts catalogs, which facilitate self-service ordering. There is also an enormous explosion of highly sophisticated direct-mail and catalog selling as well as direct-response selling via order forms in newspapers and magazines and via telephone response to television solicitation. In some of these cases the significance of what is being done is that the products and the product lines are a direct consequence of the media that are available for their sale, rather than their having previously existed in a separate life of their own. Thus certain forms of life, casualty, and hospitalization insurance were created specifically for their ability to be sold via the mail, newspapers, or television. The same is true of a large number of music record albums and even of companies, such as the $164-million-a-year K-Tel Corporation, which was specifically organized for television–telephone response merchandising.

Indeed, telephone solicitation and selling has suddenly boomed into one of the great hidden forms of modern selling. In 1975 an average of seven million U.S. consumers a day picked up their telephones to hear someone who wanted to ask them, offer them, or sell them something. Nearly three million of them

—consumers or businesspeople—agreed to listen, and 460,000 completed the offered proposition then and there at an average purchase price of $60, for a total of $28 million per day, or nearly $6 billion a year.

The very first mass-marketing telephone campaign was undertaken a decade ago by Ford Motor Company and executed by Campaign Communications Institute of America, Inc. (CCI), probably the world's foremost firm specializing in offering telephone marketing services. Twenty million telephone calls were made by 15,000 housewives hired and trained to do the job right from their own homes. Following a carefully programmed script they called a million households a day to determine whether their plans made them good prospects for an automobile purchase. On the average, each call took less than one minute. They generated 340,000 leads (during the campaign period, two per day for each of Ford's 23,000 dealer salesmen), 187,000 of which were "valid" in that they proved to be actively interested in buying within six months. Sales attributable to the program were at a campaign cost ($65 per unit), considered by the company far below its many other promotional programs.

Later CCI designed and executed a telephone subscription solicitation campaign for *World* magazine, the new venture of Norman Cousins, the former editor of *The Saturday Review*. Using a very carefully selected call list and, again, a carefully programmed calling approach, telephone solicitation was tested against carefully designed direct mail solicitation. Telephones produced three committed subscriptions for each one produced by mail.[1]

The New York Telephone Company has dozens of specialists and trainers available gratis to its users for advising and training individuals and small groups in improved techniques and procedures of telephone marketing. Telephone marketing, like most things, is a craft that uses tools and techniques that can be learned. What is significant about their recent incarnation is the introduction of carefully controlled and highly structured

[1] The details of how telephone selling has been and can be industrialized are explained in Murray Roman, *Telephone Marketing* (New York: McGraw-Hill Book Co., 1976).

production-line approaches to telephone marketing. Every aspect of the task—caller recruitment, training, call programming, working conditions, and key phrases for getting results—is as carefully planned and executed as what happens on an automotive assembly line. Firms of all kinds in almost all industries increasingly use this medium, usually with the help of professional organizations specializing in its use for such purposes as selling and taking orders, qualifying leads, motivating delinquent accounts, upgrading marginal customers, follow-ups on direct mail, converting inquiries into sales, reactivating old customers, promoting store traffic, finding and screening for new business, soliciting quality credit applications, introducing new products into distribution channels, delivering taped messages to selected audiences, raising funds for institutions or public causes, and, of course, getting out the vote.

With the availability of Wide Area Telephone Service (WATS lines), FX calls, 800 numbers (inbound WATS), and declining long-distance telephone charges (particularly as postal rates and personal-selling costs rise), telephone selling that is organized with production-line rationality has become a major means for the industrialization of various kinds of selling and sales-related communications.

## End-use specialization

The computer industry has gone perhaps farther than most in specializing its activities to the requirements of specific uses and industries. Among mainframe producers specialization has centered on selling, programming, and equipment servicing, with salesmen and programmers specializing not by equipment but rather by customer industries and applications. Though it is not usually viewed as such, this division of labor represents the same kind of rational specialization I have cited as productive in other industries. The particular value of citing the computer industry is that it views "service" as a central part of the total product package, in part because, especially in the beginning, prospects and customers were almost totally uninformed about what computers could do and how to use them. Therefore "service" became an essential part of the product itself. Specialization of the sales forces, of the programming, and of the hardware services by end-user industries and by uses produced sales and customer-satisfying results in proportions far beyond those achieved by companies that did not specialize. Specialization is to service what division of labor is to manufacturing: the first step to low-cost, reliable abundance.

Cyrus McCormick pioneered the whole idea, putting demonstration salesmen to work on wheat farms and providing repairmen in the field. DuPont pioneered with applications specialists in the textile and garment industries. In all these cases, the "product" that was offered by the "salesmen" consisted less of what was manufactured in the factory than of what was provided by way of practical help and advice in the field. "Service" *was* the product, and still today in many situations it remains more *the* product than meets the eye. Customers don't buy things, they buy tools to solve problems. Specialists who know the customer's problems are more likely to help fulfill the expectation of solution than those who know only the equipment.

The idea of specialization is actually more common than we are aware. We have become so accustomed to seeing savings and loan institutions standing cheek-by-jowl with commercial banks that we fail to note that each is a separate financial institution organized specifically to specialize in respect to separate markets: savings and loans largely to provide mortgage financing to residential home buyers; commercial banks to provide a wider range of short-term money-related services.

Dozens of examples abound: specialty retail stores (shoes, health and beauty aids, books, sporting goods); specialty service stores (some already mentioned, like shoe repair and muffler replacement, others like dry cleaning, insurance, realty); oil exploration companies like drillers, seismic testing firms, core analysis firms; a vast variety of computer software, computer data-base, and computer processing firms, many specializing in each case in a limited variety of applications; chemical and medical testing firms; investment advisory and fulfillment firms, from those that serve only small individual investors to those that serve only large institutional clients, from those that provide a full range of investment services to boutiques that do only executions. The list is varied and, in recent years, is in explosive expansion. These facts are trying to tell us something. They are trying to say that specialization has a virtue that transcends the simple obvious fact that narrow functional specialization tends to focus energy and attention rather than let them be whirled centrifugally into uncontrolled and uncontrollable bits and pieces where management attention and talent are spread too thin over too much.

About two hundred years ago Adam Smith gave a name to the kind of specialization and concentration I have been talking about. It has traveled in manufacturing and economics ever since under one name: division of labor. The difference in the cases cited above is that this division has become embodied in separate institutions and products, firms specializing in the "labors" into which they divided themselves, and products created around those divided "labors." Thus, what we witness is nothing particularly new. What *is* new is the suggestion that the accidents of evolution which created these institutional specialists and product specializations in service can be explained and contemplated in the theoretical context of what I have called "industrialization." The managerial rationality embodied in the practical imagination we see exercised so effectively everywhere in manufacturing can, given the effort, be applied with similarly munificent results in the service industries. We are only now seeing the practical possibilities of the industrialization of service, which in fact has existed in some form for thousands of years but has recently been pressing forward with accelerating tempo. It's like Lavoisier's discovery in chemistry. Everybody had seen that "air" helps things burn, but until Lavoisier discovered the role of oxygen in combustion, this phenomenon was a mystery. Once explained, this phenomenon that had existed since Prometheus became the foundation of modern chemistry. Now that we understand the underlying reason for the success and growth of these institutions and products, now that

70

we see that they have a common and explicable rationality, this understanding has the potential of having in the world of commerce and industry the revolutionizing impact of Lavoisier's insight in chemistry and life.

So it may very well be with the concept of "industrialization." It is an explanation of what the historic and now accelerating specialization in service is, practically speaking, all about. Man lives not by bread alone, but mostly by catchwords. What he believes and feels in his mind and emotions is more deterministic than what's in his possession. What's in his mind, like love, hate, anger, joy, fear, jealousy, alienation, loyalty, or ideology, religion, causation, consequences—all these are, finally, deterministic. They shape and control his actions. To understand and get into our minds that the kinds of successful specializations of effort in the non-goods-producing sectors of our world that I have so briefly described represent a uniquely organized set of processes, that these are in fact the *industrialization* of activities long thoughtlessly assumed to be uniquely inaccessible to the functional rationality that has produced so much low-cost abundance in the goods-producing sectors of the world's more advanced economies—to recognize and understand this phenomenon for what it practically is—is to introduce a potentially emancipating new cognitive mode and operating style into modern enterprise. "Industrialization in service," like "oxygen in combustion," once it enters our minds, though we have unknowingly lived with it since the beginning of mortal time, can transform how we behave, what we do, and where we go. It can generate liberating new solutions to intractable old problems. It can bring to the increasingly service-dominated economies of the future the same kinds of vaulting advances in productivity and living standards as did the newly created goods-producing factory economies brought to the world in the past.

# 4

---

# Differentiation—of Anything

There is no such thing as a commodity. All goods and services can be differentiated and usually are. Though the usual presumption is that this is true more of consumer goods than of industrial goods and services, the opposite is the actual case.

The only exception to this proposition is in the minds of people who profess that exception. In the market place differentiation is everywhere. Everybody—whether producer, fabricator, seller, broker, agent, merchant—engages in a constant effort to distinguish his offering in his favor from all others. This is true even of those who produce, deal in, or buy primary metals, grains, chemicals, plastics, or money.

In fabricated consumer and industrial goods, competitive distinction is visibly sought via distinctive product features, some visually or measurably identifiable, some cosmetically implied, and some rhetorically claimed by reference to real or suggested hidden attributes that promise results or values different from those of competitors.

So too with consumer and industrial services—what I shall call, to be accurate, "intangibles."

Though it is true that on the commodities exchanges dealers in metals, grains, pork bellies, and the like trade in totally undifferentiated generic products, what they "sell" is the claimed distinction of their execution—how well they make transactions in behalf of their clients, how responsive they are to inquiries, the clarity and quickness of their confirmations, and so on. In short, the "offered" product is differentiated, though the "generic" product (say, Treasury Bill futures, gold bullion, or No. 2 winter wheat) is identical.

It is precisely when the generic product is undifferentiated that the "offered" product makes the difference in getting customers, and the "delivered" product in keeping them. When the enormously knowledgeable senior partner of a well-known Chicago brokerage firm appeared at New York banks in a tight-fitting lime-green polyester suit and Gucci shoes soliciting trading business for financial instrument futures, the outcome was predictably poor. The unintended offering implied by his sartorial appearance contradicted the intended offering of his carefully prepared presentation. No wonder that Thomas Watson the elder insisted so uncompromisingly that his salesmen be "properly" attired in their famous IBM "uniform." Though clothes may not make the man, they may help make the sale. And if they do, the customer is buying something beyond the generic product that the salesman offers. That is what is meant by "differentiation."

The usual presumption about so-called undifferentiated commodities is that they are exceedingly price sensitive. A fractionally lower price gets the business. That's seldom true except in the imaginary world of economics textbooks. In the actual world of real markets, nothing is exempt from other considerations, even when price competition is virulent. The fact that price differences are, prima facie, measurable becomes the usual, and usually false, basis for asserting their powerful primacy.

Price is, of course, powerful. But to be powerful is not automatically to be sufficient, no matter how narrowly price negotiations get hardened or to what minuscule fractions price bids are driven.

During periods of sustained surplus, excess capacity, or unrelieved price wars, when all attention seems firmly riveted on nothing but price, it is precisely because price is so visibly objective (i.e., measurable) and so potentially devastating in its effects that it deflects attention from the possibilities for successful extrication from ravaging price competition. So compelling are the price pressures that other possibilities get proportionately slighted. Nor are these "other possibilities," even in the short run, confined simply to "nonprice competition," such as harder personal selling, intensified or enhanced advertising, or what's loosely called more or better "services."

To see fully what these "other possibilities" are, it is useful first to remind ourselves more firmly exactly what a product is.

## WHAT IS A PRODUCT?

Some things are easy enough to see and have been often noted. Products may be tangible and intangible. Often they are combinations of both. An automobile is not simply a tangible machine for movement, visibly or measurably differentiated by design, size, color, options, horsepower, or miles per gallon. It is also a complex symbol denoting status, taste, rank, achievement, aspiration, and, these days, being "smart"—that is, buying economy rather than display. But the customer buys even more than these. The enormous efforts of the auto companies to cut the time between placement and delivery of an order and to select, train, supervise, motivate, and enhance their dealerships suggest that these too are integral parts of "the product" people buy and are therefore ways by which they may be differentiated.

In the same way a computer is not simply a machine for data storage, processing, calculation, or retrieval. It is also an operating system with special software protocols for use and special accompanying possibilities for and promises of maintenance and repair.

Carbon fibers are chemical additives that enhance flexuous stiffness, reduce weight, fight fatigue and corrosion, and cut fabrication costs when combined with certain other materials. But they have no value for an inexperienced user without the heavy design and applications help that only the experienced seller can provide.

Securities underwriters deliver money to the issuers but also promises to the buyers. The promises are carefully packaged in prospectuses of awesome length and detail, only part of whose contents are prescribed by law. The rest is a portentous advertisement for the offering, on the tombstone page of which the members of the underwriting syndicate are listed in a ritual hierarchical order that itself represents a constant battle for advertised image supremacy by the syndicate members themselves. As in the case of thousand-page major-contract proposals to the National Aeronautics and Space Administration or five-page consulting proposals to industrial clients, "the product" is a promise whose commercial substance resides as much in the proposer's carefully curried reputation (or "image") and in the proposal's meticulous packaging as it does in its substantive content.

When the substantive content—the generic product—of competing vendors is scarcely differentiable, sales power migrates to all other differentiating ways in which buyers are likely to be influenced. In this regard there is scant substantive difference between what's done by Morgan Stanley & Co., by Lockheed, McKinsey & Co., and by Revlon. Though each will, in public, vigorously proclaim commanding generic distinctions vis-à-vis competitors, in practice each is profoundly preoccupied with packaging, that is, representing itself as unique. And, indeed, each may be unique. But its uniqueness in relation to its competitors resides precisely in things that transcend its generic offerings. All four offer "products" that extend beyond what is at their generic core. The reason is clear enough: The generic core seldom has competitive viability by itself. It must be differentiated from competitive offerings, because people understandably respond to differentiation, and they respond differently to different kinds of differentiation.

When I say "people" respond, I mean nobody is exempt, not even the chief executives of the world's largest and best-managed corporations or the Ph.D. scientists in their laboratories. "One eminent [U.S. investment banking] house has entrances on two streets, with a different set of stationery printed for each entrance. One door is intended to be more exclusive than the other, and a visitor supposedly can tell the firm's assessment of his importance by the entrance indicated on the letterhead of the stationery he receives."[1] Obviously, the distinctions being made are selling devices based on the assumption that VIP treatment of some visitors at reception will convince them that they will get a VIP product.

As for how Ph.D. corporate laboratory scientists make vendor decisions, a carefully controlled study of purchasing behavior regarding complex new industrial materials showed that

> . . . technically sophisticated technical personnel seem to be influenced by the seller's reputation to a point that is unexpectedly higher than the influence of that reputation on such technically less sophisticated personnel as purchasing agents. . . . In . . . trying to sell such products to technically trained personnel it may not be wise to rely so unevenly on the product's inherent virtues and on making strong technical product presentations. Technical personnel are not human computers whose purchasing and product-specification decisions are based on cold calculations and devoid of less rigorously rational influences.[2]

People buy products (whether purely tangible products, purely intangible products, or hybrids of the two) in order to solve problems. Products are problem-solving tools. If the buyer won't buy for lack of help in design and application, it's not a product, because it does not fulfill a problem-solving need. Certainly it is incomplete. If he won't buy because it is styled unsuitably, its delivery is uncertain, its sales terms are un-

[1] This is from page 147 of a highly prescient study on the workings of image and other forms of competition among investment-banking firms, Samuel L. Hayes, III, "Investment Banking: Power Structure in Flux," *Harvard Business Review*, March/April 1971, pp. 136–52.

[2] Theodore Levitt, *Industrial Purchasing Behavior: A Study of Communications Effects* (Boston: Division of Research, Graduate School of Business Administration, Harvard University, 1965), pp. 26–27.

acceptable, its maintenance difficult, the salesperson is officious, the proposal has misspellings or lacks clarity, the store smells, or the supplier's general reputation is questionable or only slightly inferior to that of another—if all or any of these keep the prospect from buying, then clearly the prospect thinks of a product as more than the generic engineering "thing" that's made in the factory, the generic benefit bundle that's described in the proposal, or the generic item that's on display.

A product is, to the potential buyer, a complex cluster of value satisfactions. The generic "thing" or "essence" is not itself the product. It is merely, as in poker, the table stake, the minimum necessary at the outset to allow its producer into the game. But it's only a "chance," only a right to enter play. Once entry is actually attained, the outcome depends on a great many other things. Mostly it depends on how the entrant plays the game, rather than on the table stake (the generic product) that entitles one to play. In business, as in poker, there is competition, but in business it is for the patronage of solvent customers. Customers attach value to products in proportion to the perceived ability of those products to help.solve their problems. Hence a product has meaning only from the viewpoint of the buyer or the ultimate user. All else is derivative. Only the buyer or user can assign value, because value can reside only in the benefits he wants or perceives.

Nothing demonstrates this more clearly than the supreme clarity with which the Detroit auto companies buy sheet steel. Detroit buys to exceedingly tight technical specifications, but it specifies more than the qualities of the steel itself. It also specifies a vast variety of delivery conditions and flexibilities, price and payment conditions, reordering responsiveness, and the like. Employing multiple suppliers, the Detroit companies shift from year to year the proportions of steel they buy from their various suppliers on the basis of elaborate grading systems by which they measure the performance of their suppliers on each of the specified conditions.

Clearly Detroit views "the product" as more than the specified sheet steel alone. It buys a bundle of value specifications of which sheet steel, the generic product, is only a small proportion. If other parts of the product it buys—the delivery conditions and flexibilities, for example—are not fulfilled, or if they are fulfilled erratically, grudgingly, or only partially, the customer is not getting "the product" he expects. If one supplier gets, on a ten-point scale, a lot of sixes and sevens for the dimensions on which he gets graded, while another supplier gets mostly nines and tens, next year the latter will get more of the business. His "product" is better; he delivers more value. Although the steel is absolutely identical, the customer knows that "the products" are different, and the difference, in all probability, is greater than the housewife is able to discern between coffees from Maxwell House and Folger. Detroit sees with supreme clarity that No. 302, 72-inch hot-rolled strip carbon steel is not a commodity. It is a measurably differentiated product. It is never just steel, wheat, subassemblies, investment banking, engineering consultancy, industrial maintenance, newsprint, or even 99 percent pure isopropanol.

What a product is in its customer-getting and customer-satisfying entirety can be managed. But it seldom is. Things just happen, often entirely too serendipitously. To see how it can be managed, it is helpful to look in some graphic detail at how it might be visualized.

Visually, one can describe a product as having the range of possibilities shown in Figure 1, which is explained below.

*The generic product*

The "generic product" is the rudimentary substantive "thing" without which there is no chance to play the game of market participation. It is the "table stake" of the game. For the steel producer it is the steel itself. In the case of a bank, it is loanable funds. For a realtor, it is "for sale" properties. For a machine tools maker it is the lathe, milling, shaping or other equipment in whose production he may specialize. For a retailer it is a store with a certain mix of vendables. For a lawyer it's having passed the bar exam. For a producer of chemical feed stocks it is those feed stocks themselves.

FIGURE 1.   THE TOTAL PRODUCT CONCEPT

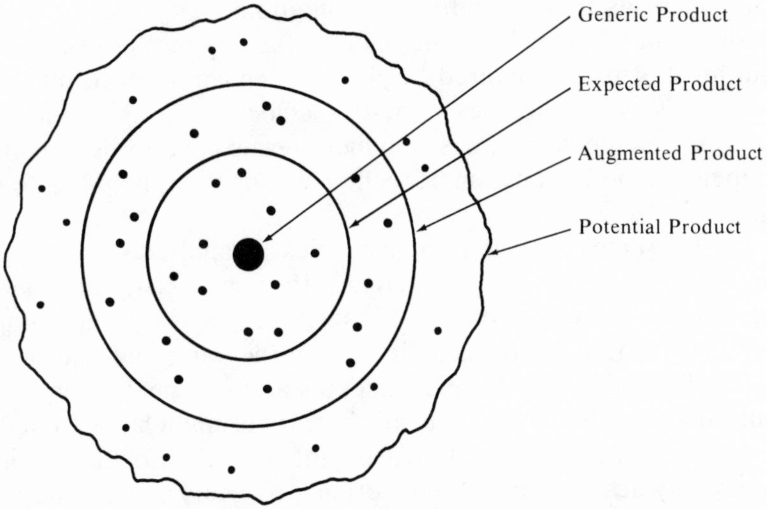

Generic Product

Expected Product

Augmented Product

Potential Product

*Note:* The dots inside each ring represent specific activities or tangible attributes. For example, inside the "Expected Product" are delivery conditions, installation services, postpurchase services, maintenance, spare parts, training, packaging convenience, and the like.

To be a producer of chemical feed stocks, say, benzene (the "Generic Product" depicted by the solid black center in Figure 1), is not automatically to be a seller of benzene, certainly not a successful seller. The customer, as we saw in the Detroit example, expects more than the generic product when he pays, nominally, for that product. Unless his other expectations are minimally fulfilled, there will be no sale. And if it is not sold, there is no "it." Commercially speaking, there is no product when what there "is" has no takers. The customer expects more.

*The expected product*

Figure 1 represents the "Expected Product" as everything inside the smallest circle, including the "Generic Product." This represents the customer's minimal expectations. Though these

79

vary by customers, conditions, industries, and the like, every customer has minimal purchase conditions that exceed the generic product itself. Benzene must not simply be "priced right" but must also be delivered "right," which can refer to minimal quantities and schedules and to specific locations in varying amounts at specified times. Payment terms have to be "right." Depending on the customer, technical support or help has to be "right."

The same general principles clearly apply to everything everywhere. A shabby brokerage office may cost the realtor access to a customer for his "for sale" properties. Even though the lawyer performed magnificently in the bar exam and occupies offices of prudential elegance, his abrasive personality may put off a potential client. The machine tools might have the most sophisticated of numerical controls tucked tightly behind an impressively designed panel, but certain prospects may not buy, in spite of all else being "right," because the machine's output tolerances are more precise than necessary or usable. The customer may actually expect and want less. For him, more is not better, not even at a competitive price.

Not even in such a putatively homogeneous product as wheat does the customer buy only the generic product itself. Indeed there are in the United States three kinds of wheat: winter wheat, which represents about 30 percent of U.S. production; spring wheat; and so-called specialty wheats, like durum. Durum itself comes in its own subspecialties, the most abundance of which is semolina, which is used almost exclusively for making pastas. About 90 percent of all U.S. durum is grown in three counties in Eastern North Dakota. Yet prices vary substantially, even for identical grades of semolina. The county elevator operators to whom most semolina farmers sell will pay premiums or take discounts from previously agreed-to or currently quoted prices, depending on the results of protein and moisture tests made on each delivery. The wheat users ("buyers"), like Prince Spaghetti Company, make additional tests for farina and gluten content, which result in additional price adjustments. Premiums and discounts for quality differences in a given year have been known to vary from the futures price on the commodity exchanges by amounts greater than the futures price fluctuations themselves during that year.

There are also variations in the expected product. Elevator operators require bulk delivery in truckload quantities. Before elevator operators installed their own truck-lifting facilities, delivery generally had to be in trucks equipped with their own hydraulic lifts to facilitate dumping. In recent years many of the larger farmers have installed their own storage elevators. Using very large trailer trucks, they bypass county elevators for direct shipment to the receiving elevators of large users. Besides avoiding middleman storage discounts, this gives them better access to quality premiums paid by buyers.

Similarly county elevator operators in the Great Plains increasingly try to organize themselves to take advantage of unit-train shipments to the Gulf Coast. Single offerings of ten-carload shipments qualify for substantial rail tariff discounts. This affects the quantities and schedules by which county elevators prefer to buy and take delivery from growers, which in turn affects how the growers manage their delivery capabilities and schedules.

Thus, not even specific types or grades of wheat are a commodity. They can be, and are generally expected by their buyers to be, differentiated. Clearly, when we know enough about a business it becomes clear that its "product" is much more than what's generically at the core of what's expected by the customer and offered by the seller.

When the customer expects more than the generic product, the generic product can be sold only if those expectations are met. The different means by which competing sellers seek to fulfill these expectations distinguish their offerings from one another. In this way, differentiation follows expectations.

*The augmented product*

But differentiation is not exhausted merely by giving the customer what he expects. What he expects may be augmented by offering him more than what he thinks he needs or has become accustomed to expect. When the selling manufacturer of, say, computers implants a software diagnostic module inside his computers which automatically locates the source of failure or breakdown (as some now do), that seller has augmented the product beyond what was required or even expected by the buyer. When a securities brokerage firm includes with its customers' monthly statements a current balance sheet for each customer and an analysis of sources and disposition of funds, that firm has augmented its product beyond what was required or even expected by the buyer. When a manufacturer of health and beauty aids offers warehouse-management advice and training programs for the employees of its distributors, that firm too has augmented its product beyond what was required or even expected by the buyer.

These voluntary or unprompted "augmentations" to the expected product are depicted in Figure 1 by the band that surrounds the "Expected Product." The "augmented product" comprises what's in this band plus everything that it surrounds. The process of providing these augmentations can, in time, educate the buyer about what is reasonable for him to expect from the seller. Just as one seller's more attractive delivery or payment terms raise the customer's expectations from all sellers, so also do all the other ways in which sellers surround the generic and the expected product with an expanding variety of customer-benefiting attributes designed to attract and hold customers. Again, customer expectations rise to what has been shown to customers to be possible.

The size and content of a product therefore consists, first, of the generic product and the customer-originated expectations regarding the conditions that must be fulfilled in order for him to buy it, and of the seller-originated augmentations with which additional competitive advantage is sought. Augmentations are a means of product differentiation. Nearly everybody employs them, though they are seldom developed as part of a conscious or systematic program of product differentiation.

Not all customers for all products and under all circumstances can be attracted by an ever widening bundle of these differentiating "value satisfactions." Some customers may prefer lower prices to more augmentations. Some cannot use certain offered augmentations. For example:

—A retailer who is large enough to take store-door delivery rather than buy from a distributor or operate his own distribution center cannot use or benefit from the kinds of distribution-center operating or training aids mentioned above.

—In the case of maturing products, the passage of time may result in the buyer's becoming so thoroughly expert in the use of the "generic product" that he no longer needs or wants applications or engineering support. Thus the rapid growth of independent steel distribution centers has paralleled the declining need of steel-using customers for mill-originated applications help. Meanwhile, independent steel distribution centers, whose "product" has always been distinguished from the mill-originated product by greater delivery speed on standard grades and sizes, a wider item mix, and ability to handle small orders, have augmented their product by doing more minor fabricating and adding certain specialty-steel applications services.

The rule can be laid down that the more successfully a seller expands the market by teaching and helping customers to use his product, the more vulnerable the seller becomes to the loss of those customers. When a prospect no longer needs the help that converted him into a customer, he becomes free to shop around for things he values more than that help. Often this is price. But the booming U.S. growth of independent steel distribution and fabrication centers suggests that price is not the only thing that attracts and holds the buyer.

It is precisely when the buyer has become less dependent on the technical help or brand support of the originating supplier that greater attention may be beneficially focused on a systematic program of finding customer-benefitiating and therefore customer-keeping product augmentations. It is also a time when increasing effort should be focused on possible cost and price reductions. Thus arises the irony of product maturity: Precisely when price competition gets more severe and therefore cost reduction becomes more important is when one is also likely to benefit by incurring the additional costs of special new product augmentations.

The augmented product is uniquely a condition of relatively mature markets or of relatively experienced or sophisticated customers. Not that more experienced or sophisticated customers cannot benefit or will not respond to augmented offerings; but when a customer knows or thinks he knows everything and can do anything, it is up to the seller to test those assumptions lest he be condemned to the purgatory of price competition alone. The way to "test" the customer's assumption that he no longer needs or wants all or any part of the augmented product is to consider what's potentially possible to offer.

### The potential product

The "potential product" consists of everything potentially feasible to attract and hold customers. Whereas the "augmented product" means everything that has been or is being done, the "potential product" refers to what may remain to be done, that is, what is possible.

What may be possible is not strictly a matter of what is purely imaginable on the basis of what is known or knowable about customers and competitors. It generally depends heavily on changing conditions. That is why people in business so seldom any longer greet each other with the old rhetorical question, How's business? Instead they ask the more substantively information-seeking question, What's new? That helps describe what has changed, and this helps define the potential product with which to compete more effectively under the changed conditions. When American independent steel distributors saw the declining reliance of steel users on mill-originated technical support, they began buying increasingly from overseas mills, expanded their facilities to carry larger inventories for even faster deliveries, and increased their fabrication capabilities. The response of American mills was to integrate forward by expanding their own distribution and fabrication centers, in some cases actually buying part of their requirements from competing overseas mills.

All this was succinctly described in 1976 by Professor E. Raymond Corey of the Harvard Business School:

1. "... the form of a product is a variable, not a given, in developing market strategy. Products are planned and developed to serve markets."
2. "... the 'product' is what the product does; it is the total package of benefits the customer receives when he buys. ... Even though a product might, in the most narrow sense, be indifferentiable, an individual supplier may differentiate his product from competitive offerings through service, product availability, and brand image. And differentiation in one respect or another is the basis for developing a market franchise."
3. "... the product, in this broad sense, will have different meaning to different customers. This consideration is important with regard to both market selection and pricing."[3]

This final point about "market selection and pricing" leads us to another form of differentiation, for which all that's been said till now is prologue.

## DIFFERENTIATION VIA MARKETING MANAGEMENT

The way a company manages its marketing can become the most powerful form of differentiation. When Professor Corey writes of the options regarding "market selection and pricing" available to sellers, he refers, in effect, to how the marketing process is managed. Indeed, that may be how industrial-product

[3] E. Raymond Corey, *Industrial Marketing: Cases and Concepts* (Englewood Cliffs, N.J., Prentice-Hall, 1976), pp. 40–41.

companies vary most from one to another and therefore may constitute their most important forms of differentiation.

Brand management and product management are managerial tools of marketing that have demonstrable advantages over simple catchall functional modes of management. The same is true of market management, a system widely employed when a specific industrial tangible or intangible is used by many different kinds of industries. Putting somebody in charge of a product that's bought and used essentially in the same way by a large segment of the total market (as in the case, say, of packaged detergents sold through retail channels) or in charge of a specific market for a product that's bought and used in essentially different ways in different industries (as in the case, say, of isopropanol sold directly to manufacturers or indirectly via distributors) so clearly focuses attention, responsibility, and effort that clear competitive advantage generally goes to firms so organized.

A great many generically undifferentiated consumer goods are operationally differentiated by means of branding, packaging, advertising, at times stylized features, and even pricing. Differentiation by pricing is, however, derivative. If nothing else is done (at the minimum, with packaging), price differentiation alone generally fails.

The list of highly differentiated consumer products that not so long ago were sold as essentially undifferentiated or minimally differentiated commodities is long: coffee, soap, flour, beer, sugar, salt, oatmeal, pickles, frankfurters, rice, bananas, chickens, pineapples, potatoes, and lots more. Among consumer intangibles, in recent years there has been an intensification of brand or vendor differentiation in banking, insurance of all kinds, auto rentals, credit cards, stock brokerage, airlines, travel agencies, realtors, beauticians, entertainment parks, small-loan companies, mutual funds, bond funds, and lots more. Among consumer hybrids the same thing has occurred: fast foods, theme restaurants, opticians, food retailers, and specialty retailers in a burgeoning variety of categories—jewelry, sporting goods, books, health and beauty aids, pants and jeans, musical records and cassettes, auto supplies and parts, ice cream shops, home improvement centers, and lots more.

In each of these cases, especially those of consumer tangibles, the general assumption among the less informed is that their competitive distinction rests largely on packaging and advertising. Even substantive differences in the generic products are presumed to be so minimal that what really count are the ads and the packages.

This presumption is one of the most palpably wrong of all the many wrong presumptions that parade so abundantly as wisdom among even insiders in the affected industries. It is not simply their ads or packages that account for the preeminence of General Foods and Proctor & Gamble in so many of their product categories. Nor is it their superior generic products that explain the greater successes of IBM, Xerox, ITT, and Texas Instruments. If either were so, executive recruiters would be less successful in attracting raw material to these outstanding companies.

Their real distinction lies heavily in how they manage. In the case of P&G, General Foods, IBM, and Xerox, it is especially in how they manage marketing. The amount of careful but hidden analysis, control, and field work that characterizes their management of marketing is masked by the enormous visibility of their advertising or presumed generic product uniqueness.

The branded grocery products companies advertise heavily, just as the auto companies do. But they don't have franchised dealers. They have wholesale and retail "distributors," and, depending on which firm we talk about, they work as hard and as closely with their distributors as do the auto companies. Indeed, often they work with them even harder, because their "distributors" handle many competing brands, and the distribution channels are longer and more complex.

Most retail grocery stores handle a number of more or less competing brands of the same generic (or functionally undifferentiated) product. There are more than two dozen national brands of powdered laundry detergent. They are sold to retail buyers mostly in supermarkets or small convenience stores, which get them either from a supermarket chain warehouse or the warehouse of a cooperative wholesaler, a voluntary wholesaler, or an independent wholesaler. Each of these warehouses generally carries a full line of competing brands. Though the national brands try through advertising and promotion to create consumer "pull," they are heavily involved as well in trying to create retailer and wholesaler "push." At retail they regularly seek more advantageous shelf space and more advertising support from the retailer directly. At wholesale they do other things. Some years ago General Foods did a massive study of materials handling in distribution warehouses, making its results and recommendations available to the trade through a carefully trained crew of specialists who helped the trade implement those recommendations. The object, obviously, was to curry special favor with the distributive trades for General Foods' products. The company did something similar for retailers: It made a major study of retail space profitability and then offered retailers a new way of space-profitability accounting. The assumption was that if they helped retailers better manage their space, retailers would favor General Foods products in their merchandising activities. The program was specifically aimed at supermarkets.

At the same time Pillsbury devised Creative Marketing Systems, a program designed specifically to help small convenience stores to operate and compete more effectively. The object was, of course, to obtain preferential "push" treatment for Pillsbury products in these stores.

There is, moreover, a continuous process of improved logistical and material-handling interfacing between suppliers, distributors, and retailers. Deliveries are often scheduled to arrive at specific hours and dates, much as they are for auto assembly plants by parts suppliers. The form in which they are delivered —pallets, dollies, bulk, and the like—are often customized, and retailer preference as to particular shippers are quickly honored. All this is in the service of gaining preference over competitors. The "product" that's bought for the home at retail is one thing, but the same thing is an equally different "product" bought by the store, and still different when bought by the wholesaler. In each case the originating seller tries to achieve some positive differentiating advantages over his competitors.

Nor does the matter stop there. When Heinz packages, sells, and delivers ketchup to institutional purveyors who supply hospitals, restaurants, hotels, prisons, schools, and nursing homes, it not only operates otherwise than when it deals with cooperative wholesalers but also seeks to operate differently in some advantage-producing fashion from Hunt Foods when it deals with the same purveyors. An example of how far this can go is provided by General Foods, whose Institutional Food Service Division some years ago provided elaborate theme-meal recipes for schools, "safari" meals that included such delectables as "Groundnut Soup Uganda," and "Fish Mozambique." General Foods provided "decorations to help you go native" in the cafeteria, including travel posters, Congo face masks, pith helmets, tiger tails, lotus garlands, and paper monkeys. These were merchandised by and through the purveyors in order to raise demand for the General Foods products in the menus.

Such examples abound in consumer-goods marketing, although the visible superstructure of heavy advertising and special packaging often leads people engaged in other industries to the erroneous view that the latter is what marketing is most about in consumer goods, that that's mostly how they differentiate.

It's not. That's only what's easily seen. What's not so easily seen is how they manage their marketing. All four companies referred to before (General Foods, P&G, IBM, Xerox) are organized along product or brand-management lines for their major generic products, and in the case of IBM and Xerox these are complemented with market managers as well. What differentiates them from others is how well they manage marketing, not just what is visibly marketed. It is the *process,* not just the product, that is uniquely differentiated.

Consider the case of a large manufacturer of isopropyl alcohol, commonly called isopropanol. It is a moderately simple, totally undifferentiated generic product chemically synthesized via a well-known process from gas recovered in petroleum refining. It comes in two grades: crude, which is 9 percent water, and refined, which is 1 percent water. In 1970, 1.9 million pounds were produced in the United States, 43 percent being used as a feed stock to make acetone, which had a variety of uses including as a solvent for protective coatings, as a process solvent, and in manufacturing plastics, synthetic fibers, pharmaceuticals, and other chemicals. Isopropanol is also used to make intermediate chemicals such as isopropyl acetate and isopropyl amine, which are used to make plastics, synthetic fibers, and paints and other protective coatings. Isopropanol is also used in large amounts for making various lacquers and protective coatings. Some of it is used by its producers themselves, who are vertically integrated to make some of the above products but also sell it directly to other manufacturers and to distributors.

Because of the introduction of the new cumene process for making acetone, in 1970 isopropanol was in vast oversupply. Prices were deeply depressed and were expected to remain so for some five years until demand caught up to the supply. One of the larger isopropanol producers in 1970 sold 310 million pounds of acetone and isopropanol into the so-called merchant market—that is, direct to a large number and variety of manufacturers. The distribution of these sales was represented by the Sales Department as follows:

| Industry or Use | Million lb |
|---|---|
| Acetone | 124 |
| Other intermediates | 20 |
| Agri-biochemical | 31 |
| Coatings | 86 |
| Other | 49 |
| Total | 310 |

Though the so-called prevailing prices per pound for both acetone and isopropanol were exceedingly low (as low as 4 cents for acetone and 6.7 cents for isopropanol), a careful analysis of this producer's invoices showed wide variations around these prices for sales made to different customers on precisely the same days. Two possible conclusions follow: (1) Not all buyers were identically informed about what indeed were the "prevailing" prices on each of those days, and (2) not all buyers were equally price sensitive. Further analysis showed that these price variations tended often to cluster by industry category and by customer size, but not geographically. A further breakdown of industry categories revealed yet other "price segments." Different kinds of coatings manufacturers exhibited different clusterings of prices they had paid. There were substantial relative differences in prices paid between most agricultural chemical producers and different types of biochemical producers. The category called "other" showed many different price clusters.

Had the marketing process been managed reasonably properly, there might have been a product manager who would have requested the types of analyses the results of which I've just mentioned. Inevitably, the revealed differences in invoice prices and price clusterings would have led a moderately intelligent and inquisitive product manager to ask:

1. Who seem to be the least price aware or price sensitive among the various industry user sectors to which we sell? What is their size distribution? Who exactly are the companies?
2. Who are the most and the least vendor "loyal"—that is, who buy regularly from us, regardless of price fluctuations? Why? And who buy from us occasionally, largely apparently because of price?
3. Who can use or needs our applications help most? Who least?
4. Who will respond most to our offer for help?
5. Where and with whom might we selectively raise prices? Selectively hold prices?
6. How should all this be communicated to the sales organization and be employed to manage the sales forces?

Consider the economics of the situation. Suppose that by careful management of the sales force these generically undifferentiated products (acetone and isopropanol) had been sold largely to the less informed or less price-sensitive industry sectors or customers? Suppose each of the broadly defined customer segments had yielded higher prices of as little as .1 cents per pound, .2 cents per pound, or .5 cents per pound? What would have been the immediate cash contribution to our company? The following table suggests some answers.

| Industry or Use | Million lb | Additional Cash Contributions, by Price Premiums | | |
|---|---|---|---|---|
| | | .1¢ | .2¢ | .5¢ |
| Acetone | 124 | $124,000 | $248,000 | $620,000 |
| Other intermediates | 20 | 20,000 | 40,000 | 100,000 |
| Agri-biochemical | 31 | 31,000 | 62,000 | 155,000 |
| Coatings | 86 | 86,000 | 172,000 | 430,000 |
| Other | 49 | 49,000 | 98,000 | 245,000 |
| Total | 310 | $310,000 | $620,000 | $1,550,000 |
| If 50% had been sold at the premiums | | $155,000 | $310,000 | $775,000 |
| If 10% had been sold at the premiums | | $31,000 | $62,000 | $155,000 |

Thus if only 10 percent of total sales had been sold for only one-tenth of a penny more than they were, the pretax contribution would have risen $31,000. If 50 percent of sales had been raised by this minuscule amount, it would have yielded an extra $155,000; $310,000 if 50 percent had been raised by .2 of one cent.

Given the analysis of markets and users explained above, some such increases seem highly probable. How much would it have been worth to expand the market analysis function into an on-the-spot, on-line activity that would have guided the sales organization to get these results? Obviously a lot. By doing precisely this, this producer would have differentiated itself from its competitors in a manner that one could reasonably expect would have yielded highly profitable differential results.

It is precisely this and related kinds of attention to marketing details that characterizes the work of product managers and market managers. Among producers of generically undifferentiated products—particularly products sold as ingredients to industrial customers—*the management of the marketing process can itself be a powerful differentiating device.* This device is constantly and assiduously employed in the better-managed branded consumer packaged goods companies, which are so often falsely viewed as differentiating only what they sell, not how they manage what is sold.

Differentiation is possible everywhere, and one of its more powerful hidden forms is how the marketing process is managed. In this may reside for many companies, especially those selling what they think of as commodities, the opportunity to escape the commodity trap.

# 5

# Marketing Intangible Products and Product Intangibles

Is the marketing of "services" different from the marketing of "goods"?

The answer, as in most things, is equivocal: The principles may be the same, but translation into practice may be profoundly different.

To understand the difference, it helps to change the words we use. Instead of talking of "goods" and of "services," it is better to talk of "tangibles" and "intangibles." To understand the distinction is to appreciate its practicality.

Tangible products can usually be directly experienced—seen, touched, smelled, tasted, and tested. Often this can be done before you buy. You can test drive a car, smell the perfume, work the numerical controls of a milling machine, inspect the seller's steam-generating installation elsewhere, pretest an extruding machine. Intangible products (like transportation, freight forwarding, insurance, repair, consulting, computer software, investment banking, brokerage, education, health care, accounting) can seldom be experienced or tested in advance.

The significance of modern times is, however, that even the most tangible and experienceable of products cannot, in fact, be reliably tested or experienced in advance. To inspect a vendor's steam-generating plant in advance at another location and to study thoroughly his detailed proposal and design are not enough. Like a successful computer installation, a great deal more is involved than product features and physical installation alone. Though a customer may "buy" a product whose generic tangibility (like the computer or the steam plant) is as palpable as the primeval rocks, and though he may have agreed after great study and extensive negotiation to a cost that runs into the millions of dollars, the process of getting it built on time, installed, and then smoothly operational involves an awful lot more than the generic tangible product itself. What's more crucially at stake are usually a lot of complex, slippery, and difficult intangibles that can make or break the "product's" success. That's true even of mature consumer goods like dishwashing machines, shampoos, and frozen pizza. If a shampoo is not used as prescribed or a pizza not heated as intended, the results can be terrible. So it makes sense to say that all products are in some crucial respects intangible. No matter how diligently designed in advance and carefully constructed in the factory, if installed or used "incorrectly" they'll fail or disappoint in use. The significance of all this for their marketing can be profound.

There are exceptions to the distinctions that separate tangible from intangible products. You can't taste in advance or even see sardines in a can or soap in a box. This is commonly so of frequently purchased moderate- to low-priced consumer goods. To make buyers more comfortable and confident about tangibles that can't be pretested, companies go beyond the literal promises of specifications, advertisements, and labels to provide reassurance. Packaging is a common tool. Pickles are put into see-through glass jars, cookies into cellophane-windowed boxes, canned goods get strong appetite-appealing pictures on the labels, architects make elaborately enticing renderings, and proposals to NASA are packaged in binders that match the craftsmanship of Tyrolean leatherworkers. In all cases the idea is to provide reassuring tangible (in these examples, visual) surrogates for what's promised but can't be more directly experienced till consumption.

Exceptions in intangible products are also frequent. You *can* see a hotel room before you rent and use it. You *can* study a computer software program, and samples of its output, before you buy. But, more than even canned goods, intangible products force buyers to depend on surrogates to assess what they're likely to get. They can look at gloriously glossy pictures of elegant rooms in distant resort hotels set by the shimmering sea. They can consult current users to see how well a software program performs or how well the investment banker or the oil well drilling contractor performs; they can ask experienced customers regarding engineering firms, trust companies, lobbyists, professors, surgeons, prep schools, hair stylists, consultants, repair shops, industrial maintenance firms, shippers, franchisers, general contractors, funeral directors, caterers, environment management firms, construction companies, and on and on.

When prospective customers can't taste, test, feel, smell, or watch the product in operation in advance, what they are asked to buy are, simply, promises of satisfaction. Even tangible, testable, feelable, smellable products are, before they're bought, largely promises.

Satisfaction later in consumption or use can seldom be quite the same as earlier in trial or promise. Some promises promise more than others. It depends on product features, design, degree of tangibility, type of promotion, price, and differences in what customers hope to accomplish with what they buy. Of some products less is expected than what is explicitly or symbolically promised. The right kind of eye shadow properly applied may promise to transform you into an irresistible tigress in the night. But not even the most eager buyer literally believes the metaphor. Still, the metaphor makes the sale. Neither do you literally expect the proposed new corporate headquarters, so artfully rendered by the winning architect, automatically to produce all those cheerfully productive employees the renderings show lounging with casual elegance at lunch in the verdant courtyard.

Yet the metaphor helps win the assignment. When prospective customers can't taste, test, feel, smell, watch, or properly try the promised product in advance, the necessity of metaphorical reassurances to the marketing effort becomes amplified. Promises, being intangible, have to be tangibilized in their presentation, hence the tigress and the lounging employees. Metaphors and similes become surrogates for the tangibility that cannot be provided or experienced in advance.

This accounts for the solid, somber, Edwardian decor of downtown law offices; for the prudentially elegant and orderly public offices of investment banking houses; for the confidently articulate consultants in dark vested suits; for engineering and project proposals in "executive" type and leather bindings; for the elaborate pictorial documentation of the performance virtuosity of newly offered machine controls. It explains why insurance companies pictorially offer "a piece of the rock," put you under a "blanket of protection," under an "umbrella," or in "good hands."

Not even tangible products are exempt from the necessity of using symbol and metaphor. A computer terminal has to look "right." It has to be "packaged" to convey an impression of reliable modernity—based on the assumption that prospective buyers will translate appearance into confidence about performance. In that respect, the marketing ideas behind the "packaging" of a $1-million computer, a $2-million jet engine, and a half-million-dollar numerically controlled milling machine are scarcely different from the marketing ideas behind the "packaging" of a $50 electric shaver or a $1.50 tube of lipstick.

Common sense tells us, and research confirms, that people use appearances to make judgments about realities. It matters little whether the products are high-priced or low-priced, whether they are technically complex or simple, whether the buyers are supremely sophisticated in the technology of what's being considered or just plain ignorant, or whether they buy for themselves or for their employers. Everybody always depends to some extent on appearances, on external impressions.

Nor is the importance of impressions limited only to the "generic" product itself—that is, to the technical offering, such as the speed, versatility, and precision of the lathe, the color and creaminess of the lipstick, or the taste and size of the lobster thermadore. Consider investment banking. No matter how thorough and persuasive a firm's recommendations and assurances about a proposed underwriting, no matter how pristine its reputation for integrity and performance, somehow the financial vice president of the billion-dollar client corporation would feel better had the bank's representative not been quite so youthful and apple-cheeked. The offered products will be judged in part by who personally offers it—not just "who" the vendor corporation is but also "who" the corporation's representative is. The vendor and the vendor's representative are both inextricably and inevitably part of "the product" that the prospect must judge before he buys. The less tangible the generic product, the more powerfully and persistently the judgment about it is shaped by the "packaging"—how it's presented, who presents it, what's implied by metaphor, simile, symbol, and other surrogates for reality.

So too with tangible products. They do not stand alone on their generic essence. The sales engineers assigned to work with an electric utility company that will ask for competitive bids on a $100-million steam boiler system for its new plant are as powerfully a part of the offered product (the "promise") as the investment banking firm's partner.

The reason is easy to see. In neither case is there a product until it's delivered. You don't know how well it works until it's put and kept at work.

In both investment banking and big boilers, to become the designated vendor requires successful passage through several successive gates, the stages in the sales process. It is not unlike courtship. Both customers know that a rocky courtship spells trouble ahead. If the suitor is not sufficiently solicitous during courtship, if he's insensitive to moods and needs, unresponsive or wavering during stress or adversity, there will be problems in the marriage. But unlike a real marriage, there can be no divorce. Once the deal is made, marriage and gestation have simultaneously begun. After that things are often irreversible. In investment banking, it may take months of close work with the client's organization before the underwriting can be launched, before the baby is born. In the construction of an electric power plant it takes years, through sickness and health. But as with babies, birth presents new problems. All babies must be carefully coddled to see them through early life. Relapse is to be avoided or quickly corrected if it happens. Stocks or bonds should not go quickly to deep discounts. The boiler should not suddenly malfunction after several weeks or months; if it does, it should be rapidly restored to full use. Understandably, the client will, in courtship, note everything carefully, judging always what kind of husband and father the eager suitor is likely to make.

In that sense, the way the product is packaged (how the promise is depicted in brochure, letter, design appearance) and how it is presented and by whom all become parts of the product itself, because they are elements of what it is that the customer finally decides to buy or reject.

A product is more than a tangible thing, even a huge thing like a $100-million boiler. From the buyer's viewpoint, the product is a promise, a cluster of value expectations of which its nontangible parts are as integral as its tangible parts. Certain conditions must be satisfied before the prospect buys. If they are not satisfied, there is no sale. There would have been no sale in the cases of the investment banker and the boiler manufacturer if their representatives had been improperly responsive or insufficiently informed about the customers' special situations and problems during the prebidding (courtship) stages of the relationship. The reason there would have been no sale is that in each case the promised product—the whole product—was not satisfactory. It is not that it was incomplete; it was not right. Changing the "salesman" in midstream is not likely to have helped. In each case the selling organization by then would already have "said" the wrong thing about itself, its product. If, during the courtship, the prospective customer got the impression that there might be aftermarket problems in execution, in timeliness, in the postsale support necessary for smooth and congenial relations, then the customer got a perfectly complete message of what the product would be. It would be bad.

What makes intangible products unique is that they are entirely nonexistent before being bought, entirely incapable of prior inspection or review. For that reason, the customer is forced to make judgments far more on the basis of what's asserted or implied about the product than with tangible products. Assertions and implications must therefore be more carefully managed than with tangible products. Still, in some cases the distinction between the marketing needs of tangible and those of intangible products is negligible. Tangible products that may require considerable or continuing after-sale buyer–seller interaction, or ones that perform functions vital to the continuing effectiveness of the buyer's company (such as, for example, a data processing installation), depend heavily for sales success on assertions and implications made in advance. That is particularly so when tangible products require considerable maintenance help, parts availability, postpurchase adjusting, and application support.

What therefore becomes crucial for sales success is how competitors differentiate themselves from each other. Competing firms offering tangible products differentiate each other by design, operating features, and special-purpose applications. Competing intangible products do so more commonly by surrogates. While similarities abound, the differences are crucial. When offering minicomputers for the international departments of commercial banks, Digital Equipment Corporation (DEC) emphasizes a software package oriented to what it believes are the special needs of those departments. Its major competitors emphasize software oriented to the bank's total information processing and cash management needs. Digital believes that the department, operating as a profit center, is more attracted to a product that *it* can "control" for getting its customer-serving jobs done than to a product (which includes software) that might be preferred by the bank's central data center, whose main concern is record-keeping, or the bank's corporate managers, whose main concern is bankwide cash management. DEC has therefore shifted the battle for competitive advantage not simply away from the capabilities of the computer itself but more significantly to the institutional incentives of its specific users in the customer organization. It has positioned itself in a different competitive quadrant—asserting and implying superior capability of meeting the needs of the users rather than simply of the "corporation" (the bank) that will sign the check. DEC tangibilizes its distinction with software, brochures, and other indicative evidence of its special understanding of and responsiveness to the needs and practices of the bank departments on which it calls.

So much, briefly, for making a sale, for getting a customer. Keeping a customer is quite another thing, and on that score intangible products have very special problems.

Intangible products are by nature highly people-intensive in their production and delivery. Corporate financial services of banks are, in this respect, not so different from hairdressing or consultancy. The more people-intensive a product, the more room there is for personal discretion, idiosyncrasy, error, and delay. Once a customer for an intangible product is sold, the customer can be easily unsold as a consequence of his expectations having been underfulfilled. A tangible product, being manufactured under close supervision in a factory and generally delivered through a planned network of orderly transmission, is much more likely than an intangible product to fulfill the promised expectation. Consider the contrast:

"Goods are produced, services are performed," wrote John M. Rathwell.[1] A tangible product is designed, generally, by design professionals working under conditions of benign isolation, having received guidance from market intelligence experts, scientists, and others. The product will be manufactured by another group of specialists in a facility and with equipment specifically designed for that purpose, generally under conditions of close supervision that facilitate relatively reliable quality control. Installation and use by the customer is guided within a relatively narrow range of possibilities dictated by the product itself.

Intangible products present an entirely different picture.

[1] John M. Rathwell, *Marketing in the Service Sector* (Cambridge, Mass.: Winthrop Publishers, 1974), p. 58.

The computer software designer must do his own research on the customer's premises, trying to understand complex networks of interconnecting operations. Then he designs the system and the software. Having designed it, he has manufactured it. Unlike tangible products, for intangible products design and manufacturing is simultaneous and generally done by the same people. Often they are done by one person alone, like a craftsman at a workbench. Moreover, manufacturing the product is generally indistinguishable from its actual delivery. In situations such as consultancy, from the client's viewpoint, the delivery *is* the manufacturing. If the delivery is an oral presentation that's intended to effect change (as is often the case in consultancy and other expert advisory work), though the study may have been excellent, if the delivery is poor, it will be viewed as having been badly "manufactured." It's a faulty product. So too with the work of brokers of all kinds, restaurants to a considerable extent, educators and trainers, accounting firms, engineering firms, architects, orthodontists, transportation companies, hospitals and clinics, government agencies, banks, trust companies, mutual funds, car rental companies, insurance companies, repair and maintenance operations, and on and on. For each, delivery and production are virtually indistinguishable.

Because these are highly people-intensive operations, there is an enormous problem of quality control. Quality control on an automobile assembly line is in some respects automatic, built into the system. If a yellow door is hung on a red car, somebody on the line will quickly ask if that's what was intended. If the left front wheel is missing, the person next in line, especially if the task is to fasten the lug bolts, will stop the line. But if a commercial banker misses an important feature of a financing package or doesn't do it well, his lapse may never be found or may be found too late. If the ashtrays aren't cleaned on a rented car, discovery is provocative, not preventive: It will annoy or irritate the already committed customer. Repeat business is jeopardized.

No matter how well trained or motivated, people make mistakes, forget, commit indiscretions, at times get hard to handle. Hence the search for alternatives to dependence on people. Automatic telephone switching is not simply cheaper than manual switching, it is far more reliable. Chapter 3 suggests a variety of ways to reduce people dependence in the so-called service industries via what I have called "the industrialization of service." This means substituting "hard," "soft," or "hybrid" technologies for totally people-intensive activities. Examples of a "hard" technology, as noted before, are automatic direct dialing to replace operator-assisted telephone dialing, credit cards replacing repetitive credit checking, and continuous computerized monitoring rather than batch testing of industrial processes. A "soft" technology is the substitution of division of labor for one-person craftsmanship in production—as, for example, organizing the work force that cleans an office building so that each worker specializes in one or several limited tasks (dusting, waxing, vacuuming, window cleaning) rather than have each person do all these jobs alone. Insurance companies long ago went to extensive division of labor in their applications processing—registering, underwriting, actuarying, policy issuing. "Hybrid" technologies combine the soft and the hard. The floor is waxed by machine rather than by hand. French fries are precut and portion-packed in a factory for finishing in a fast-food restaurant in specially designed deep fryers that signal when the process is completed. A computer automatically calculates and makes all entries in an Internal Revenue Service form 1040 after a relatively modestly trained clerk has entered the raw data on a console.

Industrializing systems help control quality and cut costs. To get those results it is important to see what's involved. Instead of depending on people to work better, industrialization redesigns the work so that people work differently. Thus there is applied to service (the production, creation, and delivery of largely intangible products) the same modes of managerial rationality that were first applied to goods production in the nineteenth century. The real significance of the nineteenth century is not the Industrial Revolution, with its shift from animal to machine power, but the managerial revolution, with its shift from the craftsman's functional independence to the manager's rational routines. In successive waves, the mechanical harvester, the sewing machine, and then the automobile epitomized the genius of the century. Each was rationally designed so as to become an assembled rather than a constructed machine, a machine that depended not on the idiosyncratic artistry of a single craftsman but on simple standardized tasks performed to simple routine specifications by unskilled workers. This required detailed planning and enormous managerial enterprise so that interchangeable parts would be properly designed, manufactured, ordered, and arranged via lifts and jigs for assembly on moving conveyors, and so that large numbers of people would be at the right places at the right times to do the right simple jobs in the right ways. Then, with massive output, distribution and aftermarket training and service systems had to be created and kept going so that the massive output of goods would itself be justified.

What's been largely missing in nontangible goods production is the kind of managerial rationality that produced the Industrial Revolution. That is why the quality of nontangible goods tends to be less reliable than it might be, the costs higher than they should be, and customer satisfaction lower than it need be.

While I have referred to the enormous progress that has in recent years been made on these matters and suggested ways to make still more, there is one characteristic of intangible products that requires special attention for holding customers. Unique to intangible products is that the customer is seldom aware when he's being served well. This is especially so in the case of intangible products that, for the duration of the contract, are consumed almost constantly, such as certain banking services, cleaning services, freight hauling, energy management, maintenance services, telephones, and the like.

Consider an international banking relationship, an insurance relationship, an industrial cleaning relationship. If all goes well, the customer is virtually oblivious to what he's getting. Only when things don't go well or a competitor suggests they could go better does the customer become aware of the product's existence or nonexistence: when a letter of credit is incorrectly drawn; when a competing bank proposes better arrangements; when the annual insurance premium notice arrives or a claim is disputed; when the ashtrays aren't cleaned or a favorite pen holder is missing after the cleaning crew has left.

The most important thing to know about intangible products is that the *customer usually doesn't know what he's getting until he doesn't*. Only when he doesn't get what he bargained for does he become aware of *what* he bargained for. Only on dissatisfaction does he dwell. Satisfaction is, as it should be, mute. Its prior presence is affirmed only by its subsequent absence.

And that's dangerous, because the customer will be aware only of failure, of dissatisfaction, not of success or satisfaction. That makes him terribly susceptible to the blandishments of competitive sellers. A competitor can always structure a more interesting corporate financing deal, can always propose a more imaginative insurance program, can always find dust on top of the picture frame in the office, can always cite small visible failures that imply big hidden ones and vendor neglect.

Thus, while in *getting* customers for intangibles it becomes important to create surrogates or metaphors for tangibility— how we dress, how we speak, write, design and present proposals, work with prospects, respond to inquiries, initiate ideas, show how well we understand the prospect's business—in *keeping* customers for intangibles it becomes important regularly to remind the customers of what they're regularly getting. If that's not done, the customer will not know. He'll only know when he's *not* getting what he bought, and that's all that's likely to count unless, in the interval, he's been made so regularly and persuasively aware of what he's been getting all along that occasional failures fade in relative importance.

To keep customers for regularly delivered and consumed intangible products, they have to be regularly reminded of what they're getting. The promises that were made in order to land the customer must be regularly reinstated when the promises are fulfilled. Even the source of the delivered product has to be regularly reinstated in the customer's consciousness lest he forget who his anonymous and silent vendor is.

When an insurance prospect is heavily romanced and finally accepts marriage, the subsequent silence and inattention can be deafening. Most customers seldom recall for long what kind of life insurance package they bought, often forgetting as well the name of both underwriter and agent. To be reminded a year later via a premium notice reminds one only of the disjunction between the loving attention in courtship and the long cold silence in marriage. No wonder the lapse rate in personal life insurance is so high.

Once a relationship is cemented, equity is created for the seller. He has a customer. To help keep him, the equity in that relationship must be enhanced lest it decline and become jeopardized by competitors.

There are innumerable ways to do that, and some of these can be industrialized. Periodic letters or phone calls that remind the customer of how well things are going are low-cost and surprisingly powerful equity maintainers. Newsletters or regular visits suggesting new or better or augmented product features are useful. Even nonbusiness socializing has its value, as is acknowledged and affirmed by corporations struggling in recent years with the Internal Revenue Service about the deductability of hunting lodges, yachts, clubs, and spouses attending conferences and customer meetings at exotic watering holes in distant places.

Here are some examples of how companies have strengthened their relationships with customers:

—An energy management company sends out a periodic "Update Report" on conspicuous yellow paper, advising clients how to discover and correct energy leaks, install improved monitors, and accomplish cost savings.

—A computer service bureau organizes its account managers for a two-week series of blitz customer callbacks to "explain casually" the installation of new central processing equipment that is expected to prevent cost increases next year while expanding the customers' interactive options.

—A long-distance hauler of high-value electronic equip-

106

ment (computers, terminals, mail sorters, word processors, medical diagnostic instruments) has instituted quarterly performance reviews with its shippers, some of which include customers who are encouraged to talk about their experiences and expectations.

—An insurance company sends periodic one-page notices to policyholders *and* policy beneficiaries. These generally begin with a single-sentence congratulation that policy and coverage remain nicely intact and follow with brief views on recent tax rulings affecting insurance, new notions about personal financial planning, and special protection packages available with other types of insurance.

In all these ways, sellers of intangible products reinstate their presence and performance in the customers' minds, reminding them of their continuing presence and the value of what is constantly, and silently, being delivered.

All products have elements of tangibility and intangibility. Companies that sell tangible products invariably promise more than the tangible products themselves. Indeed, enormous dedication, often in pretentious proportions, focuses on the enhancement of the intangibles—promises about bountiful benefits conferred rather than on features offered. To the buyer of photographic film, Kodak promises with unremitting emphasis just one thing, the satisfactions of enduring remembrance, memories clearly preserved. Wisely, Kodak says almost nothing about the superior luminescence of its pictures. The product is remembrance, not film or pictures. The promoted product of the automobile, as everyone knows, is certainly not transportation. Auto companies promote what people respond to most in their minds, not what the manufacturers make most effectively in their factories. Auto dealers, on the other hand, assuming correctly that people's minds have already been reached by the manufacturers' ads, focus on other considerations: deals, availability, postpurchase servicing. Neither the dealers nor the manufacturers "sell" the tangible cars themselves. They "sell" the intangible benefits that are bundled into the entire package: the total product, with considerable emphasis these days on fuel efficiency.

If tangible products must be intangibilized to add customer-getting appeal, then intangible products must be tangibilized—what Professor Leonard L. Berry calls "managing the evidence."[2] Ideally, this should be done as a matter of routine without the necessity of intervening personal promises or reassurances. It should be industrialized. Hotels do this regularly. In their bathrooms the drinking glasses are wrapped in fresh bags or film, the toilet seat has a "sanitized" paper band, the end piece of the toilet tissue is neatly shaped into a fresh-looking arrowhead. All these say with silent affirmative clarity that "the room has been specially cleaned for your use and comfort," yet no words are spoken to say it. Words, in any case, would be less convincing, nor could employees be reliably depended on to say them each time or say them convincingly. Hotels thus have not only tangibilized their promise but also industrialized its delivery. It's become a nonpersonalized routine.

Take, on the other hand, the instructive case of house insulation, a necessity most homeowners approach with understandable apprehension. Suppose you call two companies to bid on your house. The first insulation installer arrives in his car. After pacing once around the house with measured self-assurance and making quick calculations on back of an envelope, he confidently quotes $2,400 for six-inch fiberglass, total satisfaction guaranteed. Another drives up in a clean white truck with clipboard in hand. He scrupulously measures the house dimensions, counts the windows, crawls the attic, records from a source book the area's seasonal temperature ranges and wind velocities. He asks a host of questions, meanwhile recording everything with obvious diligence. He then promises to return in three days, which he does, with a typed proposal for six-inch fiberglass insulation at $2,600, total satisfaction guaranteed. From which will you buy?

The latter has tangibilized the intangible, made a promise

[2] Leonard L. Berry, "Service Marketing Is Different," *Business,* May–June 1980, pp. 24–29.

into a credible expectation. Even more persuasive tangibility is provided by an insulation firm whose representative types the relevant information into a portable intelligent printing terminal. The analysis and response are almost instant, causing one user to call it "the most powerful tool ever developed in the insulation industry." If the house owner is head of the project buying team of an electric utility company, the treasurer of a mighty corporation, the materials purchasing agent of a ready-mixed cement company, the transportation manager of a fertilizer manufacturer, or the data processing director of an insurance company, it's almost certain he will make vendor decisions in his work the same way as he did for his house. He requires the risk-reducing reassurance of tangibilized intangibles.

The practice of providing reassuring tangibilizations of the intangible—of the promise—can be effectively employed even when the generic product is itself tangible. Laundry detergents that claim special whitening capabilities make the promise credible with "blue whitener beads" that are clearly visible to the user. Proctor & Gamble's new decaffeinated instant coffee (High Point) attests to coffee genuineness with luminescent "milled flakes for hearty, robust flavor." You can *see* what the claims promise.

Getting customers for an intangible product requires the product to be tangibilized. Keeping customers for an intangible product requires the product to be reinstated, to be constantly resold while things go well lest the customer get lost when things go badly. Doing both well requires that the tasks be industrialized. The relationship with the customer has to be managed much more carefully and continuously in the case of intangible than tangible products, though it is vital in both cases. Managing the relationship is in itself another topic. It rises in importance as products become more complex and links between buyer and seller are required by the necessity of that complexity to become more intimate and stretch out over greater periods of time, often much longer than any of the parties to the transactions remain in their jobs. "Relationship management" is a special important subject all its own. It is treated separately in Chapter 6.

Meanwhile, the importance of what I've tried to say here is

emphasized by one overriding fact: A customer is an asset that's usually more precious than the tangible assets on the balance sheet. You can usually buy balance sheet assets. There are lots of willing sellers. You cannot so easily buy customers. They are far less willing than are sellers and have lots of eager sellers offering them many choices. Moreover, a customer is a double asset: First, he is the direct source of cash from the sale, and second, his existence can be used to raise cash from bankers and investors, cash that can be converted into tangible assets.

The old chestnut that "Nothing happens till you make a sale," is awfully close to an important truth. What it increasingly takes to make and keep that sale is to tangibilize the intangible, to restate the benefit and its source to the customer, and to industrialize the processes that are involved in doing these.

# 6

## Relationship Management

The relationship between a seller and a buyer seldom ends when the sale is made. In a great and increasing proportion of transactions, the relationship actually intensifies subsequent to the sale. This becomes the critical factor in the buyer's choice of the seller the next time around. This is certainly true of all financial services, consultancy, general contracting, the military and space equipment industries, capital goods, and any vendor organization involving a continuous stream of transactions between seller and buyer.

The sale merely consummates the courtship. Then the marriage begins. How good the marriage is depends on how well the relationship is managed by the seller. That determines whether there will be continued or expanded business or troubles and divorce, and whether costs or profits increase.

In some cases divorce is impossible, as when a major construction or installation project is under way. What remains is a

111

burdened and costly marriage that tarnishes the seller's reputation. Companies can avoid troubles and enhance their standing by recognizing at the outset the necessity of managing their relationship with customers.

This takes more than what comes normally in good marketing. It takes special attention geared to what uniquely characterizes a relationship. That is *time*. The economic theory of "supply and demand" is totally false in this respect. It presumes that the work of the economic system is time discrete and absent of human interactions—an instantaneous, disembodied sales transaction clears the market at the intersection of supply and demand. This was never so and is increasingly less so as growing product complexity and interdependencies among the institutions of the industrial system intensify. The buyer of automated machinery does not, like the buyer at a flea market, walk home with his purchase and take his chances. He expects installation services, applications aids, parts, postpurchase repair and maintenance, retrofitted enhancements, and vendor R & D in support of the buyer's need to stay competitive in all respects. The buyer of a continuous stream of transactions, like a frozen food manufacturer who buys cartons from a packaging company and cash-management services from a bank, is concerned not with "clearing the market" but rather with maintaining the process. With the growing complexity of military equipment, it is not surprising that 78 percent of the U.S. defense budget now goes for items in units of less than a hundred. Growing complexity and increasing costs lead to a growing need for continuous services and enhancements in order to keep the product longer in effective and state-of-the-art use.

The purchase cycles of products and major components gets increasingly stretched, and this changes the nature of what needs to be attended to. Consider the purchase cycles of the following:

| | |
|---|---|
| Oil field installations | 15–20 years |
| Chemical plant | 10–15 years |
| EDP system | 5–10 years |

| Weapons system | 20–30 years |
|---|---|
| Steel plant major components | 5–10 years |
| Paper supply contract | 5 years |

And consider the changing character of assurances under which purchases are being made:

LONG-TERM ASSURANCES

| Subject | From | → | To |
|---|---|---|---|
| Tankers | Spot | | Charter |
| Apartments | Rental | | Cooperative |
| Auto warrants | 10,000 | | 50,000 |
| Technology | Buy | | Lease |
| Labor | Hire | | Contracts |
| Supplies | Shopping | | Contracting |
| Equipment | Repair | | Maintenance |

In these conditions a purchase decision is not a decision to buy an item (to have, as in modern life, an affair), but a decision to enter a bonded relationship (to have a marriage). This requires of the would-be seller a new orientation and a new strategy. Marketing by itself is no longer enough. Consider the compelling differences between the old and the new. Consider selling:

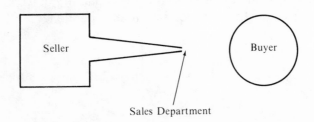

Sales Department

Here the seller, living at a distance from the buyer, reaches out with his sales department to unload onto the buyer what the seller has decided to make. This is the basis for the notion that a salesman needs charisma, because it is charisma that makes the sale rather than the product selling itself. Consider, by contrast, marketing:

113

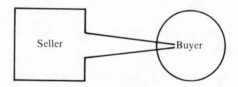

Here the seller, living closer to the buyer, penetrates the buyer's domain to learn about his needs, desires, fears, and the like, and then designs and supplies the product in all its forms. Instead of trying to get the buyer to want what the seller has, the seller tries to have what the buyer will want. The "product" is no longer merely an item but a whole bundle of value satisfactions —what in Chapter 4 I called the "augmented product."

With increasing interdependence, more and more of the world's economic work gets done through long-term relationships between sellers and buyers. It is not just that once you get a customer you want to keep him. It is more a matter of what the buyer wants. He wants a vendor who keeps his promises, who'll keep supplying and stand behind what he promised. The age of the blind date or the one-night stand is gone. Marriage is both more convenient and more necessary. Products are too complicated, repeat negotiations too much of a hassle and too costly. In these conditions success in marketing, like success in marriage, is transformed into the inescapability of a relationship. The interface is transformed into interdependence.

To be, under these circumstances, a good marketer in the conventional sense is not good enough. When it takes five years of intensive, close work between seller and buyer during which the previous signing of a contract is converted into the "delivery" of, say, an operating chemical plant or a telecommunications system, more will have to be done than in the kind of marketing that landed the contract at the outset. The buyer needs assurance at the outset that the two parties will live congenially together during the long period in which the purchase is transformed into delivery.

The seller and the buyer have different capital structures, face different competitive conditions and costs, and have different incentive structures and different purposes respecting the commitments they have made to each other. The seller has made a sale, which he expects directly to yield a profit. The buyer has bought a tool with which to produce things to yield a profit. *For the seller it is the end of the process; for the buyer the beginning.* Yet their interdependence is inextricable, inescapable, and profound. To make the dependencies of these totally different and differently motivated entities work and to keep them trouble-free requires that the relationships be understood and that their management be planned for in advance of the marriage itself. To get out the marriage manual after trouble has begun is to have done so too late.

The future will be a future of more and more intensified relationships, especially in industrial marketing, but also increasingly even in frequently purchased consumer goods. Thus Procter & Gamble, copying General Mills' Betty Crocker advisory service, has found that the installation of a consumer hotline to give advice on its products and their uses raised customer brand loyalty.

The future is best understood with reference to the past and the present. These may be best seen with respect to specific matters in industrial settings, as set forth in the accompanying table (p. 116).

The defining characteristic of the terms in the column on "Future" is time. What is labeled "Item" in the first row was, in the past, simply a product, something that was bought for its own value. More recently that simple product was not enough. What was bought was an "augmented product." In the era we are entering more will be required. It will be system contracts, characterized by a complex congeries of continuous contacts and evolving relationships that surround the systems. The "Sale" will be a system over time, not just a system itself. The

| Category | Past | Present | Future |
|---|---|---|---|
| Item | Product | Augmented product | System contracts |
| Sale | Unit | System | System/time |
| Value | Feature advantage | Technology advantages | System advantages |
| Lead time | Short | Long | Lengthy |
| Service | Modest | Important | Vital |
| Delivery place | Local | National | Global |
| Delivery phase | Once | Frequently | Continuous |
| Strategy | Sales | Marketing | Relationship |

"Value" that is at stake will pertain to the advantages of that total system over time. As the customer gains more experience with it over time, the technology will decline in importance relative to the system of benefits in which the technology is embedded. More important than technology will be the other benefits and interactions, like services, delivery, reliability, responsiveness, and the quality of the human and organizational interactions between seller and buyer over time.

The management of industrial marketing contracts deals with coexistence and communications over time. The object is to fulfill the customer's expectations so as to earn his loyalty and thus his continued patronage, preferably at a level of satisfaction that will be reflected in above-average margins.

The more complex the system, and the more "software" it requires (such as its operating procedures and protocols, its management routines, its service components), and the longer it takes to implement the system, the greater the customer's anxieties and expectations. *Expectations* are what people buy, not things. They buy the expectations of benefits promised by the vendor. When it takes a long time to fulfill the promise (such as the delivery of a new custom-made automated work station), or if fulfillment is continuous over a long period (such as banking services, fuel to run your facilities, or components for your assembly operations), the buyer's anxieties build up after the purchase decision is made. Will the delivery be prompt? Will it be smooth and regular? Did we select the best vendor?

When downstream realities loom larger than up-front promises, what do you do before, during, and after the sale? Who will be responsible for what?

To answer these questions it helps to understand how the customer's expectations are shaped by the promises and behavior of the vendor before the sale is made. If you promise the moon, it is reasonable for the customer to expect it. If those who do the selling and the marketing, however, operate on commissions paid out before the customer gets everything he bargained for, or if they sell against high quotas, they're not likely to feel any strong compulsion to assure that the moon actually gets fully and reliably delivered. After the sale they'll rush off to pursue other prey. If marketing plans the sale, sales make it, manufacturing fulfills it, and service services it, who's in charge and who feels responsible?

Problems arise not only because those who do the selling, the marketing, the manufacturing, and the servicing have different incentives and, as a result, view the customer differently, but also because organizations are themselves one-dimensional. An organization necessarily internalizes itself, even though it may depend on externals (customers) for its fate. "Inside" is where the work gets done, where the workplace is, where the penalties and incentives reside, where the budgets and plans are made, where engineering and manufacturing take place, where performance is measured, where one's friends and associates are, where things are managed and manageable and the outside is where "you can't change things," and besides, it "has nothing to do with me." Those for whom the outside clearly "has something to do with me" are the people in sales and marketing. But there are lots of disjunctions between seller and buyer regarding the object of the sale, and these differ at different stages of the sale. These may be simply stated (Table A, p. 118). When the first sale is finally made, different things happen to the seller and to the buyer. These create the basis for a lot of dissonance (Table B, p. 118).

*The fact of buying changes the buyer.* He expects the seller to remember the purchase as having been a favor bestowed on him by the buyer, not as something earned by the seller. Hence

## A. STAGES AND OBJECTS OF THE SALE

| Stage of Sale | Seller | Buyer |
|---|---|---|
| 1. Before | Real hope | Vague need |
| 2. Romance | Hot & heavy | Testing & hopeful |
| 3. Sale | Fantasy—bed | Fantasy—board |
| 4. After | Looks elsewhere for next sale | "You don't care." |
| 5. Long after | Indifferent | "Can't this be made better?" |
| 6. Next sale | "How about a new one?" | "Really?" |

## B. WHEN THE FIRST SALE IS MADE

| The Seller | The Buyer |
|---|---|
| Objective achieved | Judgment postponed, applies test of time |
| Selling stops | Shopping continues |
| Focus goes elsewhere | Focus on purchase, wants affirmation of expectations |
| Tension released | Tension increased |
| Relationship reduced or ended | Relationship intensified, commitment made |

it is wrong to assume that to have gained an account gives you an advantage by virtue of having gotten "a foot in the door." The opposite is increasingly the case. If the buyer views the sale as a favor conferred by him on the seller, then he in effect debits the seller's account. The seller owes him one. The seller is in the position of having to rebuild his relationship from a deficit position.

In the absence of good management, the relationship deteriorates because of the differences between the buyer and the seller in their needs, wants, and incentive structures and because both organizations tend naturally to face inward to their internal affairs rather than outward toward each other. Inward orientation by the selling organization leads to insensitivity and unresponsiveness in customer relations, at best to the substitution of bureaucratic formalities for authentic interactions. Thus the things that build bad relationships accumulate while good ones suffer.

The natural tendency of relationships, whether in marriage

or in business, is entropy—the erosion or deterioration of sensitivity and attentiveness. A healthy relationship maintains, and preferably expands, the equity and the possibilities that were created during courtship. A healthy relationship requires a conscious and constant fight against the forces of entropy. It becomes important for the seller regularly and seriously to ask himself, for example, "How are we doing?" "Is the relationship improving or deteriorating?" "Are our promises being fully fulfilled?" "Are we neglecting anything?" "How do we stand vis-à-vis our competitors in the relationship?" Consider the good things that might be done and the bad things that are done to affect relationships with buyers (Table C).

## C. THINGS AFFECTING RELATIONSHIPS

| Good Things | Bad Things |
| --- | --- |
| Initiate positive phone calls | Make only callbacks |
| Make recommendations | Make justifications |
| Candor in language | Accommodative language |
| Use phone | Use correspondence |
| Show appreciation | Wait for misunderstandings |
| Make service suggestions | Wait for service requests |
| Use "we" problem-solving language | Use "owe-us" legal language |
| Get to problems | Only respond to problems |
| Use jargon/shorthand | Use long-winded communications |
| Personality problems aired | Personality problems hidden |
| Talk of "our future together" | Talk about making good on the past |
| Routinize responses | Fire drill/emergency responsiveness |
| Accept responsibility | Shift blame |
| Plan the future | Rehash the past |

One of the surest signs of a bad or declining relationship is the absence of complaints from the customer. Nobody is ever *that* satisfied, especially not over an extended period of time. The customer is either not being candid or not being contacted. Probably both. Communication is impaired. The absence of candor reflects the decline of trust, the deterioration of the relationship. Bad things accumulate. The relationship depreciates. As in marriage, impaired communication is both a symptom and a cause of trouble. Things fester inside. When they finally erupt, it's usually too late, or very costly.

119

Your next sale, next product, next idea, next success depend a lot on your external relationships. A good relationship is an asset. We can invest in relationships and we can borrow from them. We all do it, but we seldom account for it and almost never manage it. Yet a company's most precious asset is its relationships with its customers. It is not "who you know" but how you are known to them. And that is a function of the nature of your relationships with them, which depends on how they have been managed.

Not all relationships can be or need to be at the same level of intimacy or of the same duration. These characteristics depend on the extent of the actual or felt dependencies between the buyers and the sellers. And, of course, those dependencies can be extended or contracted by means of various direct links that can be established between buyer and seller. Thus, when Bergen Burnswig, the booming drug and health care products distributor, puts computer terminals in its customers' offices to enable them to order directly and get instant feedback regarding their shelf movement, inventory, and other valuable information, a new dependency link has been created that helps tie the customer to the vendor. At the same time, however, there are important ways in which the seller becomes dependent on the buyer. The most obvious resides in the buyer's ability to withdraw his custom or reduce the percentage of buying he does with that vendor. Less obvious is that the buyer is, or can be, an important source of important information for the seller. How much is the buyer's own business likely to change, and therefore how will he buy in the future? What are the substitute products or materials, and what variety of prices and services is being offered to the buyer by competitors who seek his business and the business of other customers or potential customers? How well are we fulfilling the customer's needs and expectations? Is our performance in the field up to our promises from headquarters? To what new uses is the customer putting our product, or how is he using it differently?

The accuracy of forecasts regarding the buyer's intentions rests on the quality of the relationship with him. In a good relationship the buyer shares his plans and expectations with the vendor or at least makes it possible to know his intentions. Surprises and bad forecasts are symptoms of bad relationships. Everybody loses, even the buyer. With better information the vendor can better serve and therefore better hold the buyer. Everybody benefits.

Thus there is a system of reciprocal dependencies. It is up to the seller to develop the relationship beyond that supposed by the simple notion of keeping a customer merely for the contribution he makes to the seller's current revenues and profits. In a proper relationship both the buyer and the seller should have a "profit." Otherwise the relationship cannot last. Moreover, acquisition costs are rarely the only costs of what's being bought. Postpurchase costs are almost always inevitable. Somebody has to bear or share them. This means that the vendor should work at getting his customer to want to maintain the vendor's long-term profitability at an acceptable level instead of squeezing to get rock-bottom delivered prices. Nor is the low-cost producer necessarily the low-cost supplier, even when his price reflects his costs. Unless the costs of the expected postpurchase services are also somehow reflected in the price, the buyer will end up paying more—in money, in delays, and in aggravation. That is no way to build and maintain a healthy relationship, no way to keep a customer. The smart relationship manager on the vendor side will help the buyer to do long-term life-cycle costing in assessing the vendor's offering.

It is not surprising that in professional partnerships, such as law, medicine, architecture, consulting, investment banking, and advertising, individuals are rated and rewarded by the client relationships they control. Those relationships, like any other assets, can appreciate or depreciate. Their maintenance and enhancement are not a matter of good manners, public relations, tact, charm, window dressing, or manipulation. They have to do with management, and not just marketing, because it transcends what marketing uniquely does. Relationship management requires companywide programs for maintenance, investment, improvement, and also for replacement. The results can be spectacular.

Consider the case of the North Sea oil and gas fields. Norway and Britain did a great deal to urge and facilitate exploration and development. They were eager and even generous hosts to the oil companies that spent hundreds of millions to do their work. Suddenly, when oil and gas started flowing, the host countries levied taxes running to more than 90 percent of the market prices. Nobody was more surprised than the companies. Why surprised? Would having built sound relationships with the governments, by whatever means, so as to have created a sense of mutuality and partnership have reduced the size of the taxes? What would it have been worth? Nor is this an isolated situation. It applies in other similar undertakings where the vendor or coventurer is required to make heavy advance expenditures to get the account and develop the product. This is represented by the depiction in Figure 2 of cash flows to such a vendor during the life of the account. As is shown, during the customer-getting and development period, cash flows are negative, with the customer eagerly encouraging the expenditures. When the product is delivered or the joint venture becomes operative, cumulative cash flows turn up and finally become positive. In the case of the North Sea, the surprising new high taxes represent the difference between what revenues to the oil companies might have been (the upper dotted line) and what they became (the solid line). With worse relationships, they might, of course, have fallen to the lower dotted line.

Consider also the case of Gillette North America. It has four separate sales forces. There are special programs for major accounts designed to help them with their businesses and assure the rapid and smooth response of Gillette to the requirements of those businesses. But in addition there is a vice president of business relations who has among his major duties, separate from the sales organization, the cultivation of Gillette's relationships with major retailers and distributors via a vast array of ceremonial activities, ranging from hosting cocktail parties, dinners, and entertainments at twelve trade association conventions annually, to the organization of special events for major accounts in connection with the annual All-Star baseball game, the World Series, the Super Bowl, and the NCAA playoffs, and to attending special events like trade-sponsored charitable din-

FIGURE 2. CUMULATIVE CASH FLOW HISTORY OF AN ACCOUNT

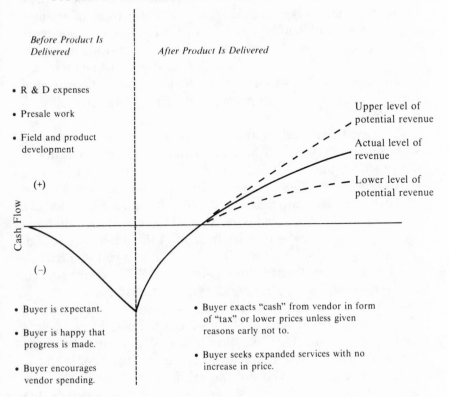

ners and retirement parties for presidents of major retail chains. Bonds are built, trust is established, and reciprocal obligations and benefits are implicitly affirmed.

Many companies do much the same. But it is only part of a more genuinely intensive effort. Many companies have specific response-sensitive and personalizing protocols and routines to handle customer inquiries, requests, and complaints. Some companies now require engineering and manufacturing people to spend time with customers and users in the field—not just to look for product and design ideas, not just for feedback regarding present products and for sensitivity enhancement for themselves, but also to get to know and to respond to customers in deeper and more abiding ways, in short, to build relationships and bonds that last. The Sperry Corporation's much advertised "listening" campaign has taken the in-house form of training large numbers of employees to listen and communicate more effectively as regards each other and their customers. Some companies have formal programs designed to enhance their customer relations. These include the requirement to take regular service initiatives and to monitor the effectiveness of all customer relations.

To get these going and keep them going well requires constant sensitivity training, because nothing degrades so easily as the practices and the behavioral routines that are and must be institutionalized. This necessary formalization of routines generally degenerates into faceless activity. It is all too easy to take action instead of spending time. It is all too easy to act first and then try to fix the relationship, instead of the other way round. It is all too easy to say, "We'll look into it and call you back," or "Let's get together for lunch sometime." These are actions of diversion and delay, not builders of relationships.

When a purchase cycle is long—as when a beer-making plant contracts with a can-making vendor to build a factory next door, or when the U.S. Air Force "buys" (commits to) a jet engine with a life of twenty to thirty years—the people in the vendor organization who did the selling and those in the customer organization who did the buying will change over the life of those "contracts." So, in all likelihood, will the entire upper levels of management on both sides. What needs to be done by the seller to assure continuity of good relations? What is expected by the customer when people who did the buying are gone and replaced?

Clearly, relationship management requires not just the care of little things day in and day out but also the cumulative constructive management of all things large and small throughout the organization. The idea is to build bonds that last, no matter who comes and goes.

The management of relationships requires the creation and constant nurturing of systems to manage them, to maintain and enhance them. As in the management of anything, this requires four familiar old steps, shopworn as they may seem.

1. *Awareness:* Show that it is a problem, and that the problem has costs. Show that it is an opportunity, and that the opportunity has benefits.
2. *Assessment:* Determine where the company now stands, especially as compared with what's necessary to get the desired results.
3. *Accountability:* Establish regular reporting on individual relationships, and then on group relationships, so that these can be weighed against other measures of performance.
4. *Actions:* Make decisions and allocations, and establish routines and communications on the basis of their impact on the targeted relationships. Constantly reinforce awareness and actions.

Checklists can, of course, be provided to help assure that all the proper things are regularly done. The problem with checklists is that they get to be mindlessly employed, thus becoming ritualized substitutes for thought and substance. Designed to achieve coverage, they require nobody to become deeply sensitized to the substance of the relationships or seriously committed to their purposes. Nobody needs seriously to look, listen, think, or get involved; one needs only to check things antiseptically off.

Relationship management can be institutionalized, but in the process it also has to be humanized. One company has regular sensitivity sessions and role-playing seminars in which members of the vendor firm assume the roles of the buyer. It also conducts in-depth debriefings on meetings with customers. Regularly with its various accounts it requires its customer-contact people (including those who make deliveries and handle receivables) to ask the seminal "relationship" questions: How are we doing in the relationship? Is it going up or down? How much are we talking with them, about what, and with whom? What have we not done lately? The emphasis on "lately" is not exceptional. It recognizes that relationships naturally degrade and have to be reinstated. If I owe you a favor, I forget, but you don't. And when I've done you a favor, you feel obliged, but not for long. You ask, "What have you done for me lately?" A relationship credit must be used, or it vanishes. It must be used soon, or it depreciates.

The institutionalization of relationship management is also possible by establishing routines that assure the right kinds of customer contacts. Consider what was done by a well-known Wall Street investment firm. It required its security analysts and salesmen to make regular constructive contacts with their institutional customers. "Constructive" was defined as conveying useful information to them. Hence the firm developed a regular Monday morning investment strategy "commentary," which analysts and salesmen could convey by telephone to their customers. In addition, each analyst was required to develop periodic industry commentaries and updates, to be either mailed or phoned to customers. Analysts and salesmen were required to keep telephone logs of these contacts, which were collected, compiled, counted, and communicated in a companywide report that was openly distributed to all salesmen and analysts each week, complete with their names and the names of the individuals and companies contacted. Low-contact salesmen and analysts were required to explain their inactions to their supervisors. End-of-year bonuses were determined not only on the basis of commissions earned from the various institutions, but on the basis of the number and types of contacts individuals had with them. Meanwhile, sensitivity training sessions were regularly conducted in order to enhance the nature of the contacts and the quality of the relationships. The results, which turned out to be highly successful, were carefully analyzed and made known to all participants, thus reinforcing their willingness to continue and the care with which they did so.

Relationship management is a special field all its own. It is as important in preserving and enhancing the intangible asset commonly known as "goodwill" as the management of hard assets. The fact that it is probably harder to do is that much more reason that hard effort be expended to do it.

# 7

---

# The Marketing Imagination

Nothing drives progress like the imagination. The idea precedes the deed. The only exceptions are accidents and natural selection, but these cannot be willed. Ideas can be willed, and the imagination is their engine. Though progress starts with the imagination, only work can make things happen. And work itself works best when fueled, again, by the imagination. An idea or a new conceptualization usually requires the imaginative application of effort to get the intended results. Thus the imagination gets the idea and then, to be effective, must help convert it into results.

The marketing imagination is the starting point of success in marketing. It is distinguished from other forms of imagination by the unique insights it brings to understanding customers, their problems, and the means to capture their attention and their custom. By asserting that people don't buy things but buy solutions to problems, the marketing imagination makes an in-

THE MARKETING IMAGINATION

spired leap from the obvious to the meaningful. "Meaning" resides in its implied suggestion as to what to do—in this case, find out what problems people are trying to solve. It is represented by Charles Revson's famous distinction regarding the business of Revlon, Inc.: "In the factory we make cosmetics. In the store we sell hope." It is characterized by Leo McGinneva's famous clarification about why people buy quarter-inch drill bits: "They don't want quarter-inch bits. They want quarter-inch holes." It leads to Professor Raymond A. Bauer's famous point that when buyers select a known vendor or known brand over another it is more meaningful to think of the choice as an act of risk reduction rather than as the expression of a brand preference.

Each of these reconceptualizations found a deeper meaning in customer behavior, thus causing marketing programs to be reshaped in ways better to attract and hold customers. To attract a customer, you are asking him to do something different from what he would have done in the absence of the programs you direct at him. He has to change his mind and his actions. The customer must shift his behavior in the direction advocated by the seller. Hence the seller must distinguish himself and his offering from those of others so that people will want, or at least prefer, to do business with him. The search for meaningful distinction is a central part of the marketing effort. If marketing is seminally about anything, it is about achieving customer-getting distinction by differentiating what you do and how you operate. All else is derivative of that and only that.

Differentiation represents an imaginative response to the existence of potential customers in such a way as to give them compelling reasons to want to do business with the originating supplier. To differentiate an offering effectively requires knowing what drives and attracts customers. It requires knowing how customers differ from one another and how those differences can be clustered into commercially meaningful segments.

If you're not thinking segments, you're not thinking. To think segments means you have to think about what drives customers, customer groups, and the choices that are or might be available to them. To think segments means to think beyond what's obviously out there to see. If everybody sees segments as obviously consisting of certain demographics, industries, user groups, buying practices, certain influencing groups, and the like, then the thinking that gives real power is thinking that transcends the ordinary. Consider the following ad:

> Men Wanted for Hazardous Journey. Small
> wages, bitter cold, long months of complete
> darkness, constant danger, safe return doubtful.
> Honor and recognition in case of success.
> —Ernest Shackleton

The ad, written by the famed polar explorer Sir Ernest Shackleton, appeared in London newspapers in 1900. It yielded an immediate response of unprecedented proportions. Its imaginative appeal was clearly to people for whom honor and recognition were, as they say, everything. Its power lay not only in the novel idea of appealing to the human desire for honor and recognition, though the risks were grave and the work terrible, but also in its deadly frankness and remarkably simple execution.

The discovery of the simple essence of things is the essence of the marketing imagination. In 1974 Milton Greenberg, chief executive of the GCA Corporation, set out to expand his company's dollar share of the various pieces of equipment used to make semiconductor devices. None of his several competitors manufactured a full line. Hence, complementary equipment from several capital goods manufacturers stood cheek by jowl in all the world's semiconductor factories, each doing a separate part of the job in the various steps of semiconductor production. To expand its share of that equipment market, GCA might have tried to displace, with superior equipment, the other suppliers whose equipment stood adjacent to its own in the production line. Instead of setting out to do that (say, make faster and cheaper equipment), GCA set out to displace existing equipment with a machine that combined several production steps in one. Its resulting DSW Waferstepper®, though slower than the competing equipment it replaced and more costly by a factor of three, was a spectacular technical and commercial success. By combining several production operations into a single piece of equipment, it reduced the amount of manual handling of the materials being processed, thus reducing contamination and thereby raising yields. By making the equipment more compact laterally but taller, it saved manufacturing floor space. By improving the lens used in the photolithographic process, it narrowed the line widths and thus raised the operating capacities of the semiconductor chips that the DSW helped produce.

Thus through a single major simplifying R&D effort that was designed to displace rather than merely improve existing equipment, it swept the DSW Waferstepper® suddenly to market dominance. That effort was based on a notion about what the market would really value. Higher yields, more capacity per chip, and better use of factory floor space became the target and the result.

Industry watchers hailed it as a prodigious technological achievement. GCA doesn't deny that. But in its corporate corridors people speak about it mostly as a great marketing achievement—not simply having done things well technologically, but having known what to do. The "what" was the result of the marketing imagination.

Imagination means to construct mental pictures of what is or is not actually present, what has never been actually experienced. To exercise the imagination is to be creative. It requires intellectual or artistic inventiveness. Anybody can do it, and most people often do—unfortunately, however, only in daydreams and fantasies, when they're not constrained by convention or conviction. To do it in business requires shedding these constraints but also discipline, especially the discipline of dissociation from what exists and what has been. It usually requires combining disparate facts or ideas into new amalgamations of meanings.

In marketing, as I have said, the object is to get and keep a customer, and also to get existing buyers to prefer to do business with you rather than your competitors. In marketing, therefore, the imagination must constantly focus on that objective.

Consider the following example from DuPont. Over the years the price for one of its materials used by medical supply manufacturers gradually fell, as did the prices of competitors producing the chemically identical materials. In plotting those prices, it was discovered that DuPont continued over those years to get a slight premium over its competitors, though the premium gap tended to narrow as the years went on. DuPont's market share remained stable. In-depth interviews with customers' design engineers, purchasing people, and manufacturing heads gradually led the DuPont investigators to the conclusion that DuPont's materials, though chemically identical to all others, were believed to be in some way purer and and that DuPont was more likely than others to come out with materials improvements. That, it was concluded, accounted for DuPont's premium.

The discovery of all this was, actually, quite imaginative. What was done with it was dramatically imaginative. DuPont created a series of trade journal advertisements and trade show demonstrations that showed how it took special care to assure the purity of its delivered products. The ads showed a series of quality assurance checks, which DuPont regularly made in the manufacturing process, using electron spectroscophy to test purity at various production stages. At trade shows electron spectroscophy test displays were erected for actual use by those attending the shows for testing batches of materials taken from various stages of the manufacturing process.

Remarkably, over the succeeding years DuPont's narrowing price premiums began to widen, and its market share rose. Follow-up trade research indicated that DuPont's reputation for product purity had risen. The marketing imagination had obviously worked.

Or consider American Express. Its green credit card ("Don't leave home without it," itself an imaginative positioning with great power) is also sold as a "Corporate Card." Corporations have been persuaded to issue it to certain classes of employees instead of giving them cash advances. This helps companies conserve cash and more closely monitor expenses. In 1982 American Express shifted the Corporate Card operations into its Travel Services Division. The Travel Services Division operated, among some other things, travel agencies, making airline and hotel reservations and procuring tickets.

131

Travel Services concluded that the larger and more geographically dispersed a corporation, the greater was the variety of its travel arrangements and the greater its per capita travel cost differences within the corporation. With airline rate deregulation and increased hotel price dealing, the less knowledgeable about prices the traveling executives, their secretaries, and in-house travel officers became. Financial officers of the corporations had little or no knowledge of the size of their annual travel costs corporatewide. The numbers were buried under other line items in the various budgets. By helping the corporation establish travel expense rules for each class of its travelers and then offering to handle all of a corporation's travel arrangements through a single dedicated American Express "travel desk" with a separate 800 telephone number dedicated to each corporation, American Express was able to help "control" travel costs corporatewide. It was able to search and bargain for the lowest possible rates, the lowest-cost routes, and the lowest-cost hotel accommodations within each class of lodging. It sent monthly systemwide travel cost analyses to the central financial officers, with flagged indicators of deviations from the travel expense rules. American Express was able to demonstrate that, even after charging its regular fees for Corporate Cards, it could save companies with normal annual travel budgets over $30 million at least 10 percent.

American Express looked at the world "out there" through the eyes of people whose needs it understood totally—the eyes of the corporate controllers of the purse strings. Controllers knew that costs of all kinds have a general tendency to creep up. They were increasingly concerned about the price of money. Knowing a lot about travel and travel-related costs, American Express asked itself simply: "How can we help the keepers of the corporate purse strings to manage costs that we know a lot about?" The rest wasn't easy but would never have been done had American Express not first done what was uniquely imaginative: combining disparate facts about its corporate customers and itself in ways that yielded new questions and previously unexperienced insights.

The essence of competition, as we have seen, is differentiation: providing something different and providing it better than your competitor. Sometimes even an obvious functional difference doesn't sell unless it is also presented or positioned differently. We know this from cosmetics and many other consumer goods. We saw it in the DuPont example. But consider computers. The explanation of Apple Computer's roaring success is not simply the enormous power it packed into minuscule size at a remarkably low price. Why would anybody, even at the price, and knowing all the horror stories of troubles with computers, buy this diminutive looking toy from this obscure company? The software available for Apple users was also usable on the minicomputers of Digital Equipment, Data General, Prime, and IBM. The genius of Apple was to avoid positioning itself as a new minicomputer, or even a microminicomputer. It did something entirely different. It called itself a "personal computer." It thus avoided having to assert itself as being yet another microminicomputer, only better, which would have required a claim of being merely superior to or cheaper than DEC, DG, or IBM. That, coming from obscurity, would have been hard to believe. Instead, Apple said, in effect, "We are an entirely new and different kind of computer—the newest new generation that the others don't have. We're different. It's a personal computer, intended for you as a normal person, not for the computer experts in your company."

Nowhere in recent years has the marketing imagination operated more powerfully to generate new customer-getting products than in financial services. Money-market mutual funds are the most spectacular example, providing access for people of modest means to balanced portfolios of high-interest-bearing and relatively secure commercial paper and making them available with enormous ease of purchase and redemption.

Another imaginative example are zero-interest, or money-multiplier, corporate bonds, issued at deep discounts from their redemption prices, requiring no periodic interest payments or related accounting costs for their issuers and incurring no tax liabilities for their owners until maturity. The remarkable ingenuity of the financial community became even more apparent when the invention of this security was almost instantly fol-

lowed by the emergence of a new category of zero-interest instruments in the form of regular bonds stripped of their coupons.

The passage of President Reagan's Economic Recovery Act
of 1981 greatly raised the investment tax credits available to
corporations. The financial community's quick ingenuity sur-
faced again. Within weeks corporations were selling their un-
used credits to others who could benefit from them.

While it may be said that designing and "manufacturing" a
new financial instrument is much easier and cheaper than designing and manufacturing a new tangible product, and even that
marketing it is relatively easier given the existence of highly
flexible and well established electronic and direct-mail channels
of distribution, two things help suggest that the American financial community is remarkably innovative nonetheless. First,
these are uniquely American innovations. The developed financial communities of Western Europe and South America, facing
high inflation for many years, did not invent any of these products. Second, neither did they invent or install the extensive
electronic and direct-mail facilities that facilitated the management and distribution of these products. Though the American
financial community does almost no market or consumer research, clearly some of its members have their own remarkably
effective way of knowing what people out there want and value.
Their way is the best way. It consists simply of letting themselves live, as it were, in their customers' shoes, talking their
language, thinking their thoughts, feeling their emotions, responding to their cues. Most members of the financial community aren't like that, obviously. But it takes only a few who think
this way to affect the entire industry. Once a new product was
successfully introduced or a new channel of distribution successfully installed, swarms of imitators rushed in to transform
everything that was done. It happened in insurance, commercial
banking, credit cards, securities brokerage, options trading,
mortgage banking, savings banking, and others.

The entrepreneurial vigor and audacity that have characterized the financial services industry in the past decade represent
a diametrical departure from its former somnambulance. Mostly
it started with the advent of new players on the scene or a
handful of old players with new ideas, most especially people

like Walter Wriston of Citicorp, Donald Regan of Merrill Lynch, and Jack Stein of the Dreyfus Fund. And there can be no doubt that it is they, as individuals, rather than their staffs or line subordinates, who personally made the revolutions associated with their companies. They had the visions, promulgated the ideas, and inspired their organizations. Besides the necessary vision and the facilitating determination and persistence, they also had the required daring. Anciently obtuse laws and regulations that stood obdurately against competitiveness and progress in the industry represented for these men things that had merely to be circumvented or changed, not, as with so many others, to be passively respected or merely criticized. Citicorp's invention of certificates of deposit and Merrill Lynch's invention of cash management accounts were end runs against obsolete and unrealistic regulations. And for neither of these firms were these isolated, one-time inventions. They were part of a continuing series of similarly shrewd and imaginative innovations. In both cases they were pieces of a transforming mosaic for their respective companies. They typify the centrality of marketing in corporate affairs. Decisions far at the top were based on shrewd insights regarding customer-getting possibilities far out in the field.

Let us repeat: The purpose of a business is to get and keep a customer. Without customers, no amount of engineering wizardry, clever financing, or operations expertise can keep the company going. To be the low-cost producer of vacuum tubes, to have the best salesmen of what's not wanted or wanted only by the few whose ability to pay won't even pay for the overhead —these can't save you from extinction. To do well what should not be done is to do badly.

What should be done can be defined only by reference to what customers do, can do, or might do in the market place. No amount of imagination can bail out companies intent on inappropriate purposes. The history of all succeeding and successful companies is a history of right purposes at the right times, executed with means right for their situations. Nor is selecting growth sectors on which to concentrate company effort a solution to the problem of stagnation. A lot of other companies are likely to have hit on the same target opportunities. The trick is to know how to convert opportunity into disproportionately opportune results. This means getting an edge over the other competitors.

The low-cost producer who gets disproportionate market share by passing part of his advantage along in the form of customer-getting lower prices has a clear and powerful advantage. But it must also be linked to doing everything else that's needed to satisfy the insatiably expanding wishes and demands of the market. In time, lower prices get taken for granted. What's usually wanted next are increasingly expanding clusters of other benefits and also often increasingly varied lines of product and service options for the customer. The strategy of price competitiveness makes sense only in the context of the larger or different clusters of things customers want and value. The trick is to combine price competitiveness with competitiveness in all other respects. In short, the trick is to provide the most competitive value.

All this is affirmed by one of the most interesting pieces of business scholarship in the last decade, by Professor William K. Hall of the University of Michigan, who is now at Cummins Engine Company. He studied the financial performance of leading firms in eight established old industries. Four were in consumer goods: automotive, major home appliances, brewing, and cigarettes; and four in industrial goods: steel, tire and rubber, heavy-duty trucks, and construction equipment. He discovered that over a significant period of time the leading firms in these industries outperformed such known growth-industry leaders as Phillips Petroleum among the oils; Xerox, Eastman Kodak, Texas Instruments, and Digital Equipment among the technology leaders; and General Electric and United Technologies among the diversification leaders. They even did better than IBM and 3M. The performance measures used by Professor Hall were average return on equity, average return on capital, and average annual revenue growth rate.[1]

[1] William K. Hall, "Survival Strategies in a Hostile Environment," *Harvard Business Review,* September/October 1980.

136

The unglamorous old basic-industry companies that did so well were National Steel, Michelin tires, Paccar trucks, John Deere farm equipment, Daimler Benz automobiles, Maytag washing machines, Heileman Brewing, and Phillip Morris cigarettes. The explanation of their superior performance was that they systematically went for meaningful differentiation in their offerings. "Differentiation" was objective both with regard to their generic products (see Chapter 4) and with respect to the rest of their total product, such as the nature and extent of such nontangible offerings as postpurchase servicing, parts availability, advisory help, delivery conditions and reliability, and the like. They understood the concept of the augmented product.

Hall further discovered that when these differentiation-oriented basic-industry high-performance companies were compared with their direct low-cost producer competitors, the former outperformed the latter. In short, meaningful differentiation is competitively more effective and enduring than low-cost production alone. When the two strategies were combined in a single company, such as by Caterpillar Tractor, the results were spectacular.

All this tells a simple and compelling story: Business success is a matter of the disproportionate and enduring attraction of certain proportions of customers at certain enduring levels of relative price. Most significantly, it is a story that defines the purpose of business in terms of marketing—once again, getting and keeping customers. This therefore installs marketing at the center of what's done in corporate strategic planning.

Strategic planning involves defining what's to be done, the allocation of resources for their maximization. Maximization is, and must inevitably be, getting the desired results in the market place. As we saw, being the low-cost producer, though enormously important, is hardly sufficient when focused on the wrong products, wrong distribution channels, and without regard to the wider wants of those segments. To decide correctly what's to be done and how to do it requires having good data about customers, competitors, and markets. Even more, it requires the imaginative conversion of these data into meaningful and usable information. The best way is to know your prospects in a way that is more fundamental and compelling than what's usually yielded by the purely metrical methods so common in market research today.

The difference between data and information is that while data are crudely aggregated collections of raw facts, information represents the selective organization and imaginative interpretation of those facts. This requires knowing, in some sort of direct and systemic way, the world with which one presumes to deal. It requires getting inside the lives and work of the people one is trying to understand. Crudely aggregated collections of data merely represent what's been serially recorded about discrete events or categories. Information represents the imposition of order, categories, and ideas on the collected data. To do this merely by means of increasingly elaborate methods of statistical and mathematical refinement and calculation, whatever their merits, loses the throbbing pulse of the reality the data sought to capture. It's like assuming you know all about sex when you've read Masters and Johnson or *The Hite Report*.

Good data about customers, converted meaningfully into good information, have the power to improve strategic decisions in the right directions. Strategic planning can be mechanistically, and therefore incorrectly, defined as deciding how to allocate resources among the possibilities of what's to be done. This definition is incorrect, because it presumes that these possibilities are self-evident. They are not. It is wrong to say that the most important and creatively challenging act of corporate decision-making is about choices regarding what's to be done. The most important and challenging work involves thinking up the possibilities from among which choices may have to be made. To select among stipulated possibilities is to make choices of preferences, not decisions about appropriateness. A possibility has to be created before it can be chosen. Therefore to think up the possibilities from among which choices might be made is to engage in acts of creative imagination.

When Milton Greenberg of GCA Corporation focused on the possibilities of making different rather than improved capital equipment, he shoved his organization in a direction profoundly different from what would have been followed without that purposeful nudge. The simple clarity of this different conceptualization as to what might be done was rooted totally in a profoundly simple and clear notion of what a large segment of the market basically wanted—even if the market itself did not know in advance exactly what it wanted. It was a strategic decision whose power resided in the creation of insightfully customer-oriented possibilities regarding what the choices were.

Strategic planning involves defining what's to be done. It is inescapably rooted in marketing matters, in the need to respond to the realities, the actualities of the market's unyielding requisites. To get done what strategic planning has decided to do requires realistic plans for implementation at the center of the competitive vortex. If the plans are not realistic, and if those who must convert the plans into action are not persuaded regarding their feasibility, the results will be disastrous. Subordinates will, perhaps grudgingly, carry out plans and programs they think are silly or wrong. But they will not seriously attempt to implement plans and programs they think are not realistic, that is, not implementable.

The Light Brigade moved obediently into the valley of death. Its own opinions regarding duty, rightness, appropriateness, or probable effectiveness were beside the point. So much for the world of the military arts. In the world of commercial affairs, duty is a lesser and less compelling calling. The plans and programs had better be reasonably right, appropriate, and compelling. They must be reasonably congruent with everyday common sense and, especially, easily understandable. In the absence of these, there is misunderstanding, resistance, and sometimes outright sabotage. People will not willingly or enthusiastically do what seems neither sensible nor suitable, and certainly not what's not understandable. They may not engage in outright opposition or sabotage, but they will drag their feet, communicate in various subtle ways to their peers and subordinates the absence of conviction or urgency, and tolerate sloppiness and slowness.

To be successful a strategy must also be simple, clear, and expressible in only a few written lines. If it is elaborate and complex, and takes a lot of space or time to communicate, few people will understand it or march to its tune. Complexity tends usually to mask a vague or unsubstantial sense of the realities that face the enterprise. The most dramatic and visible realities that so obviously destroy companies are usually fiscal: insufficient cash flow to finance debt and interest payments, to pay vendors, and the like. These usually make the headlines, because they lead so often and so obviously to bankruptcy. Often they are due to wrong decisions about purely financial affairs. Most commonly such wrong decisions are based on miscalculations or plain dumb assumptions about the market place—that sales would be sufficiently good, prices sufficiently high, accounts receivable sufficiently low and short-term. Hence, fiscal failure originates in the market place.

Marketing is inescapable in the determination of corporate results. The reason is that marketing deals with the sources and levels of the revenues that help determine the corporate fate. Since marketing means getting and keeping customers in some acceptable proportion relative to competitors, it is to the marketing imagination one must look to gain differential advantage over competitors. Assuming that the costs of what it sells are reasonably competitive, it remains the burden of the marketing imagination to find ways to attract and hold customers. It usually takes a lot of long and sweaty effort to get things done, and that itself may take a lot of imagination. But unless the decision as to what to do is appropriate, which is to say, unless it is imaginatively right, nothing can save the enterprise from disaster. Good work in pursuit of wrong purposes is more damaging than bad work in pursuit of right purposes. In business, the marketing imagination is the central tool for deciding on what the purposes are to be.

# 8

---

# Marketing Myopia

Every major industry was once a growth industry. But some that are now riding a wave of growth enthusiasm are very much in the shadow of decline. Others which are thought of as seasoned growth industries have actually stopped growing. In every case, the reason growth is threatened, slowed, or stopped is *not* because the market is saturated. It is because there has been a failure of management.

*Fateful purposes*

The failure is at the top. The executives responsible for it, in the last analysis, are those who deal with broad aims and policies: Thus:

—The railroads did not stop growing because the need for passenger and freight transportation declined. That grew. The

141

railroads are in trouble today not because the need was filled by others (cars, trucks, airplanes, even telephones), but because it was *not* filled by the railroads themselves. They let others take customers away from them because they assumed themselves to be in the railroad business rather than in the transportation business. The reason they defined their industry wrong was because they were railroad-oriented instead of transportation-oriented; they were product-oriented instead of customer-oriented.

—Hollywood barely escaped being totally ravished by television. Actually, all the established film companies went through drastic reorganizations. Some simply disappeared. All of them got into trouble not because of TV's inroads but because of their own myopia. As with the railroads, Hollywood defined its business incorrectly. It thought it was in the movie business when it was actually in the entertainment business. "Movies" implied a specific, limited product. This produced a fatuous contentment which from the beginning led producers to view TV as a threat. Hollywood scorned and rejected TV when it should have welcomed it as an opportunity—an opportunity to expand the entertainment business.

Today TV is a bigger business than the old narrowly defined movie business ever was. Had Hollywood been customer-oriented (providing entertainment) rather than product-oriented (making movies), would it have gone through the fiscal purgatory that it did? I doubt it. What ultimately saved Hollywood and accounted for its recent resurgence was the wave of new young writers, producers, and directors whose previous successes in television had decimated the old movie companies and toppled the big movie moguls.

There are other, less obvious examples of industries that have been and are now endangering their futures by improperly defining their purposes. I shall discuss some in detail later and analyze the kind of policies that lead to trouble. Right now it may help to show what a thoroughly customer-oriented management *can* do to keep a growth industry growing even after the obvious opportunities have been exhausted; and here there are two examples that have been around for a long time. They are nylon and glass—specifically, E. I. duPont de Nemours & Company and Corning Glass Works.

Both companies have great technical competence. Their product orientation is unquestioned. But this alone does not explain their success. After all, who was more pridefully product-oriented and product-conscious than the erstwhile New England textile companies that have been so thoroughly massacred? The DuPonts and the Cornings have succeeded not primarily because of their product or research orientation but because they have been thoroughly customer-oriented also. It is constant watchfulness for opportunities to apply their technical know-how to the creation of customer-satisfying uses which accounts for their prodigious output of successful new products. Without a very sophisticated eye on the customer, most of their new products might have been wrong, their sales methods useless.

Aluminum has also continued to be a growth industry, thanks to the efforts of two wartime-created companies which deliberately set about creating new customer-satisfying uses. Without Kaiser Aluminum & Chemical Corporation and Reynolds Metals Company, the total demand for aluminum today would be vastly less.

*Error of analysis*

Some may argue that it is foolish to set the railroads off against aluminum or the movies off against glass. Are not aluminum and glass naturally so versatile that the industries are bound to have more growth opportunities than the railroads and movies? This view commits precisely the error I have been talking about. It defines an industry, or a product, or a cluster of know-how so narrowly as to guarantee its premature senescence. When we mention "railroads," we should make sure we mean "transportation." As transporters, the railroads still have a good chance for very considerable growth. They are not limited to the railroad business as such (though in my opinion rail transportation is potentially a much stronger transportation medium than is generally believed.)

What the railroads lack is not opportunity, but some of the same managerial imaginativeness and audacity that made them great.

143

Even an amateur like Jacques Barzun can see what is lacking when he says:

> I grieve to see the most advanced physical and social organization of the last century go down in shabby disgrace for lack of the same comprehensive imagination that built it up. [What is lacking is] the will of the companies to survive and to satisfy the public by inventiveness and skill.[1]

## SHADOW OF OBSOLESCENCE

It is impossible to mention a single major industry that did not at one time qualify for the magic appellation of "growth industry." In each case its assumed strength lay in the apparently unchallenged superiority of its product. There appeared to be no effective substitute for it. It was itself a runaway substitute for the product it so triumphantly replaced. Yet one after another of these celebrated industries has come under a shadow. Let us look briefly at a few more of them, this time taking examples that have so far received a little less attention:

*Dry cleaning*—This was once a growth industry with lavish prospects. In an age of wool garments, imagine being finally able to get them safely and easily clean. The boom was on.

Yet here we are thirty years after the boom started, and the industry is in trouble. Where has the competition come from? From a better way of cleaning? No. It has come from synthetic fibers and chemical additives that have cut the need for dry cleaning. But this is only the beginning. Lurking in the wings and ready to make chemical dry cleaning totally obsolescent is that powerful magician, ultrasonics.

*Electric utilities*—This is another one of those supposedly "no-substitute" products that has been enthroned on a pedestal of invincible growth. When the incandescent lamp came along, kerosene

[1]Jacques Barzun, "Trains and the Mind of Man," *Holiday*, February, 1960, p. 21.

lights were finished. Later the waterwheel and the steam engine were cut to ribbons by the flexibility, reliability, simplicity, and just easy availability of electric motors. The prosperity of electric utilities continues to wax extravagant as the home is converted into a museum of electric gadgetry. How can anybody miss by investing in utilities, with no competition, nothing but growth ahead?

But a second look is not quite so comforting. A score of nonutility companies are well advanced toward developing a powerful chemical fuel cell which could sit in some hidden closet of every home silently ticking off electric power. The electric lines that vulgarize so many neighborhoods will be eliminated. So will the endless demolition of streets and service interruptions during storms. Also on the horizon is solar energy, again pioneered by nonutility companies.

Who says that the utilities have no competition? They may be natural monopolies now, but tomorrow they may be natural deaths. To avoid this prospect, they too will have to develop fuel cells, solar energy, and other power sources. To survive, they themselves will have to plot the obsolescence of what now produces their livelihood.

*Grocery stores*—Many people find it hard to realize that there ever was a thriving establishment known as the "corner grocery store." The supermarket has taken over with a powerful effectiveness. Yet the big food chains of the 1930s narrowly escaped being completely wiped out by the aggressive expansion of independent supermarkets. The first genuine supermarket was opened in 1930, in Jamaica, Long Island. By 1933 supermarkets were thriving in California, Ohio, Pennsylvania, and elsewhere. Yet the established chains pompously ignored them. When they chose to notice them, it was with such derisive descriptions as "cheapy," "horse-and-buggy," "cracker-barrel storekeeping," and "unethical opportunists."

The executive of one big chain announced at the time that he found it "hard to believe that people will drive for miles to shop for foods and sacrifice the personal service chains have perfected and to which Mrs. Consumer is accustomed."[2] As late as 1936, the National Wholesale Grocers convention and the New Jersey Retail

[2]For more details see M. M. Zimmerman, *The Super Market: A Revolution in Distribution* (New York, McGraw Hill, 1955), p. 48.

Grocers Association said there was nothing to fear. They said that the supers' narrow appeal to the price buyer limited the size of their market. They had to draw from miles around. When imitators came, there would be wholesale liquidations as volume fell. The current high sales of the supers was said to be partly due to their novelty. Basically people wanted convenient neighborhood grocers. If the neighborhood stores "cooperate with their suppliers, pay attention to their costs, and improve their service," they would be able to weather the competition until it blew over.[3]

It never blew over. The chains discovered that survival required going into the supermarket business. This meant the wholesale destruction of their huge investments in corner store sites and in established distribution and merchandising methods. The companies with "the courage of their convictions" resolutely stuck to the corner store philosophy. They kept their pride but lost their shirts.

### Self-deceiving cycle

But memories are short. For example, it is hard for people who today confidently hail the twin messiahs of electronics and chemicals to see how things could possibly go wrong with these galloping industries. They probably also cannot see how a reasonably sensible businessman could have been as myopic as the famous Boston millionaire who fifty years ago unintentionally sentenced his heirs to poverty by stipulating that his entire estate be forever invested exclusively in electric streetcar securities. His posthumous declaration, "There will always be a big demand for efficient urban transportation," is no consolation to his heirs who sustain life by pumping gasoline at automobile filling stations.

Yet, in a casual survey I recently took among a group of intelligent business executives, nearly half agreed that it would be hard to hurt their heirs by tying their estates forever to the electronics industry. When I then confronted them with the Boston streetcar example, they chorused unanimously, "That's different!" But is it? Is not the basic situation identical?

[3]Ibid., pp. 45–47.

In truth, *there is no such thing* as a growth industry, I believe. There are only companies organized and operated to create and capitalize on growth opportunities. Industries that assume themselves to be riding some automatic growth escalator invariably descend into stagnation. The history of every dead and dying "growth" industry shows a self-deceiving cycle of bountiful expansion and undetected decay. There are four conditions which usually guarantee this cycle:

1. The belief that growth is assured by an expanding and more affluent population
2. The belief that there is no competitive substitute for the industry's major product
3. Too much faith in mass production and in the advantages of rapidly declining unit costs as output rises
4. Preoccupation with a product that lends itself to carefully controlled scientific experimentation, improvement and manufacturing cost reduction

I should like now to begin examining each of these conditions in some detail. To build my case as boldly as possible, I shall illustrate the points with reference to three industries—petroleum, automobiles, and electronics—particularly petroleum, because it spans more years and more vicissitudes. Not only do these three have excellent reputations with the general public and also enjoy the confidence of sophisticated investors, but their managements have become known for progressive thinking in areas like financial control, product research, and management training. If obsolescence can cripple even these industries, it can happen anywhere.

## POPULATION MYTH

The belief that profits are assured by an expanding and more affluent population is dear to the heart of every industry. It takes the edge off the apprehensions everybody understandably feels about the future. If consumers are multiplying and also buying more of your product or service, you can face the future with considerably more comfort than if the market is shrinking. An expanding market keeps the manufacturer from having to think very hard or imaginatively. If thinking is an intellectual response to a problem, then the absence of a problem leads to the absence of thinking. If your product has an automatically expanding market, then you will not give much thought to how to expand it.

One of the most interesting examples of this is provided by the petroleum industry. Probably our oldest growth industry, it has an enviable record. While there are some current apprehensions about its growth rate, the industry itself tends to be optimistic.

But I believe it can be demonstrated that it is undergoing a fundamental yet typical change. It is not only ceasing to be a growth industry, but may actually be a declining one relative to other businesses. Although there is widespread unawareness of it, I believe that within twenty-five years the oil industry may find itself in much the same position of retrospective glory that the railroads are now in. Despite its pioneering work in developing and applying the present-value method of investment evaluation, in employee relations, and in working with backward countries, the petroleum business is a distressing example of how complacency and wrongheadedness can stubbornly convert opportunity into near disaster.

One of the characteristics of this and other industries that have believed very strongly in the beneficial consequences of an expanding population, while at the same time being industries with a generic product for which there has appeared to be no competitive substitute, is that the individual companies have sought to outdo their competitors by improving on what they are already doing. This makes sense, of course, if one assumes that sales are tied to the country's population strings, because the customer can compare products only on a feature-by-feature basis. I believe it is significant, for example, that not since John D. Rockefeller sent free kerosene lamps to China has the oil industry done anything really outstanding to create a demand for its product. Not even in product improvement has it showered itself with eminence. The greatest single improvement—namely, the development of tetraethyl lead—came from outside the industry, specifically from General Motors and DuPont. The big contributions made by the industry itself are confined to the technology of oil exploration, production, and refining.

*Asking for trouble*

In other words, the industry's efforts have focused on improving the *efficiency* of getting and making its product, not really on improving the generic product or its marketing. Moreover, its chief product has continuously been defined in the narrowest possible terms, namely, gasoline, not energy, fuel or transportation. This attitude has helped assure that:

—Major improvements in gasoline quality tend not to originate in the oil industry. Also, the development of superior alternative fuels comes from outside the oil industry, as will be shown later.
—Major innovations in automobile fuel marketing are originated by small new oil companies that are not primarily preoccupied with production or refining. These are the companies that have been responsible for the rapidly expanding multipump gasoline stations, with their successful emphasis on large and clean layouts, rapid and efficient driveway service, and quality gasoline at low prices.

Thus, the oil industry is asking for trouble from outsiders. Sooner or later in this land of hungry inventors and entrepreneurs, a threat is sure to come. The possibilities of this will become more apparent when we turn to the next dangerous belief of many managements. For the sake of continuity, because this second belief is tied closely to the first, I shall continue with the same example.

*Idea of indispensability*

The petroleum industry is pretty much persuaded that there is no competitive substitute for its major product, gasoline—or if there is, that it will continue to be a derivative of crude oil, such as diesel fuel or kerosene jet fuel.

There is a lot of automatic wishful thinking in this assumption. The trouble is that most refining companies own huge amounts of crude oil reserves. These have value only if there is a market for products into which oil can be converted—hence the tenacious belief in the continuing competitive superiority of automobile fuels made from crude oil.

This idea persists despite all historic evidence against it. The evidence not only shows that oil has never been a superior product for any purpose for very long, but it also shows that the oil industry has never really been a growth industry. It has been a succession of different businesses that have gone through the usual historic cycles of growth, maturity, and decay. Its overall survival is owed to a series of miraculous escapes from total obsolescence, of last-minute and unexpected reprieves from total disaster reminiscent of the Perils of Pauline.

### Perils of petroleum

I shall sketch in only the main episodes.

First, crude oil was largely a patent medicine. But even before that fad ran out, demand was greatly expanded by the use of oil in kerosene lamps. The prospect of lighting the world's lamps gave rise to an extravagant promise of growth. The prospects were similar to those the industry now holds for gasoline in other parts of the world. It can hardly wait for the underdeveloped nations to get a car in every garage.

In the days of the kerosene lamp, the oil companies competed with each other and against gaslight by trying to improve the illuminating characteristics of kerosene. Then suddenly the impossible happened. Edison invented a light which was totally nondependent on crude oil. Had it not been for the growing use of kerosene in space heaters, the incandescent lamp would have completely finished oil as a growth industry at that time. Oil would have been good for little else than axle grease.

Then disaster and reprieve struck again. Two great innovations occurred, neither originating in the oil industry. The successful development of coal-burning domestic central-heating systems made the space heater obsolescent. While the industry reeled, along came its most magnificent boost yet—the internal combustion engine, also invented by outsiders. Then when the prodigious expansion for gasoline finally began to level off in the 1920s, along came the miraculous escape of a central oil heater. Once again, the escape was provided by an outsider's invention and development. And when that market weakened, wartime demand for aviation fuel came to the rescue. After the war the expansion of civilian aviation, the dieselization of railroads, and the explosive demand for cars and trucks kept the industry's growth in high gear.

Meanwhile, centralized oil heating—whose boom potential had only recently been proclaimed—ran into severe competition from natural gas. While the oil companies themselves owned the gas that now competed with their oil, the industry did not originate the natural gas revolution, nor has it to this day greatly profited from its gas ownership. The gas revolution was made by newly formed transmission companies that marketed the product with an aggressive ardor. They started a magnificent new industry, first against the advice and then against the resistance of the oil companies.

By all the logic of the situation, the oil companies themselves should have made the gas revolution. They not only owned the gas; they also were the only people experienced in handling, scrubbing, and using it and the only people experienced in pipeline technology and transmission, and they understood heating problems. But, partly because they knew that natural gas would compete with their own sale of heating oil, the oil companies pooh-poohed the potentials of gas.

The revolution was finally started by oil pipeline executives who, unable to persuade their own companies to go into gas, quit and organized the spectacularly successful gas transmission companies. Even after their success became painfully evident to the oil companies, the latter did not go into gas transmission. The multibillion-dollar business which should have been theirs went to others. As in the past, the industry was blinded by its narrow preoccupation with a specific product and the value of its reserves. It paid little or no attention to its customers' basic needs and preferences.

The postwar years have not witnessed any change. Immediately after World War II the oil industry was greatly encouraged about its future by the rapid expansion of demand for its traditional line of products. In 1950 most companies projected annual rates of domestic expansion of around 6 percent through at least 1975.

Though the ratio of crude oil reserves to demand in the Free World was about 20 to 1, with 10 to 1 being usually considered a reasonable working ratio in the United States, booming demand sent oil men searching for more without sufficient regard to what the future really promised. In 1952 they "hit" in the Middle East; the ratio skyrocketed to 42 to 1. If gross additions to reserves continue at the average rate of the past five years (37 billion barrels annually), then by 1970 the reserve ratio will be up to 45 to 1. This abundance of oil has weakened crude and product prices all over the world.

## Uncertain future

Management cannot find much consolation today in the rapidly expanding petrochemical industry, another oil-using idea that did not originate in the leading firms. The total United States production of petrochemicals is equivalent to about 2 percent (by volume) of the demand for all petroleum products. Although the petrochemical industry is now expected to grow by about 10 percent per year, this will not offset other drains on the growth of crude oil consumption. Furthermore, while petrochemical products are many and growing, it is well to remember that there are nonpetroleum sources of the basic raw material, such as coal. Besides, a lot of plastics can be produced with relatively little oil. A 50,000-barrel-per-day chemical plant is a giant operation.

Oil has never been a continuously strong growth industry. It has grown by fits and starts, always miraculously saved by innovations and developments not of its own making. The reason it has not grown in a smooth progression is that each time it thought it had a superior product safe from the possibility of competitive substitutes, the product turned out to be inferior and notoriously subject to obsolescence. Until now, gasoline (for motor fuel, anyhow) has escaped this fate. But, as we shall see later, it too may be on its last legs.

The point of all this is that there is no guarantee against product obsolescence. If a company's own research does not make its product obsolete, another's will. Unless an industry is especially lucky, as oil has been until now, it can easily go down in a sea of red figures—just as the railroads have, as the buggy whip manufacturers have, as the corner grocery chains have, as most of the big movie companies have, and indeed as many other industries have.

The best way for a firm to be lucky is to make its own luck. That requires knowing what makes a business successful. One of the greatest enemies of this knowledge is mass production.

## PRODUCTION PRESSURES

Mass-production industries are impelled by a great drive to produce all they can. The prospect of steeply declining unit costs as output rises is more than most companies can usually resist. The profit possibilities look spectacular. All effort focuses on production. The result is that marketing gets neglected.

John Kenneth Galbraith contends that just the opposite occurs.[4] Output is so prodigious that all effort concentrates on trying to get rid of it. He says this accounts for singing commercials, desecration of the countryside with advertising signs, and other wasteful and vulgar practices. Galbraith has a finger on something real, but he misses the strategic point. Mass production does indeed generate great pressure to "move" the product. But what usually gets emphasized is selling, not marketing. Marketing, being a more sophisticated and complex process, gets ignored.

The difference between marketing and selling is more than semantic. Selling focuses on the needs of the seller, marketing on the needs of the buyer. Selling is preoccupied with the seller's need to convert his product into cash, marketing with the idea of satisfying the needs of the customer by means of the product and the whole cluster of things associated with creating, delivering, and finally consuming it.

In some industries, the enticements of full mass production have been so powerful that for many years top management in effect has told the sales departments, "You get rid of it; we'll worry about profits." By contrast, a truly marketing-minded firm tries to create value-satisfying goods and services that consumers will want to buy. What it offers for sale includes not only the generic product or service,

[4]*The Affluent Society* (Boston, Houghton Mifflin, 1958). pp. 152–60.

but also how it is made available to the customer, in what form, when, under what conditions, and at what terms of trade. Most important, what it offers for sale is determined not by the seller but by the buyer. The seller takes his cues from the buyer in such a way that the product becomes a consequence of the marketing effort, not vice versa.

## Lag in Detroit

This may sound like an elementary rule of business, but that does not keep it from being violated wholesale. It is certainly more violated than honored. Take the automobile industry.

Here mass production is most famous, most honored, and has the greatest impact on the entire society. The industry has hitched its fortune to the relentless requirements of the annual model change, a policy that makes customer orientation an especially urgent necessity. Consequently the auto companies annually spend millions of dollars on consumer research. But the fact that the new compact cars are selling so well in their first year indicates that Detroit's vast researches have for a long time failed to reveal what the customer really wanted. Detroit was not persuaded that he wanted anything different from what he had been getting until it lost millions of customers to other small-car manufacturers.

How could this unbelievable lag behind consumer wants have been perpetuated so long? Why did not research reveal consumer preferences before consumers' buying decisions themselves revealed the facts? Is that not what consumer research is for—to find out before the fact what is going to happen? The answer is that Detroit never really researched the customer's wants. It only researched his preferences between the kinds of things which it had already decided to offer him. For Detroit is mainly product-oriented, not customer-oriented. To the extent that the customer is recognized as having needs that the manufacturer should try to satisfy, Detroit usually acts as if the job can be done entirely by product changes. Occasionally attention gets paid to financing, too, but that is done more in order to sell than to enable the customer to buy.

As for taking care of other customer needs, there is not enough

154

being done to write about. The areas of the greatest unsatisfied needs are ignored, or at best get stepchild attention. These are at the point of sale and on the matter of automotive repair and maintenance. Detroit views these problem areas as being of secondary importance. That is underscored by the fact that the retailing and servicing ends of this industry are neither owned and operated nor controlled by the manufacturers. Once the car is produced, things are pretty much in the dealer's inadequate hands. Illustrative of Detroit's arms-length attitude is the fact that, while servicing holds enormous sales-stimulating, profit-building opportunities, only 57 of Chevrolet's 7,000 dealers provide night maintenance service.

Motorists repeatedly express their dissatisfaction with servicing and their apprehensions about buying cars under the present selling setup. The anxieties and problems they encounter during the auto buying and maintenance processes are probably more intense and widespread today than thirty years ago. Yet the automobile companies do not *seem* to listen or take their cues from the anguished consumer. If they do listen, it must be through the filter of their own preoccupation with production. The marketing effort is still viewed as a necessary consequence of the product, not vice versa, as it should be. That is the legacy of mass production, with its parochial view that profit resides essentially in low-cost full production.

*What Ford put first*

The profit lure of mass production obviously has a place in the plans and strategy of business management, but it must always *follow* hard thinking about the customer. This is one of the most important lessons that we can learn from the contradictory behavior of Henry Ford. In a sense Ford was both the most brilliant and the most senseless marketer in American history. He was senseless because he refused to give the customer anything but a black car. He was brilliant because he fashioned a production system designed to fit market needs. We habitually celebrate him for the wrong reason, his production genius. His real genius was marketing. We think he was able to cut his selling price and therefore sell millions of $500 cars because his invention of the assembly line had reduced the costs. Actually he invented the assembly line because he had concluded that at $500 he could sell millions of cars. Mass production was the *result*, not the cause, of his low prices.

Ford repeatedly emphasized this point, but a nation of production-oriented business managers refuses to hear the great lesson he taught. Here is his operating philosophy as he expressed it succinctly:

> Our policy is to reduce the price, extend the operations, and improve the article. You will notice that the reduction of price comes first. We have never considered any costs as fixed. Therefore we first reduce the price to the point where we believe more sales will result. Then we go ahead and try to make the prices. We do not bother about the costs. The new price forces the costs down. The more usual way is to take the costs and then determine the price; and although that method may be scientific in the narrow sense, it is not scientific in the broad sense, because what earthly use is it to know the cost if it tells you that you cannot manufacture at a price at which the article can be sold? But more to the point is the fact that, although one may calculate what a cost is, and of course all of our costs are carefully calculated, no one knows what a cost ought to be. One of the ways of discovering . . . is to name a price so low as to force everybody in the place to the highest point of efficiency. The low price makes everybody dig for profits. We make more discoveries concerning manufacturing and selling under this forced method than by any method of leisurely investigation.[5]

## Product provincialism

The tantalizing profit possibilities of low unit production costs may be the most seriously self-deceiving attitude that can afflict a company, particularly a "growth" company where an apparently assured expansion of demand already tends to undermine a proper concern for the importance of marketing and the customer.

The usual result of this narrow preoccupation with so-called concrete matters is that instead of growing, the industry declines.

[5]Henry Ford, *My Life and Work* (New York, Doubleday, Page & Co., 1923), pp. 146–47.

It usually means that the product fails to adapt to the constantly changing patterns of consumer needs and tastes, to new and modified marketing institutions and practices, or to product developments in competing or complementary industries. The industry has its eyes so firmly on its own specific product that it does not see how it is being made obsolete.

The classical example of this is the buggy whip industry. No amount of product improvement could stave off its death sentence. But had the industry defined itself as being in the transportation business rather than the buggy whip business, it might have survived. It would have done what survival always entails, that is, changing. Even if it had only defined its business as providing a stimulant or catalyst to an energy source, it might have survived by becoming a manufacturer of, say, fan belts or air cleaners.

What may someday be a still more classical example is, again, the oil industry. Having let others steal marvelous opportunities from it (e.g., natural gas, as already mentioned, missile fuels, and jet engine lubricants), one would expect it to have taken steps never to let that happen again. But this is not the case. We are now getting extraordinary new developments in fuel systems specifically designed to power automobiles. Not only are these developments concentrated in firms outside the petroleum industry, but petroleum is almost systematically ignoring them, securely content in its wedded bliss to oil. It is the story of the kerosene lamp versus the incandescent lamp all over again. Oil is trying to improve hydrocarbon fuels rather than develop *any* fuels best suited to the needs of their users, whether or not made in different ways and with different raw materials from oil.

Here are some things which nonpetroleum companies are working on:

—Over a dozen such firms now have advanced working models of energy systems which, when perfected, will replace the internal combustion engine and eliminate the demand for gasoline. The superior merit of each of these systems is their elimination of frequent, time-consuming, and irritating refueling stops. Most of these systems are fuel cells designed to create electrical energy directly from chemicals without combustion. Most of them use chemicals that are not derived from oil, generally hydrogen and oxygen.

—Several other companies have advanced models of electric storage batteries designed to power automobiles. One of these is an aircraft producer that is working jointly with several electric utility companies. The latter hope to use off-peak generating capacity to supply overnight plug-in battery regeneration. Another company, also using the battery approach, is a medium-size electronics firm with extensive small-battery experience that it developed in connection with its work on hearing aids. It is collaborating with an automobile manufacturer. Recent improvements arising from the need for high-powered miniature power storage plants in rockets have put us within reach of a relatively small battery capable of withstanding great overloads or surges of power. Germanium diode applications and batteries using sintered-plate and nickel-cadmium techniques promise to make a revolution in our energy sources.

—Solar energy conversion systems are also getting increasing attention. One usually cautious Detroit auto executive recently ventured that solar-powered cars might be common by 1980.

As for the oil companies, they are more or less "watching developments," as one research director put it to me. A few are doing a bit of research on fuel cells, but almost always confined to developing cells powered by hydrocarbon chemicals. None of them are enthusiastically researching fuel cells, batteries, or solar power plants. None of them are spending a fraction as much on research in these profoundly important areas as they are on the usual run-of-the-mill things like reducing combustion chamber deposit in gasoline engines. One major integrated petroleum company recently took a tentative look at the fuel cell and concluded that although "the companies actively working on it indicate a belief in ultimate success . . . the timing and magnitude of its impact are too remote to warrant recognition in our forecasts."

One might, of course, ask: Why should the oil companies do anything different? Would not chemical fuel cells, batteries, or solar energy kill the present product lines? The answer is that they would

158

indeed, and that is precisely the reason for the oil firms' having to develop these power units before their competitors, so they will not be companies without an industry.

Management might be more likely to do what is needed for its own preservation if it thought of itself as being in the energy business. But even that would not be enough if it persisted in imprisoning itself in the narrow grip of its tight product orientation. It has to think of itself as taking care of customer needs, not finding, refining, or even selling oil. Once it genuinely thinks of its business as taking care of people's transportation needs, nothing can stop it from creating its own extravagantly profitable growth.

### "Creative destruction"

Since words are cheap and deeds are dear, it may be appropriate to indicate what this kind of thinking involves and leads to. Let us start at the beginning—the customer. It can be shown that motorists strongly dislike the bother, delay, and experience of buying gasoline. People actually do not buy gasoline. They cannot see it, taste it, feel it, appreciate it, or really test it. What they buy is the right to continue driving their cars. The gas station is like a tax collector to whom people are compelled to pay a periodic toll as the price of using their cars. This makes the gas station a basically unpopular institution. It can never be made popular or pleasant, only less unpopular, less unpleasant.

To reduce its unpopularity completely means eliminating it. Nobody likes a tax collector, not even a pleasantly cheerful one. Nobody likes to interrupt a trip to buy a phantom product, not even from a handsome Adonis or a seductive Venus. Hence, companies that are working on exotic fuel substitutes which will eliminate the need for frequent refueling are heading directly into the outstretched arms of the irritated motorist. They are riding a wave of inevitability, not because they are creating something which is technologically superior or more sophisticated, but because they are satisfying a powerful customer need. They are also eliminating noxious odors and air pollution.

Once the petroleum companies recognize the customer-satisfying logic of what another power system can do, they will see that they have no more choice about working on an efficient, long-lasting fuel (or some way of delivering present fuels without bothering the motorist) than the big food chains had a choice about going into the supermarket business, or the vacuum tube companies had a choice about making semiconductors. For their own good the oil firms will have to destroy their own highly profitable assets. No amount of wishful thinking can save them from the necessity of engaging in this form of "creative destruction."

I phrase the need as strongly as this because I think management must make quite an effort to break itself loose from conventional ways. It is all too easy in this day and age for a company or industry to lets its sense of purpose become dominated by the economies of full production and to develop a dangerously lopsided product orientation. In short, if management lets itself drift, it invariably drifts in the direction of thinking of itself as producing goods and services, not customer satisfactions. While it probably will not descend to the depths of telling its salesmen, "You get rid of it; we'll worry about profits," it can, without knowing it, be practicing precisely that formula for withering decay. The historic fate of one growth industry after another has been its suicidal product provincialism.

## DANGERS OF R&D

Another big danger to a firm's continued growth arises when top management is wholly transfixed by the profit possibilities of technical research and development. To illustrate, I shall turn first to a new industry—electronics—and then return once more to the oil companies. By comparing a fresh example with a familiar one, I hope to emphasize the prevalence and insidiousness of a hazardous way of thinking.

### Marketing shortchanged

In the case of electronics, the greatest danger which faces the glamorous new companies in this field is not that they do not pay enough attention to research and development, but that they pay *too much* attention to it. And the fact that the fastest-growing electronics firms owe their eminence to their heavy emphasis on technical research is completely beside the point. They have vaulted to affluence on a sudden crest of unusually strong general receptiveness to new technical ideas. Also, their success has been shaped in the virtually guaranteed market of military subsidies and by military orders that in many cases actually preceded the existence of facilities to make the products. Their expansion has, in other words, been almost totally devoid of marketing effort.

Thus, they are growing up under conditions that come dangerously close to creating the illusion that a superior product will sell itself. Having created a successful company by making a superior product, it is not surprising that management continues to be oriented toward the product rather than the people who consume it. It develops the philosophy that continued growth is a matter of continued product innovation and improvement.

A number of other factors tend to strengthen and sustain this belief:

1. Because electronic products are highly complex and sophisticated, managements become top-heavy with engineers and scientists. This creates a selective bias in favor of research and production at the expense of marketing. The organization tends to view itself as making things rather than satisfying customer needs. Marketing gets treated as a residual activity, "something else" that must be done once the vital job of product creation and production is completed.
2. To this bias in favor of product research, development, and production is added the bias in favor of dealing with controllable variables. Engineers and scientists are at home in the world of concrete things like machines, test tubes, production lines, and even balance sheets. The abstractions to which they feel kindly are those which are testable or manipulable in the laboratory or, if not testable, then functional, such as Euclid's axioms. In short, the managements of the new glamour-growth companies tend to favor those business activities which lend themselves to careful study,

161

experimentation, and control—the hard, practical realities of the lab, the shop, the books.

What gets shortchanged are the realities of the *market*. Consumers are unpredictable, varied, fickle, stupid, shortsighted, stubborn, and generally bothersome. This is not what the engineer-managers say, but deep down in their consciousness it is what they believe. And this accounts for their concentrating on what they know and what they can control, namely, product research, engineering, and production. The emphasis on production becomes particularly attractive when the product can be made at declining unit costs. There is no more inviting way of making money than by running the plant full blast.

Today the top-heavy science-engineering-production orientation of so many electronics companies works reasonably well because they are pushing into new frontiers in which the armed services have pioneered virtually assured markets. The companies are in the felicitous position of having to fill, not find, markets; of not having to discover what the customer needs and wants, but of having the customer voluntarily come forward with specific new product demands. If a team of consultants had been assigned specifically to design a business situation calculated to prevent the emergence and development of a customer-oriented marketing viewpoint, it could not have produced anything better than the conditions just described.

*Stepchild treatment*

The oil industry is a stunning example of how science, technology, and mass production can divert an entire group of companies from their main task. To the extent the consumer is studied at all (which is not much), the focus is forever on getting information which is designed to help the oil companies improve what they are now doing. They try to discover more convincing advertising themes, more effective sales promotional drives, what the market shares of the various companies are, what people like or dislike about service station dealers and oil companies, and so forth. Nobody seems as interested in probing deeply into the basic human needs that the industry might be trying to satisfy as in probing into the basic properties of the raw material that the companies work with in trying to deliver customer satisfactions.

Basic questions about customers and markets seldom get asked. The latter occupy a stepchild status. They are recognized as existing, as having to be taken care of, but not worth very much real thought or dedicated attention. Nobody gets as excited about the customers in his own backyard as about the oil in the Sahara Desert. Nothing illustrates better the neglect of marketing than its treatment in the industry press.

The centennial issue of the *American Petroleum Institute Quarterly*, published in 1959 to celebrate the discovery of oil in Titusville, Pennsylvania, contained twenty-one feature articles proclaiming the industry's greatness. Only one of these talked about its achievements in marketing, and that was only a pictorial record of how service station architecture has changed. The issue also contained a special section on "New Horizons," which was devoted to showing the magnificent role oil would play in America's future. Every reference was ebulliently optimistic, never implying once that oil might have some hard competition. Even the reference to atomic energy was a cheerful catalogue of how oil would help make atomic energy a success. There was not a single apprehension that the oil industry's affluence might be threatened or a suggestion that one "new horizon" might include new and better ways of serving oil's present customers.

But the most revealing example of the stepchild treatment that marketing gets was still another special series of short articles, on "The Revolutionary Potential of Electronics." Under that heading this list of articles appeared in the table of contents:

- —"In the Search for Oil"
- —"In Production Operations"
- —"In Refinery Processes"
- —"In Pipeline Operations"

Significantly, every one of the industry's major functional areas is listed, *except* marketing. Why? Either it is believed that electronics holds no revolutionary potential for petroleum marketing (which is palpably wrong) or the editors forgot to discuss marketing (which is more likely and illustrates its stepchild status).

The order in which the four functional areas are listed also betrays the alientation of the oil industry from the consumer. The industry is implicitly defined as beginning with the search for oil and ending with its distribution from the refinery. But the truth is, it seems to me, that the industry begins with the needs of the consumer for its products. From that primal position its definition moves steadily backstream to areas of progressively lesser importance, until it finally comes to rest at the "search for oil."

### Beginning and end

The view that an industry is a customer-satisfying process, not a goods-producing process, is vital for all businessmen to understand. An industry begins with the customer and his needs, not with a patent, a raw material, or a selling skill. Given the customer's needs, the industry develops backwards, first concerning itself with the physical *delivery* of customer satisfactions. Then it moves back further to *creating* the things by which these satisfactions are in part achieved. How these materials are created is a matter of indifference to the customer, hence the particular form of manufacturing, processing, or what-have-you cannot be considered as a vital aspect of the industry. Finally, the industry moves back still further to *finding* the raw materials necessary for making its products.

The irony of some industries oriented toward technical research and development is that the scientists who occupy the high executive positions are totally unscientific when it comes to defining their companies' overall needs and purposes. They violate the first two rules of the scientific method—being aware of and defining their companies' problems, and then developing testable hypotheses about solving them. They are scientific only about the convenient things, such as laboratory and product experiments.

The reason that the customer (and the satisfaction of his deepest needs) is not considered as being "the problem" is not because there is any certain belief that no such problem exists, but because an

164

organizational lifetime has conditioned management to look in the opposite direction. Marketing is a stepchild.

I do not mean that selling is ignored. Far from it. But selling, again, is not marketing. As already pointed out, selling concerns itself with the tricks and techniques of getting people to exchange their cash for their product. It is not concerned with the values that the exchange is all about. And it does not, as marketing invariably does, view the entire business process as consisting of a tightly integrated effort to discover, create, arouse, and satisfy customer needs. The customer is somebody "out there" who, with proper cunning, can be separated from his loose change.

Actually, not even selling gets much attention in some technologically minded firms. Because there is a virtually guaranteed market for the abundant flow of their new products, they do not actually know what a real market is. It is as if they lived in a planned economy, moving their products routinely from factory to retail outlet. Their successful concentration on products tends to convince them of the soundness of what they have been doing, and they fail to see the clouds gathering over the market.

## CONCLUSION

Less than seventy-five years ago American railroads enjoyed a fierce loyalty among astute Wall Streeters. European monarchs invested in them heavily. Eternal wealth was thought to be the benediction for anybody who could scrape a few thousand dollars together to put into rail stocks. No other form of transportation could compete with the railroads in speed, flexibility, durability, economy, and growth potentials.

As Jacques Barzun put it, "By the turn of the century it was an institution, an image of man, a tradition, a code of honor, a source of poetry, a nursery of boyhood desires, a sublimest of toys, and the most solemn machine—next to the funeral hearse—that marks the epochs in man's life."[6]

Even after the advent of automobiles, trucks, and airplanes, the railroad tycoons remained imperturbably self-confident. If you

[6]Jacques Barzun, "Trains and the Mind of Man," *Holiday*, February 1960, p. 20.

had told them sixty years ago that in thirty years they would be flat on their backs, broke, and pleading for government subsidies, they would have thought you totally demented. Such a future was simply not considered possible. It was not even a discussable subject, or an askable question, or a matter which any sane person would consider worth speculating about. The very thought was insane. Yet a lot of insane notions now have matter-of-fact acceptance—for example, the idea of 100-ton tubes of metal moving smoothly through the air 20,000 feet above the earth, loaded with 100 sane and solid citizens casually drinking martinis—and they have dealt cruel blows to the railroads.

What specifically must other companies do to avoid this fate? What does customer orientation involve? These questions have in part been answered by the preceding examples and analysis. It would take another article to show in detail what is required for specific industries. In any case, it should be obvious that building an effective customer-oriented company involves far more than good intentions or promotional tricks; it involves profound matters of human organization and leadership. For the present, let me merely suggest what appear to be some general requirements.

### Visceral feel of greatness

Obviously the company has to do what survival demands. It has to adapt to the requirements of the market, and it has to do it sooner rather than later. But mere survival is a so-so aspiration. Anybody can survive in some way or other, even the skid-row bum. The trick is to survive gallantly, to feel the surging impulse of commercial mastery; not just to experience the sweet smell of success, but to have the visceral feel of entrepreneurial greatness.

No organization can achieve greatness without a vigorous leader who is driven onward by his own pulsating *will to succeed*. He has to have a vision of grandeur, a vision that can produce eager followers in vast numbers. In business, the followers are the customers.

In order to produce these customers, the entire corporation must be viewed as a customer-creating and customer-satisfying organism.

Management must think of itself not as producing products but as providing customer-creating value satisfactions. It must push this idea (and everything it means and requires) into every nook and cranny of the organization. It has to do this continuously and with the kind of flair that excites and stimulates the people in it. Otherwise the company will be merely a series of pigeonholed parts, with no consolidating sense of purpose or direction.

In short, the organization must learn to think of itself not as producing goods or services but as *buying customers*, as doing the things that will make people *want* to do business with it. And the chief executive himself has the inescapable responsibility for creating this environment, this viewpoint, this attitude, this aspiration. He himself must set the company's style, its direction, and its goals. This means he has to know precisely where he himself wants to go and to make sure the whole organization is enthusiastically aware of where that is. This is a first requisite of leadship, for *unless he knows where he is going, any road will take him there.*

If any road is okay, the chief executive might as well pack his attaché case and go fishing. If an organization does not know or care where it is going, it does not need to advertise that fact with a ceremonial figurehead. Everybody will notice it soon enough.

## RETROSPECTIVE COMMENTARY

Amazed, finally, by his literary success, Isaac Bashevis Singer reconciled an attendant problem: "I think the moment you have published a book, it's not any more your private property. . . . If it has value, everybody can find in it what he finds, and I cannot tell the man I did not intend it to be so." Over the past fifteen years, "Marketing Myopia" has become a case in point. Remarkably, the article spawned a legion of loyal partisans—not to mention a host of unlikely bedfellows.

Its most common and, I believe, most influential consequence is the way certain companies for the first time gave serious thought to the question of what business they are really in.

The strategic consequences of this have in many cases been dramatic. The best-known case, of course, is the shift in thinking of oneself as being in the "oil business" to being in the "energy business." In some instances the payoff has been spectacular (getting into coal, for example) and in others dreadful (in terms of the time and money spent so far on fuel cell research). Another successful example is a company with a large chain of retail shoe stores that redefined itself as a retailer of moderately priced, frequently purchased, widely assorted consumer specialty products. The result was a dramatic growth in volume, earnings, and return on assets.

Some companies, again for the first time, asked themselves whether they wished to be masters of certain technologies for which they would seek markets, or be masters of markets for which they would seek customer-satisfying products and services.

Choosing the former, one company has declared, in effect, "We are experts in glass technology. We intend to improve and expand that expertise with the object of creating products that will attract customers." This decision has forced the company into a much more systematic and customer-sensitive look at possible markets and users, even though its stated strategic object has been to capitalize on glass technology.

Deciding to concentrate on markets, another company has determined that "we want to help people (primarily women) enhance their beauty and sense of youthfulness." This company has expanded its line of cosmetic products, but has also entered the fields of proprietary drugs and vitamin supplements.

All these examples illustrate the "policy" results of "Marketing Myopia." On the operating level, there has been, I think, an extraordinary heightening of sensitivity to customers and consumers. R&D departments have cultivated a greater "external" orientation toward uses, users, and markets—balancing thereby the previously one-sided "internal" focus on materials and methods; upper management has realized that marketing and sales departments should be somewhat more willingly accommodated than before; finance departments have become more receptive to the legitimacy of budgets for market research and experimentation in marketing; and salesmen have been better trained to listen to and understand customer needs and problems, rather than merely to "push" the product.

## A MIRROR, NOT A WINDOW

My impression is that the article has had more impact in industrial-products companies than in consumer-products companies—perhaps because the former had lagged most in customer orientation. There are at least two reasons for this lag: (1) industrial-products companies tend to be more capital intensive, and (2) in the past, at least, they have had to rely heavily on communicating face to face the technical character of what they made and sold. These points are worth explaining.

Capital-intensive businesses are understandably preoccupied with magnitudes, especially where the capital, once invested, cannot be easily moved, manipulated, or modified for the production of a variety of products—e.g., chemical plants, steel mills, airlines, and railroads. Understandably, they seek big volumes and operating efficiencies to pay off the equipment and meet the carrying costs.

At least one problem results: corporate power becomes disproportationately lodged with operating or financial executives. If you read the charter of one of the nation's largest companies, you will see that the chairman of the finance committee, not the chief executive officer, is the "chief." Executives with such backgrounds have an almost trained incapacity to see that getting "volume" may require understanding and serving many discrete and sometimes small market segments, rather than going after a perhaps mythical batch of big or homogeneous customers.

These executives also often fail to appreciate the competitive changes going on around them. They observe the changes, all right, but devalue their significance or underestimate their ability to nibble away at the company's markets.

Once dramatically alerted to the concept of segments, sectors, and customers, though, managers of capital-intensive businesses have become more responsive to the necessity of balancing their inescapable preoccupation with "paying the bills" or breaking even with the fact that the best way to accomplish this may be to pay more attention to segments, sectors, and customers.

The second reason industrial-products companies have probably been more influenced by the article is that, in the case of the more technical industrial products or services, the necessity of clearly communicating product and service characteristics to prospects results in a lot of face-to-face "selling" effort. But precisely because the product is so complex, the situation produces salesmen who know the product more than they know the customer, who are more adept at explaining what they have and what it can do than learning what the customer's needs and problems are. The result has been a narrow product orientation rather than a liberating customer orientation, and "service" often suffered. To be sure, sellers said, "We have to provide service," but they tended to define service by looking into the mirror rather than out the window. They *thought* they were looking out the window at the customer, but it was actually a mirror—a reflection of their own product-oriented biases rather than a reflection of their customers' situations.

## A MANIFESTO,
## NOT A PRESCRIPTION

Not everything has been rosy. A lot of bizarre things have happened as a result of the article:

—Some companies have developed what I call "marketing mania"—they've become obsessively responsive to every fleeting whim of the customer. Mass-production operations have been converted to approximations of job shops, with cost and price consequences far exceeding the willingness of customers to buy the product.

—Management has expanded product lines and added new lines of business without first establishing adequate control systems to run more complex operations.

—Marketing staffs have suddenly and rapidly expanded themselves and their research budgets without either getting sufficient prior organizational support or, thereafter, producing sufficient results.

—Companies that are functionally organized have converted to product, brand, or market-based organizations with the expectation of instant and miraculous results. The outcome has been ambiguity, frustration, confusion, corporate infighting, losses, and finally a reversion to functional arrangements that only worsened the situation.

—Companies have attempted to "serve" customers by creating complex and beautifully efficient products or services that buyers are either too risk-averse to adopt or incapable of learning how to employ—in effect, there are now steam shovels for people who haven't yet learned to use spades. This problem has happened repeatedly in the so-called service industries (financial services, insurance, computer-based services) and with American companies selling in less-developed economies.

"Marketing Myopia" was not intended as analysis or even prescription; it was intended as manifesto. It did not pretend to take a balanced position. Nor was it a new idea—Peter F. Drucker, J. B. McKitterick, Wroe Alderson, John Howard, and Neil Borden had each done more original and balanced work on "the marketing concept." My scheme, however, tied marketing more closely to the inner orbit of business policy. Drucker—especially in *The Concept of the Corporation* and *The Practice of Management*—originally provided me with a great deal of insight.

My contribution, therefore, appears merely to have been a simple, brief, and useful way of communicating an existing way of thinking. I tried to do it in a very direct, but responsible, fashion, knowing that few readers (customers), especially managers and leaders, could stand much equivocation or hestitation. I also knew that the colorful and lightly documented affirmation works better than the tortuously reasoned explanation.

But why the enormous popularity of what was actually such a simple preexisting idea? Why its appeal throughout the world to resolutely restrained scholars, implacably temperate managers, and high government officials, all accustomed to balanced and thoughtful calculation? Is it that concrete examples, joined to illustrate a simple idea and presented with some attention to literacy, communicate better than massive analytical reasoning that reads as though it were translated from the German? Is it that provocative assertions are more memorable and persuasive than restrained and balanced explanations, no matter who the audience? Is it that the character of the message is as much the message as its content? Or was mine not simply a different tune, but a new symphony? I don't know.

Of course, I'd do it again and in the same way, given my purposes, even with what more I now know—the good and the bad, the power of facts and the limits of rhetoric. If your mission is the moon, you don't use a car. Don Marquis's cockroach, Archy, provides some final consolation: "An idea is not responsible for who believes in it."

# 9

# Exploit the Product Life Cycle

Most alert and thoughtful senior marketing executives are by now familiar with the concept of the product life cycle. Even a handful of uniquely cosmopolitan and up-to-date corporate presidents have familiarized themselves with this tantalizing concept. Yet a recent survey I took of such executives found none who used the concept in any strategic way whatsoever and pitifully few who used it in any kind of tactical way. It has remained—as have so many fascinating theories in economics, physics, and sex—a remarkably durable but almost totally unemployed and seemingly unemployable piece of professional baggage whose presence in the rhetoric of professional discussions adds a much coveted but apparently unattainable legitimacy to the idea that marketing management is somehow a profession. There is, furthermore, a persistent feeling that the life cycle concept adds luster and believability to the insistent claim in certain circles that marketing is close to being some sort of science.[1]

[1]For discussions of the scientific claims or potentials of marketing, see George Schwartz, *Development of Marketing Theory* (Cincinnati, Ohio: South-Western Publishing Co., 1963); and Reavis Cox, Wroe Alderson, and Stanley J. Shapiro, eds. *Theory in Marketing* (Homewood, Ill.: Richard D. Irwin, Second Series, 1964).

The concept of the product life cycle is today at about the stage that the Copernican view of the universe was three hundred years ago: a lot of people knew about it, but hardly anybody seemed to use it in any effective or productive way.

Now that so many people know and in some fashion understand the product life cycle, it seems time to put it to work. The object of this article is to suggest some ways of using the concept effectively and of turning the knowledge of its existence into a managerial instrument of competitive power.

Since the concept has been presented somewhat differently by different authors and for different audiences, it is useful to review it briefly here so that every reader has the same background for the discussion which follows later in this article.

## HISTORICAL PATTERN

The life story of most successful products is a history of their passing through certain recognizable stages. These are shown in Figure 3 and occur in the following order:

—*Stage 1. Market development:* This is when a new product is first brought to market, before there is a proved demand for it and often before it has been fully proved out technically in all respects. Sales are low and creep along slowly.
—*Stage 2. Market growth:* Demand begins to accelerate and the size of the total market expands rapidly. It might also be called the "takeoff stage."
—*Stage 3. Market maturity:* Demand levels off and grows, for the most part, only at the replacement and new-family formation rate.
—*Stage 4. Market decline:* The product begins to lose consumer appeal and sales drift downward, such as when buggy whips lost out with the advent of automobiles and when silk lost out to nylon.

Three operating questions will quickly occur to the alert executive:

174

—Given a proposed new product or service, how and to what extent can the shape and duration of each stage be predicted?

—Given an existing product, how can one determine what stage it is in?

—Given all this knowledge, how can it be effectively used?

A brief further elaboration of each stage will be useful before dealing with these questions in detail.

### Development stage

Bringing a new product to market is fraught with unknowns, uncertainties, and, frequently, unknowable risks. Generally, demand has to be "created" during the product's initial *market development stage*. How long this takes depends on the product's complexity, its degree of newness, its fit into consumer needs, and the presence of competitive substitutes of one form or another. A proved cancer cure would require virtually no market development; it would get immediate massive support. An alleged superior substitute for the lost-wax process of sculpture casting would take lots longer.

While it has been demonstrated time after time that properly customer-oriented new product development is one of the primary conditions of sales and profit growth, what have been demonstrated

FIGURE 3.   PRODUCT LIFE CYCLE—ENTIRE INDUSTRY

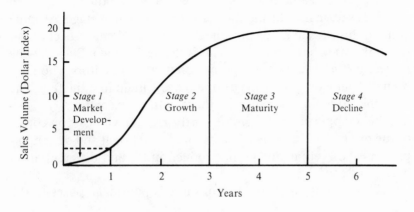

175

even more conclusively are the ravaging costs and frequent fatalities associated with launching new products. Nothing seems to take more time, cost more money, involve more pitfalls, cause more anguish, or break more careers than do sincere and well-conceived new product programs. The fact is, most new products don't have any sort of classical life cycle curve at all. They have instead from the very outset an infinitely descending curve. The product not only doesn't get off the ground; it goes quickly under ground—six feet under.

It is little wonder, therefore, that some disillusioned and badly burned companies have recently adopted a more conservative policy—what I call the "used apple policy." Instead of aspiring to be the first company to see and seize an opportunity, they systematically avoid being first. They let others take the first bite of the supposedly juicy apple that tantalizes them. They let others do the pioneering. If the idea works, they quickly follow suit. They say, in effect, "The trouble with being a pioneer is that the pioneers get killed by the Indians." Hence, they say (thoroughly mixing their metaphors), "We don't have to get the first bite of the apple. The second one is good enough." They are willing to eat off a used apple, but they try to be alert enough to make sure it is only slightly used—that they at least get the second big bite, not the tenth skimpy one.

### Growth stage

The usual characteristic of a successful new product is a gradual rise in its sales curve during the market development stage. At some point in this rise a marked increase in consumer demand occurs and sales take off. The boom is on. This is the beginning of Stage 2—the *market growth stage* At this point potential competitors who have been watching developments during Stage 1 jump into the fray. The first ones to get in are generally those with an exceptionally effective "used apple policy." Some enter the market with carbon copies of the originator's product. Others make functional and design improvements. And at this point product and brand differentiation begin to develop.

The ensuing fight for the consumer's patronage poses to the

originating producer an entirely new set of problems. Instead of seeking ways of getting consumers to *try the product*, the originator now faces the more compelling problem of getting them to *prefer his brand*. This generally requires important changes in marketing strategies and methods. But the policies and tactics now adopted will be neither freely the sole choice of the originating producer, nor as experimental as they might have been during Stage 1. The presence of competitors both dictates and limits what can easily be tried—such as, for example, testing what is the best price level or the best channel of distribution.

As the rate of consumer acceptance accelerates, it generally becomes increasingly easy to open new distribution channels and retail outlets. The consequent filling of distribution pipelines generally causes the entire industry's factory sales to rise more rapidly than store sales. This creates an exaggerated impression of profit opportunity which, in turn, attracts more competitors. Some of these will begin to charge lower prices because of later advances in technology, production shortcuts, the need to take lower margins in order to get distribution, and the like. All this in time inescapably moves the industry to the threshold of a new stage of competition.

*Maturity stage*

This new stage is the *market maturity stage*. The first sign of its advent is evidence of market saturation. This means that most consumer companies or households that are sales prospects will be owning or using the product. Sales now grow about on a par with population. No more distribution pipelines need be filled. Price competition now becomes intense. Competitive attempts to achieve and hold brand preference now involve making finer and finer differentiations in the product, in customer services, and in the promotional practices and claims made for the product.

Typically, the market maturity stage forces the producer to concentrate on holding his distribution outlets, retaining his shelf space, and, in the end, trying to secure even more intensive distribution. Whereas during the market development stage the originator depended heavily on the positive efforts of his retailers and distributors

177

to help sell his product, retailers and distributors will now frequently have been reduced largely to being merchandise displayers and order takers. In the case of branded products in particular, the originator must now, more than ever, communicate directly with the consumer.

The market maturity stage typically calls for a new kind of emphasis on competing more effectively. The originator is increasingly forced to appeal to the consumer on the basis of price, marginal product differences, or both. Depending on the product, services and deals offered in connection with it are often the clearest and most effective forms of differentiation. Beyond these, there will be attempts to create and promote fine product distinctions through packaging and advertising and to appeal to special market segments. The market maturity stage can be passed through rapidly, as in the case of most women's fashion fads, or it can persist for generations with per capita consumption neither rising nor falling, as in the case of such staples as men's shoes and industrial fasteners. Or maturity can persist, but in a state of gradual but steady per capita decline, as in the case of beer and steel.

*Decline stage*

When market maturity tapers off and consequently comes to an end, the product enters Stage 4—*market decline*. In all cases of maturity and decline the industry is transformed. Few companies are able to weather the competitive storm. As demand declines, the overcapacity that was already apparent during the period of maturity now becomes endemic. Some producers see the handwriting implacably on the wall but feel that with proper management and cunning they will be one of the survivors after the industry-wide deluge they so clearly foresee. To hasten their competitors' eclipse directly, or to frighten them into early voluntary withdrawal from the industry, they initiate a variety of aggressively depressive tactics, propose mergers or buy-outs, and generally engage in activities that make life thanklessly burdensome for all firms and make death the inevitable consequence for most of them. A few companies do indeed weather the storm, sustaining life through the constant descent that now clearly characterizes the industry. Production gets concentrated into fewer hands. Prices and margins get depressed. Consumers get bored. The only cases where there is any relief from this boredom and gradual euthanasia are where styling and fashion play some constantly revivifying role.

## PREPLANNING IMPORTANCE

Knowing that the lives of successful products and services are generally characterized by something like the pattern illustrated in Figure 3 can become the basis for important life-giving policies and practices. One of the greatest values of the life cycle concept is for managers about to launch a new product. The first step for them is to try to foresee the profile of the proposed product's cycle.

As with so many things in business, and perhaps uniquely in marketing, it is almost impossible to make universally useful suggestions regarding how to manage one's affairs. It is certainly particularly difficult to provide widely useful advice on how to foresee or predict the slope and duration of a product's life. Indeed, it is precisely because so little specific day-to-day guidance is possible in anything, and because no checklist by itself has ever been very useful to anybody for very long, that business management will probably never be a science—always an art—and will pay exceptional rewards to managers with rare talent, enormous energy, iron nerve, and great capacity for assuming responsibility and bearing accountability.

But this does not mean that useful efforts cannot or should not be made to try to foresee the slope and duration of a new product's life. Time spent in attempting this kind of foresight not only helps assure that a more rational approach is brought to product planning and merchandising; also, as will be shown later, it can help create valuable lead time for important strategic and tactical moves after the product is brought to market. Specifically, it can be a great help in developing an orderly series of competitive moves, in expanding or stretching out the life of a product, in maintaining a clean product line, and in purposely phasing out dying and costly old products.[2]

---

[2]See Philip Kotler, "Phasing Out Weak Products," *Harvard Business Review*, March/April 1965, p. 107.

*Failure possibilities . . .*

As pointed out above, the length and slope of the market development stage depend on the product's complexity, its degree of newness, its fit into customer needs, and the presence of competitive substitutes.

The more unique or distinctive the newness of the product, the longer it generally takes to get it successfully off the ground. The world does not automatically beat a path to the man with the better mousetrap.[3] The world has to be told, coddled, enticed, romanced, and even bribed (as with, for example, coupons, samples, free application aids, and the like). When the product's newness is distinctive and the job it is designed to do is unique, the public will generally be less quick to perceive it as something it clearly needs or wants.

This makes life particularly difficult for the innovator. He will have more than the usual difficulties in identifying those characteristics of his product and those supporting communications themes or devices which imply value to the consumer. As a consequence, the more distinctive the newness, the greater the risk of failure resulting either from insufficient working capital to sustain a long and frustrating period of creating enough solvent customers to make the proposition pay, or from the inability to convince investors and bankers that they should put up more money.

In any particular situation, the more people who will be involved in making a single purchasing decision for a new product, the more drawn out Stage 1 will be. Thus in the highly fragmented construction materials industry, for example, success takes an exceptionally long time to catch hold; and having once caught hold, it tends to hold tenaciously for a long time—often too long. On the other hand, fashion items clearly catch on fastest and last shortest. But because fashion is so powerful, recently some companies in what often seem

---

[3]For perhaps the ultimate example of how the world does *not* beat such a path, see the example of the man who actually, and to his painful regret, made a "better" mousetrap in John B. Matthews, Jr., R. D. Buzzell, Theodore Levitt, and Ronald E. Frank, *Marketing: An Introductory Analysis* (New York: McGraw-Hill, 1964), p. 4.

the least fashion-influenced of industries (machine tools, for example) have shortened the market development stage by introducing elements of design and packaging fashion to their products.

What factors tend to prolong the market development stage and therefore raise the risk of failure? The more complex the product, the more distinctive its newness, the less influenced by fashion, the greater the number of persons influencing a single buying decision, the more costly, and the greater the required shift in the customer's usual way of doing things—these are the conditions most likely to slow things up and create problems.

## . . . vs. success chances

But problems also create opportunities to control the forces arrayed against new product success. For example, the newer the product, the more important it becomes for the customers to have a favorable first experience with it. Newness creates a certain special visibility for the product, with a certain number of people standing on the sidelines to see how the first customers get on with it. If their first experience is unfavorable in some crucial way, this may have repercussions far out of proportion to the actual extent of the under-fulfillment of the customers' expectations. But a favorable first experience or application will, for the same reason, get a lot of disproportionately favorable publicity.

The possibility of exaggerated disillusionment with a poor first experience can raise vital questions regarding the appropriate channels of distribution for a new product. On the one hand, getting the product successfully launched may require having—as in the case of, say, the early days of home washing machines—many retailers who can give consumers considerable help in the product's correct utilization and thus help assure a favorable first experience for those buyers. On the other hand, channels that provide this kind of help (such as small neighborhood appliance stores in the case of washing machines) during the market development stage may not be the ones best able to merchandise the product most successfully later when help in creating and personally reassuring customers is less important than wide product distribution. To the extent that channel decisions during this first stage sacrifice some of the requirements of the market development stage to some of the requirements of later stages, the rate of the product's acceptance by consumers at the outset may be delayed.

In entering the market development stage, pricing decisions are often particularly hard for the producer to make. Should he set an initially high price to recoup his investment quickly—i.e., "skim the cream"—or should he set a low price to discourage potential competition—i.e., "exclusion"? The answer depends on the innovator's estimate of the probable length of the product's life cycle, the degree of patent protection the product is likely to enjoy, the amount of capital needed to get the product off the ground, the elasticity of demand during the early life of the product, and many other factors. The decision that is finally made may affect not just the rate at which the product catches on at the beginning, but even the duration of its total life. Thus some products that are priced too low at the outset (particularly fashion goods, such as the chemise, or sack, a few years ago) may catch on so quickly that they become short-lived fads. A slower rate of consumer acceptance might often extend their life cycles and raise the total profits they yield.

The actual slope, or rate of the growth stage, depends on some of the same things as does success or failure in Stage 1. But the extent to which patent exclusiveness can play a critical role is sometimes inexplicably forgotten. More frequently than one might offhand expect, holders of strong patent positions fail to recognize either the market-development virtue of making their patents available to competitors or the market-destroying possibilities of failing to control more effectively their competitors' use of such products.

Generally speaking, the more producers there are of a new product, the more effort goes into developing a market for it. The net result is very likely to be more rapid and steeper growth of the total market. The originator's market share may fall, but his total sales and profits may rise more rapidly. Certainly this has been the case in recent years of color television; RCA's eagerness to makes its tubes available to competitors reflects its recognition of the power of numbers over the power of monopoly.

On the other hand, the failure to set and enforce appropriate quality standards in the early days of polystyrene and polyethylene drinking glasses and cups produced such sloppy, inferior goods that it took years to recover the consumer's confidence and revive the growth pattern.

But to try to see in advance what a product's growth pattern might be is not very useful if one fails to distinguish between the industry pattern and the pattern of the single firm for its particular brand. The industry's cycle will almost certainly be different from the cycle of individual firms. Moreover, the life cycle of a given product may be different for different companies in the same industry at the same point in time, and it certainly affects different companies in the same industry differently.

## ORIGINATOR'S BURDENS

The company with most at stake is the original producer—the company that launches an entirely new product. This company generally bears most of the costs, the tribulations, and certainly the risks of developing both the product and the market.

### Competitive pressure

Once the innovator demonstrates during the market development stage that a solid demand exists, armies of imitators rush in to capitalize on and help create the boom that becomes the market growth, or takeoff, stage. As a result, while exceedingly rapid growth will now characterize the product's total demand, for the originating company its growth stage paradoxically now becomes truncated. It has to share the boom with new competitors. Hence the potential rate of acceleration of its own takeoff is diminished and, indeed, may actually fail to last as long as the industry's. This occurs not only because there are so many competitors, but, as we noted earlier, also because competitors often come in with product improvements and lower prices. While these developments generally help keep the market expanding, they greatly restrict the originating company's rate of growth and the length of its takeoff stage.

All this can be illustrated by comparing the curve in Figure 4

183

FIGURE 4.    PRODUCT LIFE CYCLE—ORIGINATING COMPANY

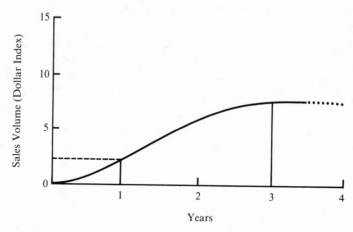

with that in Figure 3, which shows the life cycle for a product. During Stage 1 in Figure 3 there is generally only one company—the originator—even though the whole exhibit represents the entire industry. In Stage 1 the originator is the entire industry. But by Stage 2 he shares the industry with many competitors. Hence, while Figure 3 is an industry curve, its Stage 1 represents only a single company's sales.

Figure 4 shows the life cycle of the originator's brand—his own sales curve, not that of the industry. It can be seen that between Year 1 and Year 2 his sales are rising about as rapidly as the industry's. But after Year 2, while industry sales in Figure 3 are still in vigorous expansion, the originator's sales curve in Figure 4 has begun to slow its ascent. He is now sharing the boom with a great many competitors, some of whom are much better positioned now than he is.

*Profit squeeze*

In the process the originator may begin to encounter a serious squeeze on his profit margins. Figure 5, which traces the profits per unit of the originator's sales, illustrates this point. During the market development stage his per-unit profits are negative. Sales volume is too low at existing prices. However, during the market growth stage

184

FIGURE 5.  UNIT-PROFIT-CONTRIBUTION LIFE CYCLE—
ORIGINATING COMPANY

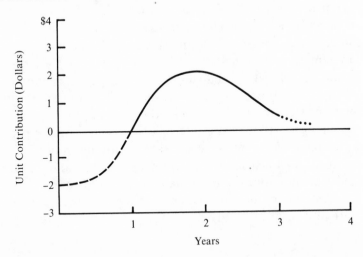

unit profits boom as output rises and unit production costs fall. Total profits rise enormously. It is the presence of such lush profits that both attracts and ultimately destroys competitors.

Consequently, while (1) industry sales may still be rising nicely (as at the Year 3 point in Figure 3), and (2) while the originating company's sales may at the same point of time have begun to slow down noticeably (as in Figure 4), and (3) while at this point the originator's total profits may still be rising because his volume of sales is huge and on a slight upward trend, his profits per unit will often have taken a drastic downward course. Indeed, they will often have done so long before the sales curve flattened. They will have topped out and begun to decline perhaps around the Year 2 point (as in Figure 5). By the time the originator's sales begin to flatten out (as at the Year 3 point in Figure 4), unit profits may actually be approaching zero (as in Figure 5).

At this point more competitors are in the industry, the rate of industry demand growth has slowed somewhat, and competitors are cutting prices. Some of them do this in order to get business, and others do it because their costs are lower owing to the fact that their equipment is more modern and productive.

The industry's Stage 3—maturity—generally lasts as long as there are no important competitive substitutes (such as, for example, aluminum for steel in "tin" cans), no drastic shifts in influential value systems (such as the end of female modesty in the 1920's and the consequent destruction of the market for veils), no major changes in dominant fashions (such as the hour glass female form and the end of waist cinchers), no changes in the demand for primary products which use the product in question (such as the effect of the decline of new railroad expansion on the demand for railroad ties), and no changes either in the rate of obsolescence of the product or in the character or introductory rate of product modifications.

Maturity can last for a long time, or it can actually never be attained. Fashion goods and fad items sometimes surge to sudden heights, hestitate momentarily at an uneasy peak, and then quickly drop off into total obscurity.

*Stage recognition*

The various characteristics of the stages described above will help one to recognize the stage a particular product occupies at any given time. But hindsight will always be more accurate than current sight. Perhaps the best way of seeing one's current stage is to try to foresee the next stage and work backwards. This approach has several virtues.

—It forces one to look ahead, constantly to try to reforesee his future and competitive environment. This will have its own rewards. As Charles F. Kettering, perhaps the last of Detroit's primitive inventors and probably the greatest of all its inventors, was fond of saying, "We should all be concerned about the future because that's where we'll have to spend the rest of our lives." By looking at the future one can better assess the state of the present.

—Looking ahead gives more perspective to the present than looking at the present alone. Most people know more about the present than is good for them. It is neither healthy nor helpful to know the present too well, for our perception of the present is too often too heavily distorted by the urgent pressures of day-to-day events. To know where the present is in the continuum of competitive time and events, it often makes more sense to try to know what the future will bring, and when it will bring it, than to try to know what the present itself actually contains.

—Finally, the value of knowing what stage a product occupies at any given time resides only in the way that fact is used. But its use is always in the future. Hence a prediction of the future environment in which the information will be used is often more functional for the effective capitalization on knowledge about the present than knowledge about the present itself.

## SEQUENTIAL ACTIONS

The life cycle concept can be effectively employed in the strategy of both existing and new products. For purposes of continuity and clarity, the remainder of this article will describe some of the uses of the concept from the early stages of new product planning through the later stages of keeping the product profitably alive. The chief discussion will focus on what I call a policy of "life extension" or "market stretching."[4]

To the extent that Figures 4 and 5 outline the classical patterns of successful new products, one of the constant aims of the originating producer should be to avoid the severe discipline imposed by an early profit squeeze in the market growth stage and to avoid the wear and waste so typical of the market maturity stage. Hence the following proposition would seem reasonable: when a company develops a new product or service, it should try to plan at the very outset a series of actions to be employed at various subsequent stages in the product's existence so that its sales and profit curves are constantly sustained rather than following their usual declining slope.

---

[4]For related ideas on discerning opportunities for product revivification, see Lee Adler, "A New Orientation for Plotting a Marketing Strategy," *Business Horizons,* Winter 1964, p. 37.

In other words, advance planning should be directed at extending, or stretching out, the life of the product. It is this idea of *planning in advance* of the actual launching of a new product to take specific actions later in its life cycle—actions designed to sustain its growth and profitability—which appears to have great potential as an instrument of long-term product strategy.

## Nylon's life

How this might work for a product can be illustrated by looking at the history of nylon. The way in which nylon's booming sales life has been repeatedly and systematically extended and stretched can serve as a model for other products. What has happened in nylon may not have been purposely planned that way at the outset, but the results are quite as if they had been planned.

The first nylon end-uses were primarily military—parachutes, thread, rope. This was followed by nylon's entry into the circular knit market and its consequent domination of the women's hosiery business. Here it developed the kind of steadily rising growth and profit curves that every executive dreams about. After some years these curves began to flatten out. But before they flattened very noticeably, DuPont had already developed measures designed to revitalize sales and profits. It did several things, each of which is demonstrated graphically in Figure 6. This exhibit and the explanation which follows take some liberties with the actual facts of the nylon situation in order to highlight the points I wish to make. But they take no liberties with the essential requisites of product strategy.

Point A of Figure 6 shows the hypothetical point at which the nylon curve (dominated at this point by hosiery) flattened out. If nothing further had been done, tne sales curve would have continued along the flattened pace indicated by the dotted line at Point A. This is also the hypothetical point at which the first systematic effort was made to extend the product's life. DuPont, in effect, took certain "actions" which pushed hosiery sales upward rather than continuing the path implied by the dotted line extension of the curve at Point A. At Point A action #1 pushed an otherwise flat curve upward.

At Points B, C, and D still other new sales and profit expan-

FIGURE 6.  HYPOTHETICAL LIFE CYCLE—NYLON

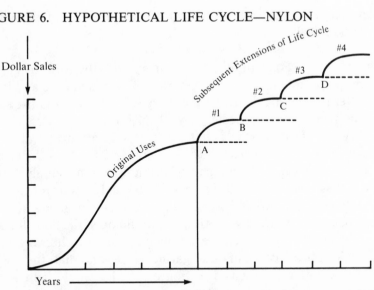

sion "actions" (#2, #3, #4, and so forth) were taken. What were these actions? Or, more usefully, what was their strategic content? What did they try to do? They involved strategies that tried to expand sales via four different routes:

1. Promoting more frequent usage of the product among current users.
2. Developing more varied usage of the product among current users.
3. Creating new users for the product by expanding the market.
4. Finding new uses for the basic material.

*Frequent Usage*—DuPont studies had shown an increasing trend toward "bareleggedness" among women. This was coincident with the trend toward more casual living and a declining perception among teenagers of what might be called the "social necessity" of wearing stockings. In the light of those findings, one approach to propping up the flattening sales curves might have been to reiterate the social necessity of wearing stockings at all times. That would have been a sales-building action, though obviously difficult and exceedingly costly. But it could clearly have fulfilled the strategy of promoting more frequent usage among current users as a means of extending the product's life.

*Varied Usage*—For DuPont, this strategy took the form of an attempt to promote the "fashion smartness" of tinted hose and later of patterned and highly textured hosiery. The idea was to raise each woman's inventory of hosiery by obsolescing the perception of hosiery as a fashion staple that came only in a narrow range of browns and pinks. Hosiery was to be converted from a "neutral" accessory to a central ingredient of fashion, with a "suitable" tint and pattern for each outer garment in the lady's wardrobe.

This not only would raise sales by expanding women's hosiery wardrobes and stores' inventories, but would open the door for annual tint and pattern obsolescence much the same as there is an annual color obsolescence in outer garments. Beyond that, the use of color and pattern to focus attention on the leg would help arrest the decline of the leg as an element of sex appeal—a trend which some researchers had discerned and which, they claimed, damaged hosiery sales.

*New Users*—Creating new users for nylon hosiery might conceivably have taken the form of attempting to legitimize the necessity of wearing hosiery among early teenagers and subteenagers. Advertising, public relations, and merchandising of youthful social and style leaders would have been called for.

*New Uses*—For nylon, this tactic has had many triumphs—from varied types of hosiery, such as stretch stockings and stretch socks, to new uses, such as rugs, tires, bearings, and so forth. Indeed, if there had been no further product innovations designed to create new uses for nylon after the original military, miscellaneous, and circular knit uses, nylon consumption in 1962 would have reached a saturation level at approximately 50 million pounds annually.

Instead, in 1962 consumption exceeded 500 million pounds. Figure 7 demonstrates how the continuous development of new uses for the basic material constantly produced new waves of sales. The exhibit shows that in spite of the growth of the women's stocking market, the cumulative result of the millitary, circular knit, and

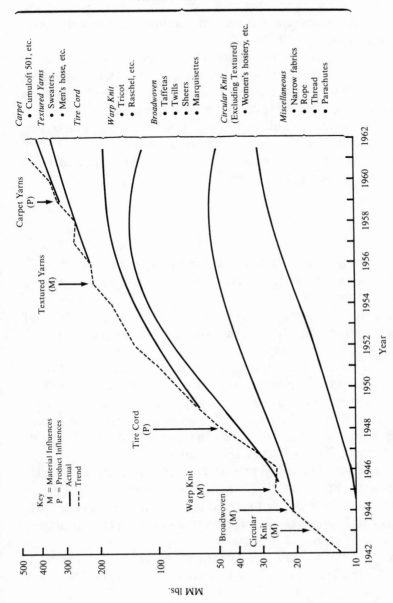

Source: *Modern Textiles Magazine*, February 1964, p. 33. © 1962 by Jordan P. Yale.

FIGURE 7. INNOVATION OF NEW PRODUCTS POSTPONES THE TIME OF TOTAL MATURITY—NYLON INDUSTRY

miscellaneous grouping would have been a flattened sales curve by 1958. (Nylon's entry into the broadwoven market in 1944 substantially raised sales above what they would have been. Even so, the sales of broadwoven, circular knit, and military and miscellaneous groupings peaked in 1957.)

Had it not been for the addition of new uses for the same basic material—such as warp knits in 1945, tire cord in 1948, textured yarns in 1955, carpet yarns in 1959, and so forth—nylon would not have had the spectacularly rising consumption curve it has so clearly had. At various stages it would have exhausted its existing markets or been forced into decline by competing materials. The systematic search for new uses for the basic (and improved) material extended and stretched the product's life.

*Other examples*

Few companies seem to employ in any systematic or planned way the four product life-stretching steps described above. Yet the successful application of this kind of stretching strategy has characterized the history of such well-known products as General Foods Corporation's "Jell-O" and Minnesota Mining & Manufacturing Co.'s "Scotch" tape.[5]

Jell-O was a pioneer in the easy-to-prepare gelatin dessert field. The soundness of the product concept and the excellence of its early marketing activities gave it beautifully ascending sales and profit curves almost from the start. But after some years these curves predictably began to flatten out. Scotch tape was also a pioneer product in its field. Once perfected, the product gained rapid market acceptance because of a sound product concept and an aggressive sales organization. But, again, in time the sales and profit curves began to flatten out. Before they flattened out very much, however, 3M, like General Foods, had already developed measures to sustain the early pace of sales and profits.

Both of these companies extended their products' lives by, in effect, doing all four of the things DuPont did with nylon—creating

[5] I am indebted to my colleague, Dr. Derek A. Newton, for these examples and other helpful suggestions.

more frequent usage among current users, more varied usage among current users, new users, and new uses for the basic "materials":

1. The General Foods approach to increasing the frequency of serving Jell-O among current users was, essentially, to increase the number of flavors. From Don Wilson's famous "six delicious flavors," Jell-O moved up to over a dozen. On the other hand, 3M helped raise sales among its current users by developing a variety of handy Scotch tape dispensers which made the product easier to use.

2. Creation of more varied usage of Jell-O among current dessert users involved its promotion as a base for salads and the facilitation of this usage by the development of a variety of vegetable-flavored Jell-O's. Similarly, 3M developed a line of colored, patterned, waterproof, invisible, and write-on Scotch tapes which have enjoyed considerable success as sealing and decorating items for holiday and gift wrapping.

3. Jell-O sought to create new users by pinpointing people who could not accept Jell-O as a popular dessert or salad product. Hence during the Metrecal boom Jell-O employed an advertising theme that successfully affixed to the product a fashion-oriented weight control appeal. Similarly, 3M introduced "Rocket" tape, a product much like Scotch tape but lower in price, and also developed a line of commercial cellophane tapes of various widths, lengths, and strengths. These actions broadened product use in commercial and industrial markets.

4. Both Jell-O and 3M have sought out new uses for the basic material. It is known, for example, that women consumers use powdered gelatin dissolved in liquids as a means of strengthening their fingernails. Both men and women use it in the same way as a bone-building agent. Hence Jell-O introduced a "completely flavorless" Jell-O for just these purposes. 3M has also developed new uses for the basic material—from "double-coated" tape (adhesive on both sides) which competes with ordinary liquid adhesives, to the reflecting tape which festoons countless automobile bumpers, to marker strips which compete with paint.

## EXTENSION STRATEGIES

The existence of the kinds of product life cycles illustrated in Figures 3 and 4 and the unit profit cycle in Figure 5 suggests that there may be considerable value for people involved in new product work to begin planning for the extension of the lives of their products even before these products are formally launched. To plan for new life-extending infusions of effort (as in Figure 6) at this preintroduction stage can be extremely useful in three profoundly important ways.

1. *It generates an active rather than a reactive product policy.*

It systematically structures a company's long-term marketing and product development efforts in advance, rather than each effort or activity being merely a stopgap response to the urgent pressures of repeated competitive thrusts and declining profits. The life-extension view of product policy enforces thinking and planning ahead—thinking in some systematic way about the moves likely to be made by potential competitors, about possible changes in consumer reaction to the product, and the required selling activities which best take advantage of these conditional events.

2. *It lays out a long-term plan designed to infuse new life into the product at the right time, with the right degree of care, and with the right amount of effort.*

Many activities designed to raise the sales and profits of existing products or materials are often undertaken without regard to their relationship to each other or to timing—the optimum point of consumer readiness for such activities or the point of optimum competitive effectiveness. Careful advance planning, long before the need for such activity arises, can help assure that the timing, the care, and the efforts are appropriate to the situation.

For example, it appears extremely doubtful that the boom in women's hair coloring and hair tinting products would have been as spectacular if vigorous efforts to sell these products had preceded the boom in hair sprays and chemical hair fixers. The latter helped create a powerful consumer consciousness of hair fashions because they made it relatively easy to create and wear fashionable hairstyles. Once it became easy for women to have fashionable hairstyles, the resulting fashion consciousness helped open the door for hair colors and tints. It could not have happened the other way around, with colors and tints first creating fashion consciousness and thus raising the sales of sprays and fixers. Because understanding the reason for this precise order of events is essential for appreciating the importance of early preintroduction life-extension planning, it is useful to go into a bit of detail. Consider:

> For women, setting their hair has been a perennial problem for centuries. First, the length and treatment of their hair is one of the most obvious ways in which they distinguish themselves from men. Hence to be attractive in that distinction becomes crucial. Second, hair frames and highlights the face, much like an attractive wooden border frames and highlights a beautiful painting. Thus hair styling is an important element in accentuating the appearance of a woman's facial features. Third, since the hair is long and soft, it is hard to hold in an attractive arrangement. It gets mussed in sleep, wind, damp weather, sporting activities, and so forth.
>
> Therefore, the effective *arrangement* of a woman's hair is understandably her first priority in hair care. An unkempt brunette would gain nothing from making herself into a blond. Indeed, in a country where blonds are in the minority, the switch from being an unkempt brunette to being an unkempt blond would simply draw attention to her sloppiness. But once the problem of arrangement became easily "solved" by sprays and fixers, colors and tints could become big business, especially among women whose hair was beginning to turn gray.

The same order of priorities applies in industrial products. For example, it seems quite inconceivable that many manufacturing plants would easily have accepted the replacement of the old single-spindle, constantly man-tended screw machine by a computerized tape-tended, multiple-spindle machine. The mechanical tending of the multiple-spindle machine was a necessary intermediate step, if for no other reason than that it required a lesser work-flow change, and certainly a lesser conceptual leap for the companies and the machine-tending workers involved.

For Jell-O, it is unlikely that vegetable flavors would have been very successful before the idea of gelatin as a salad base had been pretty well accepted. Similarly, the promotion of colored and patterned Scotch tape as a gift and decorative seal might not have been as successful if department stores had not, as the result of their drive to compete more effectively with mass merchandisers by offering more customer services, previously demonstrated to the consumer what could be done to wrap and decorate gifts.

3. *Perhaps the most important benefit of engaging in advance, preintroduction planning for sales-extending, market-stretching activities later in the product's life is that this practice forces a company to adopt a wider view of the nature of the product it is dealing with.*

Indeed, it may even force the adoption of a wider view of the company's business. Take the case of Jell-O. What is its product? Over the years Jell-O has become the brand umbrella for a wide range of dessert products, including cornstarch-base puddings, pie fillings, and new "Whip'n Chill," a light dessert product similar to a Bavarian creme or French mousse. On the basis of these products, it might be said that the Jell-O Division of General Foods is in the "dessert technology" business.

In the case of tape, perhaps 3M has gone even further in this technological approach to its business. It has a particular expertise (technology) on which it has built a constantly expanding business. This expertise can be said to be that of bonding things (adhesives in the case of Scotch tape) to other things, particularly to thin materials. Hence we see 3M developing scores of profitable items, including electronic recording tape (bonding electron-sensitive materials to tape), and "Thermo-Fax" duplicating equipment and supplies (bonding heat-reactive materials to paper).

CONCLUSION

For companies interested in continued growth and profits, successful new product strategy should be viewed as a planned totality that looks ahead over some years. For its own good, new product strategy should try to predict in some measure the likelihood, character, and timing of competitive and market events. While prediction is always hazardous and seldom very accurate, it is undoubtedly far better than not trying to predict at all. In fact, every product strategy and every business decision inescapably involves making a prediction about the future, about the market, and about competitors. To be more systematically aware of the predictions one is making so that one acts on them in an offensive rather than a defensive or reactive fashion—this is the real virtue of preplanning for market stretching and product life extension. The result will be a product strategy that includes some sort of *plan for a timed sequence of conditional moves.*

Even before entering the market development stage, the originator should make a judgment regarding the probable length of the product's normal life, taking into account the possibilities of expanding its uses and users. This judgment will also help determine many things—for example, whether to price the product on a skimming or a penetration basis, or what kind of relationship the company should develop with its resellers.

These considerations are important because at each stage in a product's life cycle each management decision must consider the competitive requirements of the next stage. Thus a decision to establish a strong branding policy during the market growth stage might help to insulate the brand against strong price competition later; a decision to establish a policy of "protected" dealers in the market development stage might facilitate point-of-sale promotions during the market growth stage; and so on. In short, having a clear idea of future product development possibilities and market development opportunities should reduce the likelihood of becoming locked into forms of merchandising that might possibly prove undesirable.

This kind of advance thinking about new product strategy helps management avoid other pitfalls. For instance, advertising campaigns that look successful from a short-term view may hurt in the next stage of the life cycle. Thus at the outset Metrecal advertising used a strong medical theme. Sales boomed until imitative competitors successfully emphasized fashionable slimness. Metrecal had projected itself as the dietary for the overweight consumer, an image that proved far less appealing than that of being the dietary for people who were fashion-smart. But Metrecal's original appeal had been so strong and so well made that it was a formidable task later on to change people's impressions about the product. Obviously, with more careful long-range planning at the outset, a product's image can be more carefully positioned and advertising can have more clearly defined objectives.

Recognizing the importance of an orderly series of steps in the introduction of sales-building "actions" for new products should be a central ingredient of long-term product planning. A carefully preplanned program for market expansion, even before a new product is introduced, can have powerful virtues. The establishment of a rational plan for the future can also help to guide the direction and pace of the ongoing technical research in support of the product. Although departures from such a plan will surely have to be made to accommodate unexpected events and revised judgments, the plan puts the company in a better position to *make* things happen rather than constantly having to react to things that *are* happening.

It is important that the originator does *not* delay this long-term planning until after the product's introduction. How the product should be introduced and the many uses for which it might be promoted at the outset should be a function of a careful consideration of the optimum sequence of suggested product appeals and product uses. Consideration must focus not just on optimum things to do, but as importantly on their optimum *sequence*—for instance, what the order of use of various appeals should be and what the order of suggested product uses should be. If Jell-O's first suggested use had been as a diet food, its chances of later making a big and easy impact in the gelatin dessert market undoubtedly would have been greatly diminished. Similarly, if nylon hosiery had been promoted at the outset as a functional daytime-wear hosiery, its ability to replace silk as the acceptable high-fashion hosiery would have been greatly diminished.

To illustrate the virtue of preintroduction planning for a product's later life, suppose a company has developed a nonpatentable new product—say, an ordinary kitchen saltshaker. Suppose that nobody now has any kind of shaker. One might say, before launching it, that (1) it has a potential market of "x" million household, institutional, and commercial consumers, (2) in two years market maturity will set in, and (3) in one year profit margins will fall because of the entry of competition. Hence one might lay out the following plan:

I. *End of first year: Expand market among current users*
Ideas—new designs, such as sterling shaker for formal use, "masculine" shaker for barbecue use, antique shaker for "Early American" households, miniature shaker for each table place setting, moisture-proof design for beach picnics

II. *End of second year: Expand market to new users*
Ideas—designs for children, quaffer design for beer drinkers in bars, design for sadists to rub salt into open wounds

III. *End of third year: Find new uses*
Ideas—make identical product for use as a pepper shaker, as decorative garlic salt shaker, shaker for household scouring powder, shaker to sprinkle silicon dust on parts being machined in machine shops, and so forth

This effort to prethink methods of reactivating a flattening sales curve far in advance of its becoming flat enables product planners to assign priorities to each task and to plan future production expansion and capital and market requirements in a systematic fashion. It prevents one's trying to do too many things at once, results in priorities being determined rationally instead of as accidental consequences of the timing of new ideas, and disciplines both the product development effort that is launched in support of a product's growth and the marketing effort that is required for its continued success.

# 10

# Innovative Imitation

We live in a business world that increasingly worships the great tribal god, *innovation*, lyrically hailing it not just as a desired, but as a necessary, condition of a company's survival and growth. This highly agitated confidence in the liberating efficacy of innovation has in some places become an article of faith almost as strong as the Natchez Indian's consuming faith in the deity of the sun. Man creates gods according to his needs. Significantly, the businessman's new demigod and the Natchez's more venerable and historic god make identical promises. They both promise renewal and life.

Yet before all our R&D energies and imaginations are too one-sidedly directed at the creation of innovations, it is useful to look at the facts of commercial life. Is innovation all that promising? Is it all that profoundly liberating? More important, how does a policy of innovation compare in promise to more modest aspirations?

In spite of the extraordinary outpouring of totally and partially new products and new ways of doing things that we are witnessing today, by far the greatest flow of newness is not innovation at all. Rather, it is *imitation* A simple look around us will, I think, quickly show that imitation is not only more abundant than innovation, but actually a much more prevalent road to business growth and profits. IBM got into computers as an imitator; Texas Instruments, into transistors as an imitator; Holiday Inns, into motels as an imitator; RCA, into television as an imitator, Lytton, into savings and loans as an imitator; and *Playboy*, into both its major fields (publishing and entertainment) as an imitator. In addition, though on a lesser scale, we see every day that private brands are strictly imitative, as are most toys and new brands of packaged foods. In fact, imitation is endemic. Innovation is scarce.

This greater abundance of imitation is perfectly understandable. Each solitary innovator sparks a wave of eager imitators. By the time a so-called new product reaches widespread visibility, it has usually been on the market for some time. Its visibility is less a consequence of its actual or temporal newness than it is of the number of its strident imitators. The newness of which consumers become aware is generally imitative and tardy newness, not innovative and timely newness.

## SIGNIFICANT DISTINCTIONS

Generally speaking, innovation may be viewed from at least two vantage points: (1) *newness in the sense that something has never been done before*, and (2) *newness in that it has not been done before by the industry or by the company now doing it.*

Strictly defined, innovation occurs only when something is entirely new, having never been done before. A modest relaxation of this definition may be allowed by suggesting that innovation also exists when something which may have been done elsewhere is for the first time done in a given industry. On the other hand, when other competitors in the same industry subsequently copy the innovator, even though it is something new for them, then it is not innovation; it is imitation. Thus:

— Bubble- or skin-packaging of small fixtures may be "new" for the hardware industry but may have been around several years in other applications (innovation).

— Or it may also be new for a given company in the hardware

201

industry but may have been around among competitors for some time (imitation).

These distinctions are not simply academic hairsplitting. They have the greatest significance for how a company develops its R&D budgets, structures its R&D efforts, and directs its product policies. A brief indication of what may be involved will—at the outset of this article—not only clarify the importance of the distinction, but help set the stage for the system proposed later.

R&D can be exceedingly costly, time-consuming, and frustrating. When it is oriented to the creation of pure newness, it can involve an enormous commitment of manpower and money—with no assurance of reasonable payout. But when a company's R&D effort is oriented largely toward trying to adapt to its industry or to its organization things that have already been done elsewhere, the character and costs of the commitment are quite different indeed. In the specific case of R&D oriented toward trying to develop for a company that which has already been done by an innovator, the situation is particularly special. There is usually a great premium on speed. One wants not just to catch up quickly with the successful innovator but, more particularly, to do so faster than other would-be imitators who are also working against the clock.

To call the purpose or character of this latter effort "innovation" is to mistake a space for a steam shovel. The steam shovel is not just a bigger version of the spade; its entire character is different. The spade's cost is miniscule; its user requires virtually no training; it has no maintenance costs; and since during a given time period many spades are required to do the work of a single steam shovel, the spade requires a management setup that is oriented toward the control and direction of many people, rather than toward the full utilization of an expensive and inanimate asset.

Similarly, R&D undertaken to create what might be referred to as "breakthrough newness" is vastly different from R&D which is imitative. The latter is little more than simple "D&D"—design and development. At best, it might be viewed as "reverse R&D"—working backwards from what others have done and trying to do the same thing for oneself.

The importance of these differences in the character of the required effort and commitment (coupled with a sometimes unreasoned faith in R&D and innovation) calls for a more careful self-examination in many companies of their competitive and growth strategies.

## NEEDED: BALANCED POLICY

Innovation, then, can be a highly productive, if often risky, road to success. In most industries today any company that is not aggressively alert to innovative possibilities is taking a competitive risk of which it ought at least to be intelligently aware. Moreover, it is likely to develop an in-company atmosphere and style of behavior on the part of its people that can be dangerously insular. The quest for innovation—particularly in new products, in new product attributes, and in customer service—is part and parcel of a company's being marketing oriented.

Hence to have a company style or posture that seeks out opportunities for innovation—whether (a) big massive ones, such as the new automobile diagnostic repair centers pioneered by Mobil Oil Company, or (b) modest innovations to extend the life cycle or broaden the market of a mature product, such as Mead Johnson's Enfamil baby formula being put into a ready-to-use measured bottle—can make a great deal of good sense.

And the sense it can make, as pointed out so well in John B. Stewart's perceptive and badly neglected article on the pattern of competitive imitation, is that innovation can be one of the most effective possible means of building a company image of progressiveness and leadership.[1]

Of course, to come out in favor of innovation these days is about as inspirational as to endorse motherhood. At the same time, to seem to come out *against* innovation is probably viewed with more alarm than to be opposed to motherhood. In an age of pills, rings, electric calendar clocks, and early sophistication, unintentional motherhood is a mark either of inexcusable carelessness or of unmanageable passion. Similarly, in an age of explosive science, engineering, market research, and rapid consumer acceptance of newness, opposition to innovation is a mark either of irretrievable naivety or of hopeless blindness.

[1]"Functional Features in Product Strategy," *Harvard Business Review*, March/April 1959, p. 65.

What is needed is a sensibly balanced view of the world. Innovation is here to stay, it is necessary, and it can make a lot of sense; but it does not exhaust the whole of reality. Every company needs to recognize the impossibility of sustaining innovative leadership in its industry and the danger of an unbalanced dedication to being the industry's innovator. No single company, regardless of its determination, energy, imagination, or resources, is big enough or solvent enough to do all the productive first things that will ever occur in its industry and to always beat its competitors to all the innovations emanating from the industry.

More important, no single company can afford even to *try* to be first in everything in its field. The costs are too great; and imagination, energy, and management know-how are too evenly distributed within industries. Of course, almost everybody implicitly knows this to be true, but my investigations lead me firmly to the conclusion that not everybody clearly acts this way.

### Reverse R&D

Once we become self-consciously aware that the possibilities of innovation within any one company are in some important ways limited, we quickly see that each organization is compelled by competition to look to imitation as one of its survival and growth strategies. Imitation is not just something which even the biggest, best-managed, most resourceful company will, by force of competitive circumstances, have to be involved in; it is something it will have to practice as a carefully developed strategy.

This means the company will, insofar as products and processes are concerned, have to actively engage in reverse R&D—will have to try to create its own imitative equivalents of the innovative products created by others. Moreover, the faster the rate at which entirely new products are launched in any field, the more urgent the need for each company in that field to develop a clear-cut imitative strategy—one that serves to guide not just the business judgments which must be made, but also the way in which the reverse R&D commitments are made.

Since in so many industries the survival and growth of individual companies dictates that they at least quickly imitate the innovator's new products, and since the speed of competitive imitation tends so quickly to cut the margins available to all competitors, the speed with which an imitator enters the market is crucial.

Yet in a recent informal survey I made of a range of strongly new-product oriented companies with strong R&D departments— companies whose products generally required one to three years from original idea conception to subsequent market launching—I found not a single one that had any kind of policy, not even informal or implicit, to guide its responses to the innovations of others. Not a single one of these companies had even given any systematic or sustained thought to the *general notion* of whether it might be useful to have some set of criteria for making commitments to reverse R&D.

This is especially surprising in view of my attendant findings that:

—Each of these companies had some sort of formal new-product planning process.
—Each at some time in the recent past had lost considerable profit opportunities because its imitations had been delayed too long.

In other words, while the companies did a very careful job of planning new product innovations, they had no criteria at all for the much bigger and more crucial job of new product imitation. Reverse R&D was neither a planned nor a careful process. It merely occurred. It was done entirely at random, and sometimes as an almost blind reaction to what others had done. And, in every recent case I examined in these companies, I found that the imitator paid a heavy price for imitating either too soon or too late—mostly the latter.

Had many of these tardy imitations been launched about a year sooner, enormous profits would have been earned. The magnitude of these profits would have reflected not simply the acquisition of sales that were otherwise lost, but also the higher prices and profit margins existing in this earlier year.

*Risk minimization*

Everybody knows that new products are risky. Predictably, they fail more often than they succeed. This unsettling fact helps explain why there is so much delay in competitive imitation. Would-be imitators sit carefully on the sidelines to watch the innovative product's fate. If it seems finally to take off, they then begin to make their own moves.

Watchful waiting is a perfectly legitimate business strategy. I have referred to it elsewhere as the "used apple policy."[2] According to this policy, a company consciously and carefully adopts the practice of never pioneering a new product. It says, in effect, "You don't have to get the first bite of the apple to make out. The second or third juicy bite is good enough. Just be careful not to get the tenth skimpy one." Hence it lets others do the pioneering. If the innovator's product is a rotten apple, the would-be imitator has lost nothing. If it's a healthy, juicy one, the imitator is prepared to move quickly and get an early and profitable piece of it.

But the trick is to be sure to get it early, when competitors are still few and margins still attractive. In some industries it is relatively easy to imitate rapidly because there are few setup problems, the capital requirement is small, and the products are relatively easily and quickly copied. The garment industry is probably the most obvious of such situations. However, when setup problems are great, when capital requirements are big, and when imitation requires lengthy reverse R&D, then getting the second or third juicy bite of the apple may involve several years' time and greatly increased risk.

Imitation of a proven product does not automatically reduce the risk; it merely changes its character. While the innovator faces the risk of his product's not finding a ready market, the would-be imitator faces the equally palpable risk of reaching the market when it is already glutted with many competitors—and often rapaciously price-cutting competitors at that. Obviously, the imitator who can substantially shrink his development gestation period below that of other imitators can gain a tremendous advantage. He will encounter fewer competitors and higher and more stable prices during the felicitous duration of his lead over other imitators.

### Purposeful imitation

In most of the larger, better-managed companies, the R&D process, or at least the product-development process, gets a great deal of careful attention. In many companies genuine product innovations are the direct consequence of carefully honed corporate

[2]See Chapter 9, "Exploit the Product Life Cycle," p. 176.

strategies. Product innovation is purposeful and planned, not random or accidental. Yet, in these same companies, product imitation tends to be almost entirely random, accidental, and reactive. It is the consequence not of what the *imitator* has planned, but of what his competing *innovator* has planned.

Because others have planned and produced the innovation, it is often, though not always, greeted with a certain amount of understandable skepticism by competitors in the same general field. For example:

> When the electric toothbrush was first brought out several years ago, a number of companies in the portable appliance and "personal care" field reacted quite predictably. Since it was "Not Invented Here," a great many highly plausible-sounding reasons were suggested as to why it would certainly fail. But the electric toothbrush caught on quickly to become one of the great new booming small-appliance products.
>
> All companies in the portable appliance field, of course, kept close watch on the new electric toothbrush's progress. Some immediately interviewed users and prospective buyers. But frequently these activities were carried out in the context of extreme skepticism, with management treating the subject with some degree of casualness, if not actual and systematic indifference. At best, in some small-appliance companies it was treated with only idle curiosity. Other "Invented Here" projects—innovations that were part of a carefully conceived and hard-won corporate plan—seemed both more urgent and more exciting.
>
> Yet had these small-electric-appliance companies had a more formal plan, program, or procedure for handling their approaches to the innovations of competitors, I think it can be shown that they would have been in the electric toothbrush business sooner and more profitably.

## SUGGESTED SYSTEM

The remainder of this article outlines a positive approach for planning and creating imitations—what I call a formal strategy for *innovative imitation*.

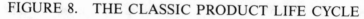

FIGURE 8.   THE CLASSIC PRODUCT LIFE CYCLE

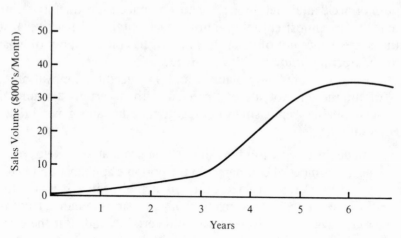

For simplicity, let us assume that the genuinely new product an innovator issues turns out ultimately to be successful, following the more-or-less classical, life-cycle curve depicted in Figure 8. The product is issued at time point "0." Competitor X becomes quickly aware of its existence. Suppose also that Competitor X has a requirement that unless the total market for a product in this price range can be expected to be at least 20,000 units per month, he will not attempt to enter the market. If it is 30,000 units, he views it as a highly attractive market.

When the innovation is first seen, the usual pattern in many Competitor X firms—whose products require heavy capital expenditures and lots of reverse R&D money and time—is similar to this:

*At Year 0*, the decision-making authorities say, "I doubt it will sell. We'll keep an eye on it." This is all that's done.

*At Year 1* (or—depending on the industry and situation—at, say, six months), the decision-making competitors may be a bit surprised that the product is still on the shelves. A typical comment at this point is "Well, it's just hanging on, but not getting anywhere. I told you so."

*At Year 2*, the story is likely to be, "They're getting a bit more business, but I hear Company Y is going into it too. There won't be enough for both of them to share. They will go broke on this one."

*At Year 3*, there is nervousness because the curve is definitely headed upward. The reaction is, "George, we'd better take a closer look at this. Get some of your people on it right away."

*Somewhere between Years 3 and 4*, a massive crash program is started.

*By Year 5*, Company X gets on the market about the same time as six other companies do.

Looking back on what happened, Company X, in effect, said at Year 0 that the chances of success for this product were 0 percent. The judgment made by Company X was zero probability in the sense that nothing was done in any positive way to get ready and launch an imitative product. Had the success probability estimates consciously been something above 0 percent, some imitative steps would have been called for, even if only tentative steps. But none were taken at this time, or at Years 1 or 2. At each point, in terms of actions taken by Company X, a zero probability was attached to the innovator's chances of success. Significantly, however, even though the Company X decision makers had gotten exceedingly nervous by Year 3, they again at that time said, in effect, that the success chances were still nil.

The reason we must say that Company X gave a zero probability to the product's chances of success even in Year 3, despite the obviously worried reaction of "George, we'd better take a closer look at this," is that no steps were taken to begin to tackle the most complex and lengthy job associated with imitation—reverse R&D. Nothing was initiated in the one area that would take the most time and most effort if the product were ever to be made. No bets were hedged because the implicit probabilities that were constantly being attached to the innovator's chances of success were still zero.

*Probability estimates*

But the obvious fact is that people, deep down inside, are seldom this sure of a genuinely new product's commercial fate. Nobody can ever be completely confident at the outset, or at Year 1 or Year 2, that a competitor's innovation will fail. Deep down, there usually is some different and more realistic weighting of probable failure or success.

I believe this attitude of doubt and tentativeness can and should be translated into sound business practice. Suppose that for every genuinely new product issued by a major innovator in its field Company X required its marketing vice-president to attach an honest and carefully thought-out coefficient to his estimate of its probable success—success by some measure of, say, unit sales volume. Hence he might in this case have come up with estimates of the chances of success, at the successive intervals at which he was required to make a judgment, that would run like this:

First at Year 0   5%
Then at Year 1   10%
Then at Year 2   15%
Finally at Year 3 50%

Let us call each of these judgments a "Success Probability Estimate" (SPE). Suppose now also that at Year 0 the policy of Company X was that the marketing vice-president must obtain a rough estimate of the reverse R&D costs involved in developing an effective imitation of the new product. Let us say, for simplicity, that the figure is $100,000, although the accompanying example applies as well for situations where it might be millions of dollars. A proper hedging policy in this case would be that at each interval during which an SPE of the competitor's new product is made, a reverse R&D appropriation is also made in proportion to that estimate (see Exhibit 2).

Thus by Year 3 half of the required reverse R&D money would have been appropriated, and some share of it would have been spent. While the economics of R&D do vary by industry and project—in some cases $5,000 could not even get a company started, so that perhaps although the Year 0 SPE is 5 percent, the appropriation would have to be, say, $10,000—and while other problems would exist in specific cases, the strategy is clear. Namely, it makes a certain kind of good competitive sense to hedge one's bets, to buy at the outset an insurance policy against the success of your competitors'

210

EXHIBIT 2. SCHEDULE OF REVERSE R&D
APPROPRIATIONS

| Year | Probability Estimate (%) | Annual Reverse R&D Appropriation (Based on $100,000 Total) | Total Appropriated to Date |
|------|------|------|------|
| 0 | 5 | $5,000 | $5,000 |
| 1 | 10 | 5,000 | 10,000 |
| 2 | 15 | 5,000 | 15,000 |
| 3 | 50 | 35,000 | 50,000 |

new activities. The face value and premiums of this policy represent an investment in reverse R&D which is designed to get an imitative product to market faster than it would get there otherwise. As time goes on, the face value and premiums would be revised year by year to reflect newly revised estimates of the likelihood of the innovator's success and also the revised estimates of the imitator's R&D costs.

## Imitator's hedge

Let us call this "insurance program" the "Imitator's Hedge" (IH). If Company X had had such a policy—in short, if its competitive strategies had included an IH—then, instead of getting to market belatedly in Year 5, when the rate of market expansion had already slackened and when competition was severe and margins depressed, it would probably have reached market at Year 4 and thus more quickly recovered its costs. Indeed, with such a clear-cut and definitive policy, chances are the whole process of auditing new products would have become so much more careful and sophisticated that the early signals of probable success or failure would have become much more obvious and meaningful. As a consequence, Company X might very well have reached the market sometime in Year 3.

There is obviously more to launching a complex (or, at least, a relatively high-technology) imitative product than reverse R&D.

Dies must be prepared, plant has to be made available, and numerous other things need time, attention, money. But the design and development process is often the most heavily time-consuming—particularly in industries where existing production lines can be modified and freed for products that have features similar to the new one. For example, a plant that makes electric shavers has considerable adaptability to making electric toothbrushes. A plant that makes pneumatic control devices has some adaptability to making laboratory process pumps. But, in either case, there will be great problems and heavy time requirements other than those of reverse R&D. Implementing an IH policy is no simple task. Good intentions will not be good enough. Neither will penury.

It is precisely because the IH often involves so many problems and such vital time considerations that interested companies should seek out all possible ways of minimizing the problems and time inputs associated with a self-conscious program of competitive imitation. We are not talking about something theoretical or arcane. Increasingly in recent years, the military establishments of technically advanced nations have had programs of precisely this kind in their weapons planning and development. For them, a moment saved may be a nation saved. For business, a moment saved may spell many dollars earned. The dollars lost as the result of early support of reverse R&D on products that end up as market failures before the would-be imitator ever produces them will be no less uselessly "lost" than the dollars spent on other forms of insurance that every prudent company very sensibly buys.

The rate of genuine new product introductions in some industries is obviously too great to justify their companies' installing the IH on each new product that comes along. On the other hand, not every company has ambitions to cover every product opportunity. Still, it is possible to be insurance-poor—to buy too many IH's. This therefore calls for the establishment of insurance criteria. It calls for criteria to select those new competitive products for which reverse R&D should be undertaken and those for which no R&D funds should be allocated. These criteria can take many forms—how close a new competitive product is to the various competences of your company, how near a substitute it is for one of your important products, how big its market potential is, how big development costs might be, how long it might take to achieve reasonable market acceptance, and so forth.

But another and different kind of criterion might usefully be attached to each of these. This might be a policy which says that, except in extreme cases of direct potential threat to one of your central major products, your company will not, during any single year within the next five years, commit itself to new IH's whose combined first-year costs exceed $Y. The company's total IH bill in any year could conceivably far exceed $Y, but the aggregate of all new, first-year projects would not exceed $Y.

Such a policy might then stipulate that the available $Y be distributed among the proposals with the highest Success Probability Estimates at Year 0. If this results in the exclusion of projects for which strong IH program demands are still being made, then this becomes an indication of the need to review either the original criteria, or the size of the company's total Imitator's Hedge budget, or both.

## CONCLUSION

Innovation; new product development; extending the lives and expanding the markets of existing products by adding new features, styles, packaging, pricing—all these inexorably belong in the arsenal of devices by which a modern company competes. And innovation is an abundant commodity in our society. But it is probably less abundant than many of us assume. We often mistake innovation for what is really imitation, the large and highly visible outpouring of an imitative product that was genuinely new several years previously when a single innovator first launched it.

Simple arithmetic tells us that there is lots more imitation than innovation. At the beginning a genuinely new product, process, or service generally has only one innovator, but later there are hordes of imitators. No single company can be, or can prudently afford to be, as constant an innovator as it is compelled to be an imitator. And while there are great recognized risks to innovation, there is not today an equivalent recognition of the risks of imitation. When

213

a company comes to market with its imitation at about the same time as the rest of the imitative horde, the risk is great indeed.

Since we live in an age of such unquestioning and often very justified faith in the virtues of innovation, there can develop in the more committed companies a strongly one-sided system of rewards. Plaudits, Brownie points, and promotions go to the clearly innovative individuals—and rightly so. But it is well to be aware of the possible negative consequences. The most unhappily negative effect may be the creation of an environment in which people who frequently suggest imitative practices get viewed as being somehow inferior or less worthy. Taking their cues from the system of rewards, people may then systematically refrain from championing the imitative strategies upon whose early implementation the continued bread-and-butter success of their companies depends.

Hence an affirmative policy of supporting a strategy of imitation in some organized fashion would have the virtue not only of getting necessary imitative activities into motion early, but of communicating to the entire organization that while innovators are valued, so are the creative imitators. It would legitimize systematic imitative thinking as much as the more glamorous innovative thinking.

It makes sense therefore to have just as clear and carefully developed a method of planning innovative imitation as of planning innovation itself. Such a policy may very well require the institution of the Imitator's Hedge—the IH factor in product policy. While the newness of this suggestion may make it sound strange and perhaps even vaguely academic, it is useful to compare it with what we already do in related areas. Take, for example, the field of insurance. The rationale and usefulness of an IH policy is no more unusual than is the rationale of liability insurance, and it is no more novel than the concept of budgeting for success and control.

Perhaps it is an overstatement to say that innovation is the false messiah and a mistake to say that imitation is the new messiah. But to behave lopsidedly as if innovation were a messiah, and especially at the awful expense of a realistic appreciation of the fructifying power of more systematic imitation, would be an even greater mistake.

# 11

# Marketing and Its Discontents

It seems impossible these days for people in marketing to gather anywhere in the world without the subject's finally turning to their troubles with the public. Everywhere marketing is maligned for its pushy, noisy, manipulative intrusions into our lives; its corruptive teachings of greed and hedonism; its relentless pursuit of the consumer's cash, regardless of consequence, save the profit of the seller.

Paradoxically, these complaints seem to rise in direct proportion to the rising practice of the marketing concept, that is, to the business implementation of the idea that success is most assured by responding in every fiscally prudent way to what people actually want and value. That is why market research is such a thriving industry.

Nothing characterizes the successful conversion in the past two decades of so many companies to the practice of the marketing concept than the rising criticism that they practice a baleful opposite. Thus, the more carefully companies try to "give the people what they want," the more surely they are attacked for trying to get people to buy what they don't want, what they don't need, and what they can't afford—and doing it with wanton waste, noise, abrasiveness, and vulgarity.

One might have assumed way back in those doleful days when Henry Ford made the famous remark, "They can have any color car they want, so long as it's black," that once business learned how to be more customer-oriented and less product-oriented, thus giving people any color they wanted, that today's greater responsiveness would create greater consumer satisfaction and certainly less criticism of business.

It hasn't worked out that way, in part for the same reason that the discovery of a new source of unlimited energy (atomic fission) has not made physics more popular. The marketing concept has spurred the professionalized study of people through market research. The psychologists, learning more about what motivates and actuates people in commercial matters than the people themselves know, have thus enabled business strategists to become what critics have called "hidden persuaders" and "captains of consciousness," turning with subterfuge and cunning to their advantage knowledge that in more innocent days we assumed would naturally produce a better world. This, too, has been the pattern in physics. Discovery becomes diabolized in use: The physicist in social action becomes seen as a sinister Dr. Strangelove, in possession of power to control the world, just as the psychologist in business becomes a devious "hidden persuader" with power to control the consumer.

About those who know a lot more than ourselves about things that can ruin our lives and ravage our pocketbooks, our defense is to attribute to them evil, or at least questionable, intent. In the case of business and marketing, the consumer's unease is understandable and perhaps even justified.

Consider again the basic premise of the marketing concept: that a company should determine what consumers need and want, and try to satisfy those wants and needs, provided that:

1. doing so is consistent with the company's strategy
2. the expected rate of return meets company objectives

Implicit in this are two further considerations:

1. A consumer need can generally be defined best in terms of a total marketing program (product, information, reassurance, distribution, attendant services, price, promotion), rather than simply the product itself.
2. Different consumers will want or need different things.

This latter idea we clarify into the concept of "market segments": that there are groups of potential customers sharing particular wants or needs (rather than that there is simply one large, gelatinous market), and that these groups are objectively identifiable.

The discovery of the idea of segments has become a powerful organizing principle in the affairs of modern business. Not that ancient business practitioners in Babylon did not know about segments—they did, selling different wares at different prices to princes than to paupers—but it never became an organizing principle that so consciously or fully dominated commercial life as it does now.

The objective difference between a prince and a pauper is in how much money each has. That is one of several demographic ways to distinguish between segments, rich and poor. It may also be the basis for social class and psychographic distinctions: elite versus mass, powerful versus powerless, self-assured versus self-doubting, psychologically independent versus dependent.

Translated into observable purchasing behavior, people may be segmented into their preferences for various product attributes. In automobiles, for example, some want a big car for the big family and some a smaller one for a small family with a limited budget; some prefer sporty speed to smooth-riding comfort; some will sacrifice certain comforts for lower operating costs; some want dual-purpose vehicles like station wagons to haul groceries and the little kids; while the teenage kids have dual purposes that are as quixotic as they are erotic.

The second category of segments deals with people's psychosocial wants and expressions—a car that reflects or affirms one's rank, position, achievement, or even aspiration, rather than his practical need (Rolls Royce, Cadillac); one that confirms a sense of power or command, one that suggests superior taste, or one that suggests freedom from susceptibility to commercial hucksterism.

These product and psychosocial segments can each be subdivided in an elaborate matrix of possibilities.

Since the marketing concept says that a company is likely to be more successful when it carefully determines and caters to the different wants and needs of different people, the practice of that concept explains a great deal that otherwise looks wasteful and baleful. If nothing else, it explains, for example, why we have so many different kinds of cars, and so many different kinds of laundry detergent with different chemical formulas, different brand names, and different advertising themes. Each targets a different little customer segment, even those detergents that are "all-purpose" and seek to appeal to the "I-don't-care, it-makes-no-difference-to-me" segment.

But for a lot of people it *does* make a difference. Some women want heavy-duty detergents that cut grease. Their husbands are automotive mechanics. Some, whose husbands are mechanics, may not want heavy-duty detergents because they degrade the fabric. Others want something that's safe for delicate underclothes, and others something that preserves or restores the original color. And, like cars, laundry detergents are also bought for psychosocial reasons. The appeal of a mild detergent may be that it affirms the buyer's self-perception of being of a superior species that has only beautifully delicate clothes, not all those tacky, tasteless rags of the lower classes. The appeal of a workhorse detergent that gets things "cleaner than clean" may affirm its user's undeviating dedication to the health and welfare of her family rather than seeming to be one of those fragile and frivolous jet-setters or one of those obsessed women's liberationists. Even the "all-purpose" buyer may in some respects simply be saying "I'm above all that advertising idiocy. They can't fool me. Soap is soap."

When five major manufacturers of laundry detergents discover the existence of the same seven consumer segments, each having three groups of people who prefer their packages in a different size, we can quickly see why the supermarket has such a prodigality of brands and packages—in the United States, about 105 (5 producers × 7 segments × 3 packages = 105). And since the store doesn't want to go to the expense of refilling the shelves every few hours (which would, besides, inconvenience the shoppers), we not only get a lot of packages but a lot of shelf space devoted to them. All this, combined with all those ads, makes things look horribly wasteful.

But looked at another way, all this is merely the understandable consequence of competing producers and sellers responding to the wants, wishes, and behavior of various market segments. Whether this great proliferation of brands, packages, and advertising themes of products that are often only marginally different from one another (if not actually functionally identical), whether these "truly" satisfy consumer needs, or whether wants are being created where no needs "really" exist, or whether it is socially or economically desirable to "create" wants where consumers perceive no need until research discovers and capitalizes on them—these are the normative questions that underlie the issues.

The answers may be easy for some to give and agonizing for others. For both, they require one to act more or less as God's ventriloquist, declaiming on these rather trivial matters what's right or wrong, enough or too much.

The fact is, few of us actually need all of what we have or want. But once we've had our fill of simple food and shelter, can it honestly be said that everything else, including especially music, art, poetry, breathtaking cathedrals built at great expense to glorify God and humble man before Him, is unnecessary and perhaps even self-indulgent? Few of us in the more "advanced" nations will be satisfied to live, as Jesus Christus, in sackcloth and sandals. Nor, it seems, is anybody else who has a better choice. When T. S. Eliot said "Humankind cannot stand too

219

much reality," he meant to explain why in so many ways we try to escape nature's rude animality with manufactured shelter, man-made possessions, entertainments, arts, and fantasies. It's what we call "civilization."

We return to the paradox that puzzles and perplexes: Precisely as the marketing concept has advanced over the years, so, perversely, has the irritation it's produced, even among its practitioners. The millions of dollars annually spent on consumer research and product development, all designed to respond so carefully to what the consumer wants, do not stem the continuing assault on precisely the companies that seem most energetically, conscientiously, and effectively to spend that money.

It should come as no surprise that in recent years a lot of money has also gone into researching the reasons for the assault. Interestingly, there is surprisingly little complaining about product failures or deliberate excesses, like shoddy products, tricky warranties, deceptive advertising, misleading packaging, or questionable selling practices. While these surely exist, they are rare among the big visible companies, precisely those which sell their products the hardest and research their consumers the most. What seems to bug people most, even though they don't usually say it outright quite this way, is encompassed by the far less tractable and more serious charge of generalized wastefulness, offensiveness, and annoyance incident to so much marketing activity—the way it pollutes our lives.

A study by Professor Stephen Greyser of Harvard (reported in the *Journal of Advertising Research*) showed that 72 percent of the 2,500 American adults he surveyed felt advertising was more irritating than ten years before. Laundry soap and detergent ads were felt to be the most irritating. The big surprise is that the survey respondents consisted entirely of business executives. Imagine the results on the campus, at the League of Women Voters, or in the literary salons of the Western world.

But the study revealed something else that explains a lot: respondents were annoyed or offended by 37 percent of the ads for products they *did not* use but only 21 percent of those for products they *did* use. In other words, irritation and annoyance is produced not by the ads themselves but by their consumers as well. And that, really, is not such surprising news. Nobody is ever irritated by anything without his own consent. Indeed, the point is driven home hard in the study's disclosures about brands. Only 7 percent of the ads for one's favorite brand were disliked, as compared with 76 percent of the ads for competing brands. Whether these dramatically contrasting numbers are cause or effect is perhaps arguable. But other evidence and logic suggest a fairly clear answer. People like what they like and don't what they don't. They are most interested in what they think is more relevant to them than in what is not. They find comfort and reassurance and even flattery in ads for brands they've selected. If your family's soiled clothing is produced entirely by a husband and wife employed at sedentary jobs in air-conditioned offices, whose manual labor consists mostly of writing checks for theater tickets and country club dues, ads for heavy-duty detergents that remove grease from mechanics' overalls and grime from children's play clothes are likely to leave you irritated—maybe even highly distracted. If you are poor, ads for Adriatic cruises and Mercedes Benz automobiles will probably leave you frustrated. If you're healthy and athletic in all respects, ads for hemorrhoid relief will be distracting and probably offensive. But if your dentures slide, ads for new adhesives may be rather informatively welcome and helpful, though irritating and offensive to others. And if you've just bought a Winnebago motor home, its ads may be strongly reassuring that you've done the right thing, dispelling the usual post-purchase dissonance that research shows follows big expenditures. (The most avid and attentive consumers of auto ads are people who've just bought the brand being advertised. To keep your customers happy and coming back the next time around, it pays to advertise to those who have just bought, not just to those who might buy.) If you're looking for Granola or Special K ready-to-eat cereal, to have to search for it on a 60-foot triple-decker gondola loaded with children's brands like Cap'n Crunch and Froot Loops may leave you not only irritated but also exhausted.

221

Thus, in the case of consumer goods, which are the source of most of the irritations, complaints, and accusations, Steven Star points out that a lot of the trouble comes from the incongruence between the people for whom specific products, brands, and messages are specifically intended and the people who are exposed to them. The hemorrhoid ad is not particularly offensive to the afflicted viewer, reader, or listener. But most people exposed to the message aren't afflicted. Most likely they're either indifferent or offended. No matter how good Special K may be, toddlers will find the ads intrusive on their television watching, though ads for Cap'n Crunch may be received as informative, exciting, or titillating. Antismoking ads will probably irritate a lot of teenagers—another case of adults bugging them. And there are always too many gasoline stations, except for the person who is running low or has actually run out. Nor should we be surprised that laundry soap and detergent ads irritated the 2,500 executives most. How many of them do that household chore?

The incongruence between the intended and the actual audience for marketing programs represents an imperfection in the connection between the sophisticated practice of the marketing concept and the communications and institutions that facilitate marketing. To appreciate fully the resulting dilemmas and frustrations, it is useful to examine the ideas of marketing programs and segments a bit more fully.

A marketing program comprises the product; how it is packaged, priced, promoted, delivered; where it is sold; and so forth. Marketing programs are directed toward market segments. Indeed, the marketing concept almost by definition divides customers into many specific segments, regardless of product class, whether consumer goods, industrial goods, durable goods, capital goods, or consumables. A segment is that part of the population that has the need in question that might be satisfied with a particular product and marketing program. But some parts of that segment are not particularly good "fits" for every part of the marketing program. For example, some members of the segment may have the need for the indicated product but not the money to buy it. Some may have both but live too far from any place where the product can be economically delivered or serviced. Some may have the need, the money, and the proximity but not the interest. But all may be exposed to the marketing program—the ads for the product, its visible presence where they shop, or its appearance in use where they visit, work, or play. Those in need who are exposed but can't afford to pay will be frustrated. Those in need who are exposed and who *can* afford to pay but have no interest may be distracted. Both may be irritated, as, indeed, will those who found the communication or program highly interesting yesterday and bought, but having bought are now exposed to redundant messages. Having made their choice, they now feel badgered.

It is thus no surprise that irritation, frustration, and distraction arise most commonly in connection with consumer goods marketing. Here is the widest and most frequent incongruity between the total audience exposed to a marketing program and the specific "best fit" proportion of the market segment being targeted. A million people may be exposed to the marketing program (the ads, the displays in the shops), though it is designed for the segment needs of only 400,000, and the "best fit" of only 100,000 of that segment. This 100,000 "best fit" becomes the actual "Program Target"—the only one that can conceivably become satisfied by the marketing program. The other 90 percent who get the message are bored, irritated, distracted, frustrated, or some combination of these. And if some proportion of the best fit 10 percent has already bought the offered product, they too will be bored or irritated.

Such incongruence and abrasion is much less likely in industrial goods. Potential customers are often relatively few, with each representing potentially large sales volume. Customers who share a particular need (a market segment) are likely to group themselves into clearly identifiable targets (say, all companies that anodize metal). Finally, there are highly specialized trade media through which to reach them: magazines, industry conventions, distribution channels. The congruence of market segment, marketing program, and program target with the audience exposed to the marketing program is likely to be considerable. Things get organized to make them that way. Thus IBM effectively divided its data processing business into sixteen major market segments (banking, distribution, aerospace, education, medical, government, and so on). A separate program was developed for each segment, and individual salesmen and sales offices were specialized by individual segments. The customer got the communications and programs suited to his special needs. Overlap and incongruence were minimal.

Not so, however, in consumer goods. All business is aware of the problem, though not often sufficiently conscious of its awareness. The big advertisers who use the mass media, and especially television, consider them the cheapest effective ways of reaching mass markets. Yet they tend generally to go to a lot of effort to mitigate the incongruities they're aware of. No children's programs are put on television at 10:00 P.M. Radio news reports, sponsored by ads for men, get heavily aired during commuting hours. Most general interest magazines in the larger countries carry regional editions whose advertising is tailored to those regions. Some general interest magazines do the same for such subscriber groups as medical doctors and teachers. Similarly, specialty stores carry only certain specialty products, like pharmaceuticals, sporting goods, and the like. All this mitigates incongruence and abrasion. But not a whole lot.

Though marketing tries increasingly to fashion products, communications, distribution channels, prices, and other components of the marketing mix to suit the special needs and capabilities of carefully defined market segments, thus giving the customer more nearly what he wants, this fashioning, notwithstanding increasingly specialized targeting activities, inescapably creates more irritated, frustrated, and distracted consumers. The best intentions, supported by the best efforts, return abrasion and hostility.

Direct marketing via mail, telephone, and cable can help mitigate this unhappy condition. In direct marketing, products, messages, and even media can be specifically tailored and even limited to their intended audiences. Best-fit program targets can be more closely matched to precise program audiences. The better this can be done, the more effective it will be as a market-

224

ing device, and the more attractive its relative costs to its user. It may cost more but still be cheaper.

Much depends on getting the fit right, of course, but the fit will almost always be better than with most mass media. Hence it has the potential of reducing social dissonance while also improving marketing effectiveness. But, as with most things, a good thing is not necessarily improved by its multiplication. An abundant daily harvest of unsolicited direct mail, no matter how interested I am in collecting stamps or improving my sexual performance, can get to be too much. The phone can ring too often and too inconveniently with invitations to ski where the skiing is best, buy where the price is lowest, and get what's not easily available elsewhere. This is not to mention the irritations of these calls when in incompetent hands, or the trickiness, pushiness, and effrontery of some of the mail.

When the marketing concept operates at full throttle, it generates products, services, and communications that target the specifically discovered needs and wants of specific narrow best-fit consumer segments. Each segment therefore has a better chance of getting what it really wants or needs than in the bad old days when Henry Ford told people they could have any color Model T they wanted so long as it was black.

But there are costs. One, production runs are shorter, distribution channels more varied and more crowded, and prices probably higher. Two, while more people are better satisfied by getting a chance to buy what's better tailored to their specific functional or psychosocial wants, an almost exactly equal number of people get frustrated, annoyed or distracted by the marketing programs of what they don't want, or can't afford but would like to have. Add to this the fact that the sheer magnitude of commercial communications is expanded as product numbers increase and that it is intensified through emulation and competitive drive. Put them all together, and one begins to see the reason for the perverse simultaneity of a triumphant marketing concept that seeks better to satisfy the public and a less satisfied public.

Or so it seems. The disjunctions, abrasions, and irritations

THE MARKETING IMAGINATION

I've referred to certainly exist. But something else also exists: the apparent insatiability of human appetites, regardless of how much better off they keep getting. Each generation everywhere seems to ask for what its predecessors asked only of God. The special condition of present times is that we have all so suddenly been immersed in such an intensively communicative world that we have become intensely conscious of all the squalor, greed, competitiveness, dishonesty, negation, and covetousness that have, in fact, characterized humankind from the beginning. A rereading of the Old Testament or the Iliad quickly reminds us of how much each told us about the awful presence in their times of these rather ignoble human traits. It takes a Geiger counter to find any alleviating traces in either book of any continuing evidence of civic virtue, honor, civility, humanity, self-denial, and decency. They surface mostly as contrasting examples of how things might or ought to be rather than how they were.

In past times we excelled not in civic virtue or nobility of character but in ignoring, hiding, disguising, and denying the prodigal existence of their infamous opposites.

Today these are harder to bury or ignore, in part because, for the moment at least, we seem to take a special masochistic pleasure in parading our imperfections in public view every hour of the day. Also, because we're doing so well, exceptions to our good fortunes become by contrast more visible as well as more irritating. In the dark and desperate 1930s, with 25 percent unemployment that lasted for ten years, and before unemployment compensation, Social Security, Medicare, HUD, and pot, good fortune was to be able to hold one's job, any job, or failing that, to get on the WPA. In the affluent 1980s, when unemployment is way less, with home ownership, auto ownership, education, medical services, and symphony attendance way up, one still hears the self-abusing insistence that "we can do better."

In those despairing 1930s the nation enjoyed the greatest effulgence of wit and humor it had ever seen—Benchley, Thurber, George Kaufman, Dorothy Parker, E. B. White, and popular funnymen like Jack Benny, Fred Allen, Eddie Cantor, Burns and Allen, Fibber McGee and Molly, Amos and Andy, Charlie McCarthy. In the affluent 1980s we are treated in contrast to a grating specter of gloom and glumness, with half the public pundits saying that decay and decadence have destroyed our spirit and our capabilities, and the other half, as I said, that "we can do better."

We have noted that nothing characterizes success so much as its attendant miseries. We now see that marketing, one of mankind's less cosmic concerns for urgent attention, may be no exception to that apparent rule. We focus in our lives and in public affairs more on what's wrong, bad, corrupt, and unfinished than on what's accomplished, good, noble, alleviating, and progressing. More than two hundred years ago Edward Gibbon wrote, "There exists in human nature a strong propensity to depreciate the advantages, and to magnify the evils of present times." It is still so. The end of the world is not at hand.

Nor is there any presumption that if we solve all our known problems and remove all basis for discontent, then we shall at last be happy. The problem is that every solution creates new problems.

# Index

# A

Acquisition costs, 121
Adler, Lee, 187n
Advertising, 86–89, 153, 162, 197, 220–222, 224
Alderson, Wroe, 171, 173n
Allegheny Ludlum Steel Corporation, 15–16
Allstate Insurance Company, 57
Aluminum, 143, 186
American Express Company, 131–132
*American Petroleum Institute Quarterly*, 163
Apple Computer, 133
ASFs (Ambulatory Surgical Facilities), 62
Assembly line, 156

Atomic energy, 163
Augmented products, 79, 81–84, 114
Automatic washing machines, 32–37, 181
Automation, 45–46
Automobiles, 55, 74, 77–78, 107, 147, 154–156, 158–160, 217–218
Ayoub, Sam, 31

# B

Barrie, Richard, 12
Bartlett, Christopher, 42n
Barzun, Jacques, 144, 165
Bauer, Raymond A., 128
Bergen Burnswig Company, 120
Bergerac, Michel C., 14, 15

# E

# F

# G

# H

# X

Xerox Corporation, 87, 89

# Y

*Years of Upheaval* (Kissinger), 45
Yugoslavia, 26

# Z

Zero-interest instruments, 133–134
Zimmerman, M. M., 145$n$